The Promise of LeBron James

The Promise of

The Rise, Fall from Grace,

LeBron James

and Redemption of Ohio's Own

Bill Livingston

 The Kent State University Press   *Kent, Ohio*

© 2024 by The Kent State University Press, Kent, Ohio 44242

All rights reserved

ISBN 978-1-60635-484-1

Published in the United States of America

Cataloging information for this title is available at the Library of Congress.

28 27 26 25 24   5 4 3 2 1

In memory of Fred McLeod and Bill Millsaps

Contents

Acknowledgments

Special thanks to Maryellen Driscoll and Tom Feran, who each gave the book a first reading. Thanks also to Fran Blinebury, Munch Bishop, Mary Schmitt Boyer, Tom Conkle, Tim Corbett, Buck Harvey, Steve Snapp, Jim Naveau, Brian Windhorst, and Branson Wright.

For Love of the Game

Kobe Bryant won an Oscar for the Best Short Animated Film in 2018 with a six-minute love letter to the game that was such a big part of his life. *Dear Basketball* tells the story of how he first fell in love with the game. In imaginary games, he rolls and then shoots at a wastebasket in his room the NBA team socks of his father, Joe "Jelly Bean" Bryant, a journeyman player with the Philadelphia 76ers.

LeBron James came to love basketball as a sock shooter, too, but with ordinary, sometimes raggedy socks, not NBA team socks. When his game grew bigger than his room and a ball replaced the socks, his target was a milk crate nailed to a telephone pole. First, he had a basket but no ball, then a ball but no basket. In an upbringing of scrimping and making do, it was always something.

He was a member of a class that is often lost in the shuffle of American privilege, prejudice and power—a Black child without a place to call home, born and raised in poverty and need by a 16-year-old unwed mother who had been deserted by his father. He was poor, but never utterly destitute, because he had basketball.

Unknowingly, he replicated the hardscrabble beginnings of a previous generation's NBA great, Elvin Hayes. Using a small rubber ball, Hayes spun and shot at a makeshift basket in his yard—a maneuver not conducive to athletic grace for a boy who grew up so poor in the cotton town of Rayville, Louisiana, that he often went barefoot and practiced in two left-footed tennis shoes he scavenged from the trash and taped to his feet. It was the fundament of his game. He eventually mastered a nearly indefensible turnaround jump shot despite the tape, tatters, and tangled choreography of a boy with two left feet, or left shoes, anyway.

Two years after winning the Oscar, Bryant, his 13-year-old daughter Gianna, and seven others died in a helicopter crash in dense fog. They were flying to a basketball game involving the team Bryant coached, of which Gianna was a member. He was gone, but his heartfelt words live on.

Every now and then, I think about the first time I knew basketball was a sport I would love, even if only to write about it as a newspaperman. I was in the fifth grade, playing shooting (a lot) guard. I caught a pass in the corner where three-pointers are launched like artillery barrages today. We were playing a 10:00 A.M Saturday game, and as I started to shoot, the sun burst through the clouds. The basket disappeared in a golden sheet of light pouring through the gym's windows. Reasoning that the basket did not move, I arched a shot into the glare, and it splashed into the net.

Many years later, when I was covering the Philadelphia 76ers, assistant coach Chuck Daly—later a two-time NBA champion coach in Detroit and the Dream Team's 1992 Olympic coach—was talking about the attraction of the game. "You can never lose that thrill you got from seeing that ball go through the basket on the playground," he said. "But it's the most powerful and dangerous part of the game. Because you have to pass the ball to your teammates too."

Yes, but . . . sinking that shot into a fireball was like lightning going through my veins. "Love you always," Bryant said at the film's end. He wasn't the only one.

First Look

Hype, the herald of celebrity, purveyor of both promise and peril, creator of curiosity, arrived on the last century's calendar in 1998, the 14th year of LeBron James's life.

It was early in LeBron James's growth trajectory, which would be measured not only in his stature but in the lumens of his basketball brilliance, the size of the newspaper headlines celebrating it, the caterwauling NBA introductions, and the roars of the fan who saw it.

At the turn of the twenty-first century in northeast Ohio and afterward for its next quarter century, both there and all over the world—wherever basketball hoops hung on garages and barn walls, on telephone poles and trees, in arenas and gyms, on playgrounds whose unadorned nets made haloed shadows on the hot concrete, on the polished hardwood floors of the NBA's pleasure palaces, in pickup games, in the Olympics when national pride was on the line, in the playoffs when everything else was, on radio and television sports talk shows and in increasingly polarized political debates—LeBron James was an inescapable athletic presence, dominating basketball and much of sports.

The coincidence that James was born on December 30, 1984, three years and three months before one of his great future rivals, Steph Curry, in the same hospital, Akron General Medical Center, led to jokes years later that there must be something in the water in Akron. For James and people like him, it wasn't a bubbling stream of opportunity. Curry, the son of the Cleveland Cavaliers' shooting guard Del Curry and the older brother of NBA player Seth Curry, had a far easier path, through patrimony.

James's mother, Gloria, gave birth to him when she was 16, a result of a casual romance with a shadowy figure named Anthony McClelland, who never had any connection with his son, never paid child support, and was simply another statistic in the mounting total of failures of the incarceration system in America.

James, along with his mother and uncles Curt and Terry, lived for a time in a rambling old house on Hickory Street, on a dirt road, literally on the wrong side of the railroad tracks that ran into downtown Akron. When Gloria went back to high school, the house, in disrepair anyway, became slovenly, with unwashed dishes spilling out of the sink, creaky, splintering floorboards.

After Gloria's mother, Freda, died, mother and son had to depend on the kindness of strangers. They lived with a neighbor, Wanda Reaves, for a while, moving five times in only three months, in what had become a municipal nomadic existence. Gloria was on welfare, so little LeBron used her food stamps for snacks, bringing all they could buy home in his small backpack. Mother and son slept together on a sofa, James tucked in with his stuffed blue elephant. Sometimes, the household became rowdy, and neighbors called police because of the noise.

At other times, Gloria, fond of the night life, simply left him alone to draw pictures of the logos of the Dallas Cowboys and Los Angeles Lakers. "There were times when I was so worried because I didn't know if my mama would come home or not," James said.

In the fourth grade, he had been without a permanent place to live for two-thirds of his life and had missed over 100 days of school. He had never played sports. It was almost inconceivable that he would become a global icon, a billionaire, a philanthropist dedicated to education in Akron, a political activist, and one of the greatest players in basketball history.

Recruiting for a youth football team on the east side of Akron, Bruce Kelker, coach of the East Dragons, coaxed James into a footrace against others his age or older. James won by 15 yards. He was only nine years old. The first time he took a handoff for the Dragons, he ran 80 yards for a touchdown.

Sometimes, even for notoriously slow starters in life, you can tell right away the weight of the expectations someone will carry, whether it is in the form of basketball, a football or a metal relay baton in track. Ohio State's former world record–holder in the 400 meters, Olympic gold and silver medalist Butch Reynolds, also of Akron, like James dashed untouched down the field for a touchdown on his first carry in youth football. Reynolds, however, grew up in a stable, two-parent household. He learned discipline and enjoyed the comforts of family life with his siblings.

Already big for his age, James was such a dominating presence at the beginner's level of football that it caused parents of players on other teams to demand a look at his birth certificate.

LeBron and his mother lived with Kelker and the coach's girlfriend for a time, then, when James was in fourth grade, moved in with a rival coach, Frank Walker, with whose son James bonded. It was the first time he had any idea of what "a real family is like," he said. James learned the comfort of a daily routine. Awakened at 6:30 every morning, he had to finish his homework, if his chores—cleaning the bathroom every other weekend and other such tasks—had prevented it. Walker taught him how to dribble and made him shoot left-handed layups, the beginning of his remarkable ambidexterity from 15 feet and closer to the rim.

James's play on a nine-year-old team led Walker to make him an assistant coach for eight-year-olds, believing coaching would accelerate his basketball learning curve. James enrolled in Portage Path Elementary, a poor, inner-city school with an aging building where roughly 90 percent of students qualified for free lunches. James's favorite classes became music, art, and gym. He had a spotless attendance record that year.

He liked football. But his lasting love came when he was introduced to basketball at Summerlake Community Center in Akron. "Five on five [scrimmages], this is a coach, this is what we're doing, we running sprints, get on the [starting] line," James said. In Texas, the conditioning exercise was called *running horses*, for reasons I never knew. And you ran to the *lines*, plural, not *line.* singular. Running from the baseline to the free throw line and back, then to half court and back, then making roundtrips to the free throw line at the other end of the floor, and finally to the distant baseline. By the end, you felt the "horse" was riding you.

James was only 14 years old, and a freshman, when he began as a starter on the St. Vincent-St. Mary basketball team in Akron, in the 1999–2000 season. He averaged 21 points and 6.2 rebounds per game. He scored 27 points against Akron's Archbishop Hoban High School in his third game, in what amounted to a siren's portent of what was to come. His near future would feature thunderous dunks, sonic salvos from cheering fans, passes delivered like a genie granting wishes, and a hype-o-rama by popularizers like Dick Vitale.

The basis of the glowing predictions was the base of James's body. At 14, he had the feet of a bigger man. Firm grounding, physically if not socially and academically, combined with the massive, chiseled shoulders he later sculpted in the weight room, let him bear the burden of almost impossible expectations. James carried the community and later civic, state, and national weight well. But he felt the expectations from the start.

"It's tough." he said in a YouTube interview with Kevin Durant, when the pair toured James's favorite Akron sites on a snowy night in 2018. "You know when you're growing up in a city where not many make it out, and they see, 'this kid right here has a lot of talent' they expect for you to save the whole city, and you don't feel it as much in the beginning, but as the years go on and on and you start to feel, you know, the pressure, and how many people are riding on you to succeed, not only for you and your family but for everyone. I definitely could feel that. It's the whole notion of like, when you grow up in an African American community it's like everyone is so happy when we're all on the same level. And as soon as you're able to become a little successful, with anything in life, even as a kid, even as a 14-year-old, 15-year-old, people envy that."

The choice of the Catholic school was controversial, setting a precedent for James's future disruptive decisions. The Black community in Akron expected the winning team to be the public school power, Buchtel High School (now the Buchtel Community Learning Center). James not only defied the community consensus but also took youth basketball teammates Dru Joyce III, Sian Cotton, and Romeo Travis with him. A few years later, Travis would become a top mid-major player at the University of Akron, leading to ugly sing-song chants of "LeBron's biiii-itch" from archrival Kent State University's fans.

The stated reason for the move was that his older friends were afraid diminutive point guard Dru Joyce would not be able to make the Buchtel team in his freshman year.

Altogether now: As if! LeBron was good enough even then to create a roster to his own liking.

At St. Vincent-St. Mary, James was not simply from a different part of town. It was almost as if he were from a different universe. The sea change from an all-Black circle of friends to white America, specifically to the even whiter America of a Catholic school, was a difficult one for young James. When he wasn't in shock at how different most of his classmates' lives were from his, he felt the isolation of being one of the black grains of pepper in a canister of salt.

"When I first went to the ninth grade, I was like, 'I'm not f—king with white people,'" James said during the premiere of his HBO show *The Shop*, which replicated the free-ranging, lively discussions in Black barbershops. "I was so institutionalized from growing up in the hood, it's like 'They don't f—k with us, they don't want us to succeed.'"

"The hierarchy was here," James once said, lifting one hand above his head. "And then we're here; matter of fact, we're underneath this chair," he continued, pointing his hand down to the floor.

His culture shock was pronounced. "Bread, cereal, chips, doughnuts, all that s—t is on the top of the refrigerator," he said of his life before exposure to white home furnishings. "When I got to high school was the first time I knew about a pantry."

James attended the predominantly white school in order to play with Cotton, Joyce, and Willie McGee, who, with James, were dubbed the "Fab Four" for their immense talent on the youth organized basketball circuit.

"I'm like, 'I'm going to this school to play ball, that's it,'" James recalled. "'I want nothing to do with white people, it's me and my boys. We're going to high school together and we're here to hoop.'"

Clearly, it took him a little while to adjust to the school. But Maverick Carter, James's longtime friend who also played on the St. Vincent-St. Mary team, said everything changed by the end of that first year. "Sports and basketball is the most unifying theme," he said. "By the end of the year, all of us were best friends. Our Black friends in the hood was coming, his white friends—and we were just all having a great time."

James's first high school coach was Keith Dambrot, a former University of Akron baseball player who literally would take one for the team—and then another one and another one and another one—setting a school record for being hit by pitches. A former college coach in the Mid-American Conference, Dambrot was a scratcher and clawer, surviving on "want-to" rather than "sure did." His name became anathema to college athletic directors after he was fired at Central Michigan University for calling some of his players the n-word in a fiery but colossally misguided motivational speech to his players.

Dambrot, a caring and compassionate coach despite his reputation, was awed by James's startling physical skills. The coach knew he had a prodigy who would only become more overpowering when he grew into the size portended by his feet. Wherever James played, fans' eyes were always on him.

And so were mine in his sophomore season, lured there by the insistence of the *Cleveland Plain Dealer*'s Canton-Akron bureau sports head, whose invariable mantra was, "You've got to see this kid play." By then, he was the No. 1 ranked high school sophomore in the country by the people who run basketball's cradle-robbing scouting sites. Even then, James knew what the focus of his life and the realization of his dreams would be. "I want to be the greatest of all time," he said. "There's my motivation." Asked how he pushed himself after receiving such a flattering review, he responded, "I push myself every day. My coach pushes me. My teammates push me. You've got to go do the work because if you stop working, someone else out there might be working to pass you up."

The first time I saw him play was in a game against Central-Hower High School, two weeks before a rematch in the state tournament district finals. Akron Central High School was built in 1884, a few years after Reconstruction following the Civil War had ended in a dirty deal that gave the disputed 1876 presidential election to Rutherford B. Hayes. Construction, demolition, and reconstruction were the school's story, too. Torn down in 1973, years after Basketball Hall of Famers Nate Thurmond and Gus Johnson played there, it rose from the ashes in a new building with a new name, Central-Hower, the second half in honor of an Akron industrialist. The school was again closed in 2006 but was repurposed as a science, technology, engineering and math (STEM) school.

Neither Thurmond, who was long retired, nor Johnson, who died in 1987, was available to help their old school's team against James. The prodigy had had a 42-point game against Cleveland Benedictine High School and was on his way to season averages of 25.2 points, 7.2 rebounds and 5.8 assists per game when he led the SV-SM Fighting Irish against Central-Hower in Rhodes Arena on the University of Akron campus.

Thurmond's was the more familiar name, as he had played for the Cleveland Cavaliers in 1976 when the team reached the NBA conference finals. The season, the "Miracle of Richfield," was named for the coliseum that was built in a sleepy village for a franchise so bereft of achievement that victory in a single playoff series was considered the equivalent of turning water into wine.

Stylistically, Johnson was more James's precursor. With a gold star incised in a front tooth, seated at the wheel of his gold-trimmed Cadillac, Johnson was a flamboyant presence around his hometown and a sensation wherever he played. In his career, he broke three backboards with savage dunks, one more than Darryl Dawkins, the self-styled "Dr. Dunkenstein" of the 1970s and '80s NBA. Johnson could shoot with either hand when ambidexterity was still rare in the NBA. He played above the rim, could tap the top of the 12-foot-high white target square above the rim, and was said, in a tall tale reminiscent of Paul Bunyan or Pecos Bill, to be capable of plucking a half-dollar off the top of the backboard and leaving a quarter in change behind. People called him "Honeycomb" for the sweetness of his game. With a little help from the hype machine that occasionally doubles as sportswriters' laptop computers, James's game would soon have all the hives in Pooh Corner humming.

James also had input in the design of SV-SM's green-and-white uniforms. But couture and accessorizing were not why the game was watched by a large crowd, sprinkled with NBA scouts—Washington's general manager, Bob Ferry, and Cavaliers' television analysts Austin Carr and Campy Russell, for example.

That season, James would become the first sophomore ever named as a USA Today's First Team All-American. Just as older strippers advised Gypsy Rose Lee in the musical Gypsy, "Ya gotta have a gimmick," so

James had one in his headband. Batman, James's favorite superhero, was inordinately fond of his cape, too. Of course, as Gypsy said, "At these prices, I'm not a stripper. I'm an ecdysiast." At the prices James would command in his contracts, he could have played in nearly anything and still been dominant.

Some games throb with competitive passion, with the lead changing hands more quickly than wallets at a pickpockets' convention, with screaming fans outward bound for the frenzy beyond the cuckoo's nest, and the thunderclap crescendo of a buzzer-beater.

This game was not like that.

SV-SM raced to a 20-point lead before the Central-Hower Eagles rallied with a pressing, trapping defense. Frankly, it never felt like the Fighting Irish would lose. A sports columnist, however, must have a "take," preferably a hot one, or else he is writing a game story by another name. This was a game in which life definitely needed a boost from art.

"Stop godding up these athletes," *New York Herald Tribune* sports editor Stanley Woodward barked to the great Red Smith. In his autobiography, Jim Murray, one of the greatest of sportswriters, admitted spicing up a column on stone-faced Roberto Clemente by changing the outfielder's words: "I am happy, but my face doesn't show it" to "I am happy, but my face doesn't know it." It read better. It gave a whimsical side to Clemente, a Puerto Rican who felt overlooked and outright snubbed by the baseball press in a time soon after the arrival of Black players had changed the game to one of speed, empowered by Black talent, provoking resentment in many corners. Most famously, sportswriter Grantland Rice had, in an apocalyptic paragraph or two, turned the Notre Dame backfield into Famine, Pestilence, Destruction, and Death. I decided that my first James column was absolutely jonesing for a little godding up and possibly even some of Rice's equestrian overreach.

The play that put the *high* back in *hype* and shattered the chance of a Central-Hower comeback occurred when two Eagles trapped James in the backcourt. Six hands clutched at the ball as James pivoted to protect it. Only two of them were SV-SM's. The ten seconds allowed to advance the ball to the front court ticked down.

It was then that James lit the candle, leaping above the defenders like something off a launch pad, twisting in midair and finding for a layup far down court a wide-open teammate. The screaming Eagles' fans were abruptly silenced. Order was restored. God was in his heaven and going by the alias of King James. It is to my discredit that the pass was really more looped than lasered, not that anyone could tell that from my breathless description. I included mention of James's interior sense of the 10-second clock, lauded his vertical lift, and fawned over his court vision.

No one knew then that James and I would, for the 11 seasons in all that he played for Cleveland, have a relationship that ranged on my part from awed to antagonistic, to amicable, and finally to admiring.

Truth be told, the arc of his pass on the day of my first encounter with him was, more than anything else, like a rainbow. In a way, it fit. Pot of gold at its end and all that.

CHAPTER 2

Losing and Learning

The week before the 2002 Ohio State High School Division II championship game, *Sports Illustrated*'s star incubator delivered, presumably upon a midnight clear, LeBron James to the world.

"The Chosen One," proclaimed the cover, becoming the first media outlet to give James biblical subtext. After winning the right to choose him first in the following year's NBA draft lottery, the Cleveland Cavaliers eventually spread the good news of their sheer dumb luck with an advertising campaign consisting of the single word *Witness*. It was a messianic message of a Second Coming. In case anyone missed the point, in the cover photograph James wore Michael Jordan's jersey number, 23. Strictly speaking, the bedraggled Cleveland franchise, having never reached an NBA Finals, had never really even had a First Coming.

Yet for every prophecy there are sure to be doubters and for every leap of faith apostates. St. Vincent-St. Mary was unbeaten, 75–0, against Ohio teams in James's four years there. Its three losses had come against loaded national powers. The Fighting Irish, however, were playing under the direction of a new coach, Dru Joyce Jr., formerly Dambrot's assistant and the father of the team's diminutive point guard, Dru Joyce III.

Dambrot, a man reborn in the glare of James's success, had become the assistant coach to Dan Hipsher, a Bobby Knight acolyte, at the University of Akron. Knight was the man in the Indiana University red sweater that snugged the ample torso bulging below a face frequently empurpled by fury at his own players' malfeasances, referees' myopia, and coverage by out-of-town media members, who frequently deviated from most Hoosier sportswriters' fawning norm. Like Knight, Hipsher did not suppress his feelings when displeased. James, like Larry Bird, did not like screaming coaches. The only reason the highly unlikely James-to mid-major–Akron rumors got any traction was Hipsher's firing and Dambrot's promotion to head coach in James's senior year. Several of the St. Vincent-St. Mary players joined their old coach at the University of Akron, setting in motion James's widespread but implausible dreams, too, creating a real-life version of Hickory High School's Cinderella team in the movie *Hoosiers*.

In a moment of reverie years later, James said that with him Akron would have become a mid-major power and "would have made some noise" in the NCAA Tournament. It never happened, of course. James turned pro straight out of high school. Akron never became a giantkiller like Texas Western, Butler, Gonzaga, or, in the closest analogy, Indiana State, led by the resplendent talents of Larry Bird.

Waiting in the state finals was Cincinnati's Roger Bacon Spartans, a team with a 24–3 record that had won its semifinal game by a record 52 points, a dozen more than SV-SM's romp in its half of the bracket. The Spartans were familiar with SV-SM after a competitive midseason 79–70 loss, in which the score had been tied at 66 with four minutes to play.

That game was played at Kent State, a university only 13 miles from Akron, making it a de facto home game for the Fighting Irish. Before the opening tip dismayed Roger Bacon, players watched James pose for photographs with the referees. At the same time, James's teammates, notable mostly for their roles as part of his retinue, signed autographs for fans. It was a variation on the derivative celebrity obtained, according to the old saying, by shaking the hand that shook the hand of John L Sullivan.

The day before the final, James gave the Spartans an emotional edge to go with the confidence they had gained in the teams' earlier meeting by guaranteeing that his team would win. The Spartans seethed over that all the way until the game began at 11:00 A.M.

In the very first seconds of play, Bacon's 6'6" Beckham Wyrick, off the opening tip, jarred James with an elbow, sending a message received with shock and awe by the tournament record crowd at Ohio State's Value City Arena of 18,375 fans. Some had paid $200 apiece for scalped tickets, an exorbitant price at the time. "I wanted him to know we weren't going to roll over for them like a lot of other teams did," said Wyrick, obviously unmoved by James's football background. For their part, the referees enforced neither the elbow nor other physical plays with anything approaching prosecutorial vim. James, moreover, had awakened with back spasms and struggled to only eight points in the first half. The game was clearly going to be a competition, not a coronation. The underdogs from the Cincinnati working-class suburb of St. Bernard were not intimidated in the slightest.

Stylistically, the first years of the new century were a time when the NBA game, which spawned imitators at every level of play, was between eras. The game had been ugly, low-scoring, and violent in the 1990s. Revised rules in the new millennium, eliminating hand checking and the grabbing and bumping of cutters, cleaned up the game. Steph Curry's transformative range and accuracy at Golden State soon ushered in the NBA's three-point revolution.

Tempting as was the shorter high school and college three-point line, the team with less talent at the teenage level sometimes relied on the NBA's Darwinian view of the '90s: basketball, like nature, was red in tooth and claw. When height, in those twilight years of the big man's dominance, could not make right all by itself, might was its willing accomplice. It was victory by natural selection. Might was the second pick in the gene pool draft after height, which, after all, could not be taught.

Bacon, however, must be given its rightful credit. The Spartans won the hustle categories with 13 offensive rebounds and had a 32–18 overall rebounding edge. Coach Bill Brewer used the 6'6" Wyrick on the 6'7" James with only occasional relief. It worked well enough to force James into seven turnovers, compared to six assists. Bacon would concede James his points, within reason, although they amounted to 32, over half the Fighting Irish's total of 63. The game plan was predicated on strangling his teammates. Although Romeo Travis played well, with 19 points before fouling out in the last minutes, Spartan Frank Phillips's choking defense limited SV-SM's diminutive point guard Dru Joyce III to only six points. Joyce had scored 21 in the teams' earlier meeting.

Most of all, the Spartans played five-man basketball. They were sound, well-coached, and as tough as Leonidas at Thermopylae. Admittedly, their play was not as memorable and uplifting as the astral plane to which James's game could ascend. But it was enough. The Irish trailed by 11 points late in the third quarter, when James, despite his cranky back, while playing with four fouls, stole the ball and Gus Johnsoned a ferocious breakaway dunk that made the building ring with thunderous cheers. Bedlam broke out moments later when James sank a buzzer-beating three-pointer from half-court to cut the deficit to six points. In the fourth quarter, James finally positioned himself in the low post and there proved stoppable only by the final buzzer. He scored 13 of his team's 17 points in the quarter.

But with all due respect for James's trust in his teammates and with empathy for the burden the magazine and his own success had thrust on his young shoulders, James, three for six on threes in the game, passed up a good look at a three-pointer in the last 30 seconds with Roger Bacon leading, 66–63. Instead he threw the ball to teammate Chad Mraz, whose virtue was that he was open in the corner, which, unfortunately, was for a reason: his aim was off all day. It was the wrong play, pure and simple. Mraz, a zone-busting outside shooting specialist, missed for the fifth time in his six shots. They were all three-pointers.

Soon afterward, the younger Joyce, as the unthinkable defeat became unavoidable lost his composure, and hurled the ball in frustration, drawing a technical foul. It allowed the Spartans to finish their 71–63 upset with a flurry of free throws.

The All-Tournament Team featured the four players with season-long double-figure scoring averages from Bacon—and James, who graciously congratulated the Spartans when the game ended.

The game afforded a peek at the problems that would dog James in the future until he orchestrated the team-jumping move to Miami in 2010. In James's first seven-year stint with the Cavaliers, he never really had a reliable sidekick who could take and make big shots available because of the defensive concentration on James.

It also revealed James's tendency to avoid the contact that came with positioning himself in the low post. Much was made of Wyrick's "message" elbow in that regard. James addressed the low post issue by assiduous work in the weight room before his final high school season, growing bigger, stronger, and more dominant than ever.

Another theory focused on James's reluctance to take punishment on his worry about his sometimes shaky free throw shooting.

And inescapably, there was the shot not taken by James and the opportunity missed by the teammate James trusted to take it. Jordan's Chicago Bulls won the 1995 NBA championship against Seattle in the final seconds of Game 6 of the Finals, when he passed out of a double team to teammate Steve Kerr. Jordan never faced second-guessing, because Kerr made the open shot and validated the decision. But Jordan also had the credibility earned by game-winning shots that went all the way back to his decisive last-minute shot in the national championship game against Georgetown University in his freshman year at the University of North Carolina.

It would take much longer to make obsolete the criticism of James for his failure in not taking the big shot. That, of course, is basketball. Coaches will live with a good look by a good shooter, come what may. Part of being the Chosen One, however, was apparently a mandate to chase the vainglory of heroic shots. Detractors would chew that over like a dog's toy. Eventually, the long past Roger Bacon game would be cited as evidence of a career-long character flaw.

Until season after season, game-winning shot by buzzer-beating miracle, James delivered his team from defeat and himself from doubt.

CHAPTER 3

LeBron and the "Un-LeBron," Maurice Clarett

LeBron James landed in the nation's living rooms on December 12, 2002, the way the "Lone Eagle," Charles Lindbergh, descended on LeBourget Airport in Paris in 1927. "Lucky Lindy" created a furor, with Parisians rushing onto the landing field, almost swarming over his fragile craft, the *Spirit of St. Louis*, everyone desperate for a glimpse of l'aigle solitaire, the lone eagle.

As for James's debut on national television, the game's great popularizer, Dick Vitale—joined by one of basketball's top analysts, Jay Bilas, and the great center Bill Walton—manned the microphones. All were eager to check out a prodigy billed the equal in basketball to Mozart in music.

But before that . . .

Through the eyes of Branson Wright, the *Cleveland Plain Dealer*'s Cavaliers beat man and the only reporter present, we return to one of the most thrilling days of James's yesteryears, May 22, 2002, the date of his secret, totally illegal, stupendously impressive "workout" (really a tryout and, more bluntly, the athletic equivalent of a job interview), conducted at the behest of then Cavaliers coach John Lucas. Just three months after the *Sports Illustrated* cover, James, still a high school junior, scrimmaged on the Cavs' practice floor, then located on the top floor of their downtown arena, against Cavs team members and college prospects whom the front office were considering in the next NBA draft. Once Wright's story hit the newsstands and the Internet, NBA executives—probably smacking their hands against their brows at the franchise's decision to let a reporter view it and go public with a bylined story—fined the team $150,000. The first hundred grand was probably in Column A on the menu of infractions, maybe for violating league rules, plus—sarcasm here, but the Cavs deserved it—bending child labor laws and exploiting a minor. The rest might as well have been for the Cavs' clueless, albeit customary, stupidity and brazen audacity.

Family adviser Chris Dennis and James's longtime father figure, Eddie Jackson, were there too. They had been meticulous in guiding James during his high school career. When James was a freshman, Dennis had shared a videotape of him with basketball camp guru and Adidas sneakers executive Sonny Vaccaro.

Said Lucas: "I went to go watch him play in some AAU games at Cleveland State. I had seen Kobe when he was young, and everyone was telling me how LeBron was a better prospect than Kobe, and I didn't believe them. So I went to watch him play, and I stayed for the rest of the day. And I remember making the comment that he might be better than [Cavaliers guard] Bimbo Coles, but I don't know. People thought I lost my mind. What I saw was that his IQ was off the charts. He obviously had to really work on his shooting. But his passing was already elite."

Lucas's son, John Lucas III, a college point guard at Baylor, who was part of the workout, had the expected reaction to his father's insistence that just down the road in Akron was a young kid who could be the next Kobe, Magic, Michael, or whoever: "Whatever, dad."

He would soon be convinced.

James had been content to pass and blend in at first. Then, Lucas goaded him. The play of the day, a keepsake the NBA veteran and coach would keep in the memory bank for the rest of his life, soon occurred. Said Lucas: "So, you don't want to play with the big boys? You're going to live off all of those damn accolades? You ain't ready."

Said Johnny Clark, a Cavs personnel department executive, "That was when the whole day just took a turn. It was like LeBron flipped on a switch. He just went off for the next two or three [scrimmage] games. He scored all the points and made all of the assists. He took over the whole workout. I was thinking to myself that I'm glad I was here to see this, because if I heard from someone telling me what he was doing, I wouldn't have believed them."

Lucas: "We put in a play called 'series,' and LeBron made the right reads and plays with our guys the whole time. One time he got the ball, split the defenders, and made that signature reverse dunk when the ball went through and it didn't hit the rim or anything. If I write a book, that day will go in my book."

But if you didn't live in Cleveland in 2002 and read the *Plain Dealer* or have Internet connectivity, this was all below your radar. Amid widespread acclaim and pockets of skepticism from those who had never seen a sports prodigy like him, James was expected—even in a team sport, in which James valued his teammates as he would have cherished the biological brothers he did not have—to stand alone and above everyone else, just as the lone eagle had when he flew.

The anticipation that attended James's televised debut reminded me of the aftermath of the NBA-ABA merger in the mid-1970s, when the debt-saddled New York Nets sold their top attraction as well as that of their entire league, Julius "Dr. J" Erving, to the team I covered, the Philadelphia 76ers. Only rarely had the league with the red, white, and blue ball, which Boston Celtics legend Bill Russell said "belonged on a seal's nose," received attention from the alphabet television networks— ABC, CBS, and NBC—that then ruled the airwaves. Dr. J was a word-of-mouth phenomenon, his skills more rumor than substance to most fans. He had gone to the University of Massachusetts, not one of the college basketball television staples, such as UCLA, Kansas, Indiana, North Carolina, Kentucky, or Georgetown. Erving's assignment was merely to do a basketball Triple Lindy, night-in and night-out, to *Star Trek* it and go where no man had ever gone before. In his first NBA season, on his first visit to each rival NBA city, a gameday news conference was held in the host team's arena before often overflowing rows of television and newspaper reporters, eager to see the man who could do never-before-seen acrobatics on the basketball floor.

As for James, he was debuting during a time of perfect synthesis among the 24-hour sports-programming giant ESPN, which would telecast this, his most electric performance, the Internet's transformative iconography through its reach and speed, the still-relevant auxiliaries of the national magazines, and the looming retirement of a fading Michael Jordan at the end of that same 2002–03 season.

The word *performance* is deliberately chosen, for it was just that: one that starred James, and not a game, at least to casual fans. No basketball fan, even though courtside seats at Cleveland State's Wolstein Center were going for $100 apiece, and no media member wanted to miss the coming-out party of the latest candidate for the savior role played so convincingly a generation earlier by Magic Johnson and Larry Bird, and then by Michael Jordan. The NBA's newfound wealth and global reach also would likely take hits without a clear line of succession to Jordan, because all who had auditioned for the role before James had drawbacks.

Allen Iverson was too small. Carmelo Anthony's greatest feat had been bringing Jim Boeheim his long-denied first national championship at Syracuse. He obviously had game, but not at James's transcendent level of strength, smarts, speed, selflessness, and spectacle. Tracy McGrady never got his team anywhere that amounted to much in the playoffs. Vince Carter was an impressive one-trick pony, a human pogo stick who once leaped completely over an upright French player who had barely bent his knees, and dunked in a game at the Olympics. Kobe Bryant couldn't win, at least at the time, until he had Shaquille O'Neal with him.

Of the candidates, Kobe, LeBron, and 'Melo (Carmelo) had the no-surnames-needed recognition that comes with the biggest celebrities like basketball's Magic and Kareem; baseball's Willie and Mickey; golf's Tiger, Arnie, and Jack; and music's John, Paul, George, and Ringo. The hype barkers insisted that James was better than Earvin Johnson had been in high school, doing so without the rabbits and wand conjured up by the "Magic" nickname, which had acted like an open-sesame to the gates of fame. "King" James might have been a nickname popular with theologians and students of Jacobean England, but it lacked the fantasy trappings Magic enjoyed.

To beat Magic, James had to distribute the ball the way Amazon does packages—and score like Jordan or Bird. He might never be as dominant defensively as Kareem Abdul-Jabbar, Yao Ming, and Shaquille O'Neal without their inordinate height (and O'Neal's incredible bulk), but he didn't have to play the way they did. The three-pointer was swiftly reducing the traditional big man to near-obsolescence. Virginia's Oak Hill Academy, the opponent, was less a high school than an elite basketball training camp with a curriculum that in some ways was an NBA 101 course. It had only one player from the year before, but its cupboard was never bare. Fresh talent flocked to the school, figuratively trailing the stars recruiting services awarded them like a comet's tail.

The stakes of the SV-SM vs. Oak Hill game were high. Oak Hill had beaten James's team in two previous meetings, one of them featuring Carmelo Anthony. Oak Hill was the previous season's mythical national champion and the country's top-ranked high school team as things stood in the middle of James's senior season. The Irish were the heirs apparent.

The hype grew collectively for both teams and individually at an even greater level for James personally. It was amped up by the hypersonic babble, hyperbole, and on-air near-hyperventilation of Vitale, who was joined by the celebrated and once-reclusive great Walton. A two-time NBA champion and Basketball Hall of Famer despite the fragile feet that shortened what would have been an even greater career, Walton had the same covenant with his teammates as James. He led, he empowered others, and, most of all, he won.

The NBA desperately needed someone to take attention away from the drug-addled reputations possessed by many players, fairly or not, and from the frequent franchise relocations. Buffalo's eventual move to San Diego set a record for scale of abandonment in sheer distance that could only be topped if, say, the Boston Celtics moved to Guam.

Player good citizenship had not always been a factor with the 76ers, who, during the six years I covered them as the beat man for the *Philadelphia Inquirer*, had acquired one John Quincy Trapp. Q. Trapp, as he was known, brought with him a reputation for missing the commercial flights by which all teams traveled in those days. Such behavior is a red flag to general managers, because drug-induced stupor is often the reason for such tardiness. Trapp, however, had devised a coping strategy: he admitted, according to the Sixers' late play-by-play man Bill Campbell, that he had once avoided a fine for the transgression with an earlier employer by the simple expedient of pulling into the parking lot of a 7-Eleven near the airport and calling in a bomb threat for the scheduled flight. Aghast, Campbell informed Trapp that he would alert authorities quicker than a bomb-sniffing dog with a suspicious package if a Sixers flight was ever delayed by such a threat.

The Oak Hill game, played on December 13, 2002, the week of the *Sports Illustrated* cover, was a prelude for what was to come. James sought to disprove the one regular criticism of his game, his streaky outside shooting, missing his first three shots, all jumpers. Would he stubbornly stick with a failing attempt to prove his point? Was it possible for such a savvy player to go down by relying on his weakest attribute?

James's sputtering start, however, only delayed the moments when Oak Hill would have to endure the effect of his return to the basics of the way he played. This consisted of a startling, if contradictory, mix of a football player's bull rushes to the basket for dunks and the flair and fluidity of his passing. But air power, not ground force, turned the game. The dunk that rocked Oak Hill seemed to have its sources in the myths of Thor's hammer and Zeus's lightning bolts. Late in the first quarter, after a steal by a teammate, James burst down the open court, like a hawk riding a heat thermal. He began to rise, high, then higher still, with his right arm cocked far back from his head, for the dunk heard 'round the gyms, arenas, and playgrounds of the basketball world.

Many outstanding players have a little P. T. Barnum in their heart of hearts. As showmen, they respond to the crowd's roars with renewed energy. That dunk seemed to liberate James from his intent to deliver a tutorial in jump shooting. He found his groove, one only he could cut so deeply into a defensive game plan. No-look assists, behind-the-back, seeing-eye, air-searing assists, touch passes, rip-roaring dunks before a partisan SV-SM crowd—he was Barnum, Bailey, lion-tamer, man on the flying trapeze, and anything else circus fans expected under the big top. The 17-year-old James finished with 31 points in the high school format of a 32-minute game, on 12-of-25 shooting, with 13 rebounds and six assists. So broken were the Oak Hill players that they managed only two points in the final quarter of a 65–45 loss.

"The three *d*s!" shouted Vitale. "Drive, draw [defenders], and dish!" That was a testament to uncommon unselfishness in such an uncommon player.

"I've seen great players," said Oak Hill coach Steve Smith, who proceeded to name them: Kevin Garnett, McGrady, Carter, Jerry Stackhouse (whom he had coached), Ron Mercer, Bernard King, Grant Hill. "This guy is the best I've ever seen."

CBS analyst Jay Bilas seconded that.

Walton, who had lobbied to do the game because he wanted to see the kid for himself, said he had high expectations that were exceeded.

A word about Walton and me: we go way back to a rainy morning in Portland in late 1975, the season before Walton led the Trail Blazers to an NBA championship, beating Erving and the 76ers in the Finals. The NBA courted reporters back then, before it got rich. When I asked when the Finals would start, for example, an NBA spokesman replied, jokingly, "When do you want them to start?"

In a scene that would be impossible today, I was allowed to interview the often-injured Walton in the trainer's room, where he was soaking in a hot tub to soothe his battered body. I found him surprisingly perceptive and witty. After his hale and hearty Trail Blazer teammates finished practice, Walton gave me a ride in his Jeep to a downtown Portland hotel, so I could catch a taxi to the airport hotel where the Sixers, who played the Blazers that night, were staying.

The Walton I knew was anything but the man as whom he was depicted: a campus radical when he was at UCLA for taking part in a protest of the Vietnam War; or a hermit; or maybe as a tall flower child who, like Coleridge's prophetess in "Kubla Khan," had fed on honeydew (and other vegan fare) and drunk the milk (OK, smoked the herb) of Paradise.

After the Oak Hill game, I approached Walton as he and Vitale sat in folding chairs at midcourt, waiting to grade James's game on camera. "Bill, got a minute?" I asked.

"Sure," he replied.

"What did you think?"

Walton, as any halfway attentive music buff knew, was a huge Dead-head, actually going on tours with the Grateful Dead. He knew me to be a wholehearted Rolling Stones fan. "The hardest thing in sports is to produce when everybody is watching you, when everybody is expecting greatness. To have the kind of game he had tonight is something only the truly great ones can do. I'm talking about Jerry Garcia, Mick Jagger, Bob Dylan, and Bill Livingston," he said merrily.

It wasn't on the air, and I didn't include myself in his quote, although I always wondered what the Richter scale might have registered at the moment so many Cleveland basketball fans who were watching the game fell off their couches in unison.

When Walton spoke to James on the air, the first word he said was *Congratulations.*

"Thanks for coming," said James.

"No," said Walton. "Thanks for having me."

Walton, however, was wrong about the hardest thing James would have to do. It wasn't maintaining perspective on the court but accepting that the divine right of kings had been relegated to history's dustbin.

James's senior season, in the wake of the Oak Hill game, became a victory tour. He scored 52 points, his pre-NBA high in a rout of Los Angeles Westchester, a team with future NBA players Trevor Ariza and Bobby Brown. The 17-year-old James, perhaps the most talked about high school player ever, including Kareem Abdul-Jabbar when he was still called Lew Alcindor at New York City's Power Memorial, finished 12-for-25 from the floor and had 13 rebounds and six assists in 32 minutes. He posted these numbers in a game that was shorter by 16 minutes, or fully a third of the 48 minutes in a regulation NBA game, against what was billed as the toughest team he would face before going to college or turning pro next season.

Next, James dominated the prestigious McDonald's All-American Game held on March 26, 2003, at the Cavs' home arena, as a favor to the King. In it, he binged on three-pointers, taunting the press table members, where sat Susan Viniella, one of the *Cleveland Plain Dealer* reporters assigned to cover him, "Keep writing that I can't" he shouted with each swished shot.

After the game, the great UCLA coach John Wooden, then 93 years old, presented James with the Most Valuable Player award after a 27-7-7 line in the East's 122–107 victory. In a telephone interview the next day, Wooden told me he thought James would be "a very good player in the NBA," then adding, "but not right away." It was the right prognosis for the grand scheme of James's professional career but far too cautious on the timeline.

In the audience, at courtside that day was Ohio State's Maurice Clarett, who, on January 3, 2003, scored the winning touchdown in Ohio State's double-overtime upset of Miami in one of the most dramatic college football championship games ever. James and Clarett were close. Clarett was from Warren, Ohio, only 50 miles from Akron. The two comets streaked across the sports section headlines and to the top of the sports segment telecasts. James would become Clarett's pass to a world in which he rubbed shoulders with rappers Snoop Dogg and 50 Cent.

They would not stay close, nor would they experience anything close to matching success.

Problems arose the week of the football game. Estranged from his teammates, openly critical of Athletic Director Andy Geiger, Clarett complained that he had not been allowed to return home for the funeral of a close friend, Juan Bell, who had been shot and killed in an incident in Youngstown involving drugs. Payment by the university for such bereavement travel requires bureaucratic paperwork. Geiger robotically repeated, "The paperwork is simply not there."

Clarett called Geiger a liar. Cleveland Browns icon Jim Brown, who was advising Clarett, called the athletic director a "slave master." Afterward, Clarett would get no mercy from Geiger, from whom the quality of mercy did not "droppeth like the gentle rain," as Shakespeare wrote in *The Merchant of Venice,* but rather rattleth and stingeth like hailstones.

Without his high school coach, Thom McDaniels, father of longtime Bill Belichick assistant coach and current Las Vegas Raiders head coach Josh McDaniels, and his college coach, Jim Tressel, Clarett had no governor on his behavior and no curb to his appetites. Never was the influence more important of the father figures who took James under their wings.

It was a lesson James carried into adulthood. "What really helped me out, becoming a parent, is what I went through as a kid. Not having a dad. I had to learn this s—t on my own, and when I had to become the man of the household at like five years old, I come from a single parent household, you know the story. Just me and my mom. Not only did I want to aspire to be a basketball player, and/or a football player, professionally, I wanted to get my mom out of the situation. I wanted to have kids early to prove to my father that the way you did it was the absolute wrong way to do it. And I wanted to break the mold to where, I wanted to be there and give him [his son] all the life skills. To tell him, you know, this is what your dad went through and this approach, this is how you go through it. And I'm learning. I got three kids, and I'm still learning how to be a better husband and how to be a better father and how to be a better son to my mom. It's all still a work in progress. It's never-ending, bro. All you can do and hope at the end of the road is that you are giving your kids enough life lessons to where when it's time for them to live their life, then they can flourish on their own" (Pablo S. Torre, "Lost LeBron Stories, Part 2," *ESPN the Magazine,* October 18, 2013).

By the spring of 2003, it was clear that college basketball was not enough of a test for James, although his suitors did not give up easily. Among his most serious and ever-hopeful admirers were Ohio State, with James's passion for the Buckeyes' football team considered an advantage; Florida, which boasted nice weather; Duke's collegiate dynasty, with a coach in Mike Krzyzewski who came right into Dean Smith's backyard and reorganized the pecking order; North Carolina and Kentucky, both the sport's grandees; and Louisville, with newly installed head coach Rick Pitino. None of them would land the greatest recruiting prize since Alcindor.

Nor, despite the cachet of football in a state where Paul Brown won everything there was to win from Massillon High School to Ohio State to the Cleveland Browns, would any football recruiter get James's name on a collegiate letter of intent. James's size, speed, and huge, supple, soft hands—hands that would be spared the calloused, hardscrabble life, menial jobs, and low pay of most people like him—caught the eye of future Ohio State head coach Urban Meyer. Then an assistant coach in charge of receivers and a fervent recruiter for Notre Dame, he was attracted by the 16 touchdowns James had scored as a wide receiver in his sophomore year. "Yeah, I was going to change his mind," Meyer said years later, adding, "he did OK without me, huh?"

James had given up football as a realistic possibility after breaking his wrist the summer before his senior year at SV-SM. The risk of injury was too great—though he did not refrain from crediting "me being a football player" as the reason he relished bruising drives to the rim in basketball. For actual contact sport toughness, NFL players considered James's comments a laughable self-delusion.

Yet, for all the care he took to protect his physical soundness, James had no problem gambling with the public perception of his character. He even seemed to enjoy baiting the Ohio High School Athletic Association suits. Of course, by Clarett's standards, it was simply high school high jinks. By his senior year, James, a kid from a broken home, the son of a single mother without marketable skills, was driving the biggest, baddest, most controversy-stirring car possible. The Hummer H2, purchased for the eye-popping price of $50,000, was paid with a loan his mother obtained contingent on the Midas money in his projected salary and endorsements.

It looked like an armored troop carrier and was as much vanity as a customized van. "King James," his self-styled nom de palais royale, was stitched on the upholstered seats. It also sported a television set. This extravagance of ego and expense was an understandable misstep by a teenager who grew up in humble circumstances. So was smoking marijuana, which he admitted to author Buzz Bissinger in the book he wrote with James, *Shooting Stars.*

Just in case the authorities missed the point about James's potential wealth and perceived immunity from penalty, he brought a remote-controlled toy Hummer to courtside before a game and sent it skittering around like a NASCAR winner, cutting "donuts" in the grass near the winner's circle. The scholastic sports rule-makers saw this as a flamboyant nose-thumbing gesture. The OHSAA suspended him for two games and forfeited a single SV-SM victory.

Before one state tournament game, James took a look at the lumbering players on the opposing Firelands team in the rural part of Lorain County and said to the official scorer, nonchalantly, "Put me down for 50." Predictably, resentment of a self-assured young Black man was the reaction in some quarters. But how many teenagers could go from poverty to guaranteed millions and not become as full of himself as the Stay-Puft Marshmallow Man? A more sympathetic and even emphatic take came in his admission to Bissinger, "Did I become too full of myself? Of course. I was a kid."

As for me, I saw only the dawn of days full of promise. I knew who was going to make basketball history, possibly in an unprecedented way, and I would write it in the pages of the *Plain Dealer.*

CHAPTER 4

The Richest Rookie Ever

These were the times that tried men's soles.

Before LeBron James ever played a minute in the NBA in 2003, he was set for life with a $90 million Nike shoe endorsement contract. One of the first people with whom he shared the news was Maurice Clarett, whose own future was past, a result of his season-long suspension, itself a result of his reliably fallible instinct for the wrong decision and voracious appetite for instant gratification. James's spectacular success and Clarett's massive failure would send the latter into a downward spiral of alcohol, antidepressants, pain killers, and, finally, guns and jail.

James, meanwhile, continued to navigate his burgeoning career on his own terms.

The vast majority of marketing executives deplored his decision to sack the highly regarded Aaron Goodwin as his agent after one season, despite how adroitly Goodwin had juggled competing offers from Adidas, Reebok, and Nike, the three companies with the biggest footprints on the boardroom battlegrounds of the sneaker wars. This was not only because Goodwin had done such a good job but also because he was a member of the club of high-profile agents, accustomed to the by-invitation-only auctions of the best and brightest athletes who were on the brink of professionalism.

James instead trusted his future to three friends from the neighborhood—Rich Paul, whom he first encountered as Paul sold T-shirts out of the trunk of his car; former SV-SM teammate Maverick Carter; and another longtime friend, Randy Mims. In 2005, James signed with Paul's boss at the time, Leon Rose of the Creative Artists Agency. Soon, James dumped Rose, too, and made Paul his agent in a fledgling company named LRMR Ventures, for LeBron, Rich, Maverick, and Randy. They called themselves "The Four Horsemen."

"Yeah, the Four Horsemen," said Goodwin, sardonically. "Well, they sure rode my ass of out of town." Goodwin had been at James's side, along with LeBron's mother, Gloria, when Reebok offered a staggering $100 million contract. Reebok's offer included $10 million up front. But the devil is the details.

"When Reebok slid the check down the table, they said, 'Listen, you take this right now, you just promise me you won't go talk to Nike or Adidas. You know, you can take this right now,'" James said on an episode of the *Uninterrupted* podcast, "Kneading Dough," with Maverick Carter.

"And I was lost for words at the beginning. I mean, I flew in from Akron, Ohio, out of Spring Hill, from the projects. I mean, our rent was like $17 a month. And now I'm looking at a $10 million check—and I go back to high school and go back to the classroom the next day. I was going to homeroom the next morning, I'm like, 'Holy s—t.'"

The "Catch-$10 million" was that James had to promise to spurn his other suitors. How many teenagers, much less those from an impoverished background like James, would turn it down? Hell, how many young professionals, seasoned CEOs, or well-funded senior citizens would say to such an offer, "None for me, thanks"? James did just that, reasoning that on learning of the offer Nike and Adidas might counter with $20 million or even $30 million more.

Wrote former *Plain Dealer* Cavs' beat man and current ESPN NBA insider Brian Windhorst in *LeBron Inc.: The Making of a Billion-Dollar Athlete*:

"In the final paperwork from Adidas headquarters in Germany, the company had balked and offered significantly less money guaranteed. There were incentives and royalty offerings that could have made it more than $100 million under certain circumstances, but the guarantee was for less than $60 million. Before Reebok, this would have been an awesome offer. After Reebok, it didn't measure up. Everyone knew it. The air went out of the room.

"Sonny Vaccaro personally apologized to LeBron and his mother. He was crestfallen and demoralized not just because he knew he wasn't going to land LeBron but because he'd looked bad in the process, his bosses didn't back him up. He decided that day he was going to leave Adidas. Within two months he resigned. LeBron flew home thinking about Reebok and that $100 million."

That left Nike. In thinly disguised postgraduation workouts that amounted to another job interview, featuring Michael Jordan, the man with the avaricious sole and the airborne soles, James had impressed one and all. The Nike pitch was massive and included the work of more than 100 employees. Still, the offer wasn't as strong as Reebok—it came in around $70 million.

LeBron, the entrepreneur, left Nike without a deal.

Windhorst: "So, Reebok sent lawyers and executives to LeBron's hometown, thinking they had won the deal. The two continued to negotiate the details, and Reebok even increased its offer to a reported $115 million.

"But at the last moment, Phil Knight gave Nike executives the go-ahead to increase their bid, and LeBron James signed a record-breaking seven-year, $87 million deal that included a $10 million signing bonus."

James's life was changed forever. So was the Cavs franchise. "You have to think of the back end," LeBron later told Windhorst. "I was going to be making a deal for life. You don't think about the first check; you think about all of them."

John Milton wrote in a sonnet about the loss of his sight, "They also serve who only stand and wait." Patience is a virtue. Sometimes, it is more effective to discipline your eagerness, to be forbearing and composed, than to anxiously plunge into the give-and-take of contractual bargaining. Unlike former Seattle power forward Shawn Kemp, who signed an enormous Cavs contract only to quickly turn his body into a facsimile of a Macy's Thanksgiving Day parade balloon, James took the money and worked out ferociously. Unsatisfied with a life of "whipped cream and satin sheets," as the press-box icon Jim Murray wrote (in a column about Muhammad Ali) of the lives of the rich, famous, and well-coordinated,

James instead became the driving force in four NBA championships for three different franchises.

As for the James Gang, Paul now heads the influential Klutch Sports mega-agency. James soon was worth well over $500 million from his endorsements and business ventures alone. Some of the commercials he approved had endearing touches of cleverness. They were designed to highlight different aspects of his personality, most memorably in the "three LeBrons," his alter-ego amigos Young LeBron, Business LeBron, and Old Guy LeBron.

In one memorable vignette, Business LeBron stands at the end of a diving board and, fully clad in a tasteful business suit, closes a deal on his cell phone before executing a dive into a swimming pool of which Olympic champion Greg Louganis would have been proud.

The tsunami of his accomplishments in the NBA that began in 2003, however, meant we ain't seen nothin' yet.

CHAPTER 5

"I Went to the Sorriest Team in the League"

The Cleveland Cavaliers' Ricky Davis was not yet a teammate of LeBron James on March 16, 2003. The draft lottery had not been held. But Davis did let James know what he was in for.

With six seconds remaining in a 122–95 victory over Utah at what was then called Gund Arena, the team's home court, "Wrong Rim" Ricky took an inbounds pass, dribbled away from his bewildered teammates, and deliberately shot at the wrong basket, carefully bumping the ball off the rim for a rebound.

"Wrong Rim" Ricky was an alliterative coinage of which I was quite proud, recalling, as it did, "Wrong Way" Roy Riegels's disoriented run in the Rose Bowl, granting him eternal life on blooper reels. Wrong Rim labored under the mistaken belief that retrieving the deliberately missed field goal attempt would give him the single rebound he needed for his first-ever completion of the statistical rarity of double figures in points, rebounds, and assists—a triple double. The whole misbegotten endeavor was a rim shot, recalling the way the drummer in a band might rap the cymbals after a groaner of a joke. The Cavaliers were themselves a punch line in those days.

The old "Cadavaliers" nickname, coined after the expansion team's 0–15 start in 1970, was exhumed. Undead but unmourned, the same spirit of pie-fight farce rose again in "Wrong Rim's" run to ridicule and revulsion. Suffice it to say, the 2003–04 Cavs were hardly the team the Chosen One would have chosen, had he been able to.

Jerry Sloan, the Utah coach, so old school his plays were probably diagrammed on a hornbook, praised one of his players, DeShawn Stevenson, for retaliating with a hard foul on Davis, which, alas, was not hard enough to knock some sense into him.

"I'm glad DeShawn fouled him. I'd have knocked him on his ass," said the still-simmering Sloan afterward. Sloan's flinty, physical, give-no-quarter defense for the Chicago Bulls had defined toughness. The NBA ruled after the game that the ludicrous rebound would not have counted toward a triple double.

Students of selfish and asinine behavior can debate whether Robert "Bubbles" Hawkins, who played at Illinois State with the estimable Sixers' guard Doug Collins limboed lower than "Wrong Rim" when, racing up behind Collins on a fast break, he stole the ball from his own teammate. Collins said of Hawkins, "Bubbles never shot unless the ball was actually in his hands."

Sixty-seven days later, on May 22, the Cavaliers won the draft lottery and quickly said James would be their number one pick when the selections were made on June 26.

For his part, Roy Riegels does not deserve comparison to a fool like Davis. Riegels, an All-American, had played on both offense and defense for Cal in the 1929 Rose Bowl against Georgia Tech. (The Big Ten champions' now customary berth as the Rose Bowl's visiting team was not even a gleam in the Big Ten commissioner's eye in the 1920s.) Comical as his play was, however, Riegels did not deliberately set sail toward his own goal, unlike Davis toward his own basket; instead, he got turned around after he scooped up a fumble at Georgia Tech's 30-yard-line.

Riegels was tackled 69 yards later on Cal's 1-yard-line, a stride from scoring a two-point safety for Georgia Tech, which does not make for the most flattering assessment of the spatial acuity of the swarm of Yellow Jackets in hot pursuit of him. As it was, a blocked punt from the end zone, set up by the perilous field position Riegels' dash created, gave the southern school an 8–7 victory. Years later, after Jim Marshall, a Minnesota Viking defensive lineman, scored a safety against his own team when he ran the wrong way with a recovered fumble, Riegels sent him a sympathetic letter, which began, "Welcome to the club."

The problem for James was that he was joining a club of knaves and, literally, court jesters. Locked in a race to the bottom with the Cavs for the top pick in a talent-saturated draft, the Denver Nuggets gave it their worst, winning only seven games in the second half of the season, to finish 17–65. The Cavaliers, still ensconced in the league basement by a game despite the Nuggets' bungee jump sans bungee, went into the last night of the regular season at 16–65.

"It was a must-lose game. Naturally, the Cavaliers won," I wrote. The only possible explanation of the 96–86 victory over Toronto seemed that any attempt to explain how odds worked or to instill common sense in the Cavs' players and front office deep thinkers had been, as usual, rebuffed at the hairline.

Instead of having the most ping-pong balls in the Hopper of Happiness or Heartbreak, the Cavs and Nuggets had an equal number because of their tie in fecklessness, the Nuggets having docilely and prudently lost in their finale. The Cavs' victory before a sparse, bemused crowd in Cleveland was the most inopportune display of competence since the Philadelphia Eagles won their way out of the O. J. Simpson derby in 1969.

For pure, dumb luck—emphasis on *dumb*—it was hard to beat the Cavaliers that season. The ping-pong ball bounce that allowed the Cavs to select the best player of a generation marked the first time a team with the worst record, either alone or shared, had won the lottery since 1991.

That night, Austin Carr, a standout on the "Miracle of Richfield" Cavs team of the bicentennial year wept when he heard the result. "Mr. Cavalier," a swell fellow despite his reliance on catchphrases in lieu of much actual analysis on the team's telecasts, now had the giddy prospect of nearly unlimited opportunities to shout that James "throws the hammer down!" Nowhere nearly as often, given James's inconsistent outside shooting, would he get to shout after a made James three-pointer, "from deep! deep! In the [insert name of arena]."

Not a lot was seen of James after he signed with the Cavs until exhibition games began. He did, however, in an ill-considered overreach, agree to take batting practice with the Indians the day after he signed with the Cavs.

James fanned on eight of first nine swings at the slow and slower speed of the batting practice offerings of Cincinnati Reds coach Tom Hume.

The Indians' opponents that night did the batting practice chores. The Indians wanted no chance of injuring James with their own practice pitchers. James nicked one ball robustly enough for it to spin, like a top, in the batting box dirt. Finally lofting a foul ball into the left field stands at Texas Leaguer depth, James theatrically pointed to the distant wall, of which he was about 100 feet short, in a self-deprecating gesture that won most of the fans over, despite the stunt's weak results.

Like Michael Jordan with his anemic .202 batting average during his, ahem, hiatus from basketball—which (wink, nudge) had absolutely nothing to do with Jordan's gambling proclivities, just ask any NBA poohbah, so help him, David Stern—James could pass time far more profitably in games other than the national pastime. Indians' officials, once they got a look at James's swing, were simply glad he did not get hit by the dawdling pitches.

Expectations were so high and crushing that a Nike commercial shot in the Sacramento Kings' arena, the site of James's coming NBA debut, featured not only James and then teammates DeSagana Diop, Dajuan Wagner and Carlos Boozer, who flew with him to the California capital on a private jet. In the commercial, James, guarded by Sacramento guard Mike Bibby, freezes under the pressure of the moment. The camera captures his teammates' worried looks and Bibby's surprise and finds the Sacramento owners, the Maloof brothers, in their courtside seats. Suddenly, James's competitive gears mesh, and he surges toward the basket. The last words come from NBA icon George "Iceman" Gervin, also seated in the stands, who nods approvingly and murmurs praise for the "young fella."

James's first exhibition game was a shoddy one. Nothing that happened in the game at Detroit could surpass the opening seconds when the Cavs inbounded at half court after a Pistons turnover, and the pass went to "Wrong Rim." Demonstrating the hand speed of a three-card-monte dealer and proudly displaying the selfishness and defiance of norms from the triple-double that wasn't, Davis flipped up a wild shot with fully 23 seconds remaining on the clock.

I remembered a similar "Take that!" shot by the Sixers' Joe Bryant, Kobe's father, who, disgruntled with his playing time, launched the ball barely after shucking off his warm-ups and setting foot on the court. It was effectively Bryant's last shot with his hometown team.

The Cavs tolerated Wrong Rim for 22 games before sending him packing to Boston. Any time the Cavs played there that season, Davis would be sicced on James and react like "a mad dog in a meat market," in the words of a Cleveland Browns scout's overblown reaction to a "so what?" linebacker named Mike Junkin. The problem was that James, wearing Michael Jordan's number 23 as he had in high school, had been inoculated against rabid envy.

The Cavs' Island of Misfit Toys included Kevin Ollie, who would coach an NCAA championship team at his alma mater, Connecticut, yet as a guard almost never saw James on the fast break despite television play-by-play man Michael Reghi, howling at his chair at midcourt, "Flight 23, cleared for takeoff!"

Ira Newble was another headscratcher on the roster. He was a Mid-American Conference player from Miami of Ohio, whose mere presence on the floor for the Cavaliers in San Antonio's NBA Finals sweep in 2007 was a clear example of the talent disparity between the loaded Spurs and the Cavs. A fan of music unappreciated by the older generation, Newble once strolled away from coach Paul Silas in mid-tirade as the pair stood in a corridor of Gund Arena. His veins bulging, Silas shouted at Newble in the vicinity of several interested reporters: "Come back here, you hip-hop motherf—r!"

The Cavs also presented their prized rookie another high school–to–NBA player in Darius Miles, who, with the Clippers in 2001, became the first such player to make the first team all-rookie squad. By the time he was acquired for solid point guard Andre Miller, Miles's play was not at the same lofty level. In fact, trading Miller, even if only for a bag of magic beans, was a move to outright tank the season for more lottery ping-pong balls.

Miles had an odd gesture after scoring baskets, tapping both fists against his forehead. Suspicions that this was a signal to the mothership waiting to whisk him to the Andromeda galaxy proved unfounded. Actually, since Miles was too young to go clubbing with his former San Diego Clippers teammates, it was his tribute to the same gestures made by Bobby Brown and Trevor Ariza, his age-group running mates at Los Angeles's Westchester. James had destroyed both of Miles's old pals in his last high school season.

Miles also did not measure up. With hit-and-mostly-miss three-point range, he once so exasperated Cavs' television analyst Matt Guokas, a former NBA head coach, that he said, "He's shooting 27 percent on threes. Why would you even get yourself open there?"

Yet another screwball in the comedy of errors was Jeff McInnis, who, late in the season, upset about playing time, salary, not enough cream in his coffee, or something, put his practice jersey on inside-out and declared himself an "independent contractor."

When the season was over, Carlos Boozer, a member of the previous year's All-Rookie Team, had earned "Early Bird" free agency rights, despite playing only two years. The term comes from the Larry Bird exception. Usually granted after three seasons, Early Bird rights allow a team to exceed the salary cap to retain a free agent.

Boozer swore eternal fealty to the Cavs, even though he wanted to explore the free market to get some idea of his worth. The Cavs, however, lowballed him with their offer, and, when Utah proposed to strap a Brink's truck on the burly power forward's back, he was gone.

I thought Boozer was selfish from the start, not helping out on defense of an opponent driving to the rim and instead staying on the weak side, the one away from the ball, to claim stat-padding rebounds if the opponent's shot went long. After the defection, I got some mileage out of Pinocchio references to Boozer, once wondering how many lies it would take for his nose to reach Salt Lake City from Cleveland.

I also later enjoyed looking at videos of the Knicks' Jason Richardson putting the playground in a play during the Rookies–Sophomores Game on All-Star Weekend by bouncing the ball squarely off the head of his defender, Boozer. "Right between the eyes!" as Kevin Harlan often shouted for swished shots.

All of these skeevy guys were acquired by general manager Jim Paxson, who, in six years at the helm of the listing Cavaliers, had acquired players whose overall record was 185–307 (a 37.6 percent "winning" clip), better than Jordan's batting average, but not even close to mediocre by any reasonable standard.

It was Paxson, for example, who finally okayed the needless risk of exposing Boozer to other teams' offers. "Why does Jim Paxson still have a job?" I said in the lede to an angry column after Boozer's defection.

Paxson never really supported James adequately. In the future, James would note that he had been drafted by "the sorriest team in the league." That went on Paxson, of course. He once solemnly intoned, in feigned fear of the thought of his teenaged son newly seated behind the wheel of a car, "It is my duty to note that my son passed his driver's test today. Be warned. He . . . is . . . on . . . the . . . road."

The real problem was the kid's father was at the wheel of the Cavaliers' organization.

None of it mattered—not the self-doubt and nerves stressed in the Nike commercial, not the nomads, ne'er-do-wells, and never-weres Paxson had collected and with whom he surrounded James. Unlike the Nike commercial, James's Sacramento debut was an individual success from first to last, as he scored 12 of his 25 points in the first quarter of the Cavs' loss. Twelve times, James scored at least 30 points against the grown men, many of them resentful of the teenager and eager to punish him. He scored 41 against the then New Jersey Nets. He had thirteen double-doubles. He was 18 years old when the season started. "This is just unreal," said Chicago's Jamal Crawford, of the way the teenager was dominating grown men.

After Jordan's retirement, LeBron James was possibly the most publicized player in the NBA. I recalled the criticism crusty *New York Daily News* sports columnist Dick Young made of women's Olympic gymnastics when teenager Olga Korbut won multiple gold medals and Nadia Comaneci scored the first perfect 10. Young wondered what kind of sport this was that little girls could so dominate.

Still, it is important to remember exactly how much of a one-off LeBron was as a prom-to-pros figure. Fresh out of high school, he was not just in the rotation but starting; not just starting but starring. Occasionally, sportswriters who should have known better postulated that a very good college team could beat a very bad NBA team. When the Sixers went 9–73, the case for Houston's Phi Slamma Jama collegians was made. It was also made during the Cavs' bumbling in the interregnum between King James's stays that Ohio State, a top-ranked NCAA team going into March Madness, had as its best player Jared Sullinger, a freshman. The Phi Slams, even with future NBA great Clyde Drexler, would have gotten the treatment regrettably advocated in *Private Lives,* Noel Coward's comedy of manners: "Certain women should be struck regularly, like gongs."

Had Ohio State wooed James—who was a huge Buckeyes fan, was heavily recruited by then coach Thad Matta, and was later granted a locker room stall with his nameplate on it to fascinate potential recruits—we might have seen who were the hammers and who the gongs.

Kevin Garnett made the jump to the NBA in 1995. As a big man in the years before the three-point shot became paramount, much was expected of bigs, assumed to be as masterful in the paint as Dutch or Italians with palettes, oils, and canvases. Garnett's rookie per-game stats were 17.8 points, 10.0 rebounds, and 3.7 assists. Minnesota improved by five games from the previous season, finishing 26–56.

Tracy McGrady's line was 7.0, 4.2, 1.5 in 1997–98. Toronto lost 14 more games than in its previous paltry 30-win season. It was 14 years before McGrady was on a team that won a single playoff series.

Kobe Bryant played for a longtime power, the Los Angeles Lakers, who won 56 games in 1996–97 and could afford to bring him along slowly, as his 7.6, 1.9, 1.3 points, rebounds, assists line shows.

In a close vote, James, the first draft pick, edged Carmelo Anthony, taken with the third by Denver, for Rookie of the Year honors. (In between was Detroit's pick in the second spot, a flop of international proportions, Darko Milicic of Serbia). Except in sharing the ball, Anthony's numbers were slightly better than James's. Also, Denver improved by 26 games to a 43–39 winning season. With James, the Cavaliers improved by 17, finishing at 34–48.

The novelty would wear off, but the prodigy would become more prodigious. James was unique. But, given the difference in the Nuggets and Cavs seasons, it is impossible to discount the effect of the hype that surrounded James.

And yet . . . after Jordan's retirement, James was probably the most publicized player in the NBA. But no one in the more than century since James Naismith hung the peach baskets in the YMCA gym in Springfield, Massachusetts, had come so far so fast so soon. It was close to science fiction, with Han Solo in the Millenium Falcon going to the dimension that perfectly described the LeBron James Experience—hyperspace.

Meanwhile, back on this planet, the Czech Republic's Jiri Welsch joined the Cavs the next season. He averaged a negligible 2.9-points per game but made himself memorable by the misguided missile he launched from the corner one night. It bent in majestic splendor, like a sweeping curveball in baseball or a long putt in golf, bouncing anemically in the lane, a few feet from the rim, behind a scrum of players jostling for a possible rebound, none of whom it so much as grazed.

"What the f—k was that?" asked James, voicing the question many of us, in a much larger sense, wondered about the whole Cavaliers' organization.

CHAPTER 6

Payment Due

Of all the rib joints in all the world, they came into James Albert London "Bubba" Baker's.

LeBron James, a season after he was named NBA Rookie of the Year and Braylon Edwards, the first pick of the Cleveland Browns and third overall in the 2005 NFL draft, brought their expectations of celebrity treatment to the Bubba's-Q restaurant in suburban Cleveland. They also brought their closed wallets and, with all due respect to the pork ribs that were the restaurant's signature item, that's where the beef was.

"We'll have a bottle of champagne," James grandly told Brittani Baker, Bubba's daughter.

"This is a barbecue restaurant," Brittani said. "We have beer, iced tea, and soda pop. That's all."

Improvising, she ducked out the door, drove to a nearby state liquor store, and bought an expensive bottle of champagne on her credit card.

The two bon vivants settled for it as the best she could do.

Her father, Bubba Baker, was out of town, attending a food show, spreading the gospel of the good eating that entailed neither muss nor fuss: the restaurant's signature item, boneless ribs, could be eaten with a knife and fork.

Normally, Bubba would have been watching over the family recipes, posing with memorabilia from his playing career and for selfies with customers, and in busy times, he would have been waiting on tables himself. His wife and children waited tables and ran the cash register.

None of them was given anything, not even Bubba, with the leverage of his NFL reputation. They all worked hard. Bubba took meat preparation courses online from Texas A&M University and scouted the famous Central Texas Barbecue Trail with former Houston Oilers' Hall of Fame running back Earl Campbell. When Baker returned from the trip and said he had finally discovered how to make his brisket exactly right, he was as excited as in a game in which he sacked a depth chart full of opposing quarterbacks like bushels of potatoes headed for the market.

After eating as much as members of a wheat-threshing crew might have, James and Edwards balked at the bill. "I don't pay when I'm in town," James said, offended by the very thought of such a lack of gratitude for his presence and Edwards's, the latter to a lesser degree, of course.

Meanwhile, back at the food show, Bubba did not take news of the developments at home well. "They damn sure are going to pay," he snapped.

"My father is a really big man who played in the NFL for a long time," Brittani told the recalcitrant pair. "You do not want to mess with him."

Eventually, Edwards put the bill on his credit card. James never reached for anything but another rib.

The anecdote is regrettable enough in its own right. It would have been understandable in the straitened circumstances of his upbringing, but not with the Nike money in endorsements. Furthermore, it was Black-on-Black exploitation of hardworking people trying to make an honest living. It also figured. James's reputation around town was of a man who didn't pick up checks or put down tips.

Why was he like that? A guess is fear, fear that it could all go away with a snapped tendon, fear that lying crumpled on the floor after a devastating injury could leave him without all he had counted on, the same way he had felt when his mother would vanish for long, desolate days from the bewildered little boy's life. Fear of losing so much when security was so near at hand occasionally brought Gloria James from courtside to storm the barricades.

As a baby boomer who grew up in Texas and—like James for most of his life—as an only child, I knew that memories of the hunger and hardship of the Dust Bowl and the Great Depression never completely left my mother. Widowed at the age of 51, she was always frugal, buying cheap, off-brand canned and packaged foods. When she was dying, she handed me some scissors and had me carefully slit the thick folds at the bottom and sides of the dining room drapes. She had hidden literally hundreds of dollars in them. It had been 30 years since my dad died, in 1965, and 65 years since the banks failed, but if it happened once, it could happen again. She never forgot that it could be gone in a flash. All of it.

I believe that is why James spent so much time and effort establishing a business empire in Los Angeles, including appearances in two movies.

The champagne incident was typical of him as a young player, but not now. Regarding James's fortune, a resentful fan once asked me how much money one man could need. Given where he had been, too much had never been even a theoretical concept.

CHAPTER 7

The Seat He'd Never Sat In

Crickets chirped in a shrill drone in the weeds beside a narrow road under a fierce sun on the outskirts of Megara, Greece, a city almost a marathon's 26-mile distance from Athens. Two men fidgeted beneath the sky's pitiless glare. One was John Tripoulas, an Athenian doctor whose Greek American dual citizenship reflected his youth in Rocky River, Ohio, a Cleveland suburb. I was the other.

Soon in the distant heat haze, a runner crested a hill, holding a blazing torch aloft, followed by two nondescript black cars, all of them headed for John, who was to take the handoff of the 2004 Olympic torch, like a sprinter with a relay baton. In tribute to his grandfather, who had won a bronze medal in the 800 meters at the 1896 revival of the Olympics in Athens, Tripoulas was to run a leg of the torch relay. Noting my unexpected presence, several humorless Greeks, members of the relay's security force, burst from the cars. In the excited gabble of their voices, I realized, although I spoke no Greek, that the authorities wanted to know who I was, where I was from, and what I was doing on that restricted road. John tried to explain that I was a newspaperman, doing a story on him because we both hailed from the same city in America. The cops were uninterested in John, but I was the object of all law enforcement eyes.

Panicking, I began to shout the names of prominent Ohio sports teams, starting with "Cleveland Browns!" Unfortunately, they were not up to speed on the prospects of Jeff Garcia taking over as the NFL team's quarterback. "Ohio State football!" I babbled next, pretending to throw a forward pass, a play on which, as the famous Buckeye coach Woody Hayes once said, "Three things can happen, and two of them are bad." As far as I was concerned, bad was breaking out all over. A security guy had reached the hand-on-top-of-head, insert-miscreant-in-Black-Maria moment. Then I yelped with inspiration born of desperation, "LeBron James! Cleveland Cavaliers!"

"Ooh! I love NBA!" one of the cops whooped. "What is LeBron like?"

And that was my introduction to Worldwide LeBron, teenaged super-hero, a phenomenon the world was waiting to see. Unfortunately, USA Men's Basketball coach Larry Brown was a guy who would tie Pegasus to a hitching post. In the world of the modern athlete and the modern media, with the egos of the former and the voracious appetite of the latter, Brown took the shortest path to discontent. He played James so sparingly that the last part of the box score notation "DNP–CD," meaning "Did Not Play–Coach's Decision," could have been changed to "Coach's Dereliction."

LeBron James had briefly flirted with the idea of turning pro as a high school junior. In any context, by any interpretation, patience was something for others to exercise while waiting for his Highness to show up. It did not go the other way around. A collision was inevitable between James's habitual tardiness and Larry Brown, a man obsessed by punctuality as a result of his college coaching by North Carolina's Dean Smith. Smith had what amounted to a clock fetish. He also coached a chart-everything, don't-color-outside-the-lines style of basketball. His system was so inflexible in substitutions that the joke was "only Dean Smith could hold Michael Jordan below 20 points." That was true in terms of the three seasons Jordan spent in Chapel Hill before making the jump to the NBA, finishing with a collegiate average of 17.7 points per game. But he did hit 20.0 in his second season as a Tar Heel. Still, the image of Smith's program was one of a strict system, rigidly enforced.

In his book, *The Carolina Way*, Smith denounced the selfishness of people who are habitually late, charging that they "think their time is more important than that of everyone else." When I called him to do a column on the book, his phone was busy at the appointed hour. I called it again and again, once every minute, until he answered six minutes after the time we had agreed on for the interview. "Coach, I tried to call you, but your line was busy. I tried again and again," I said.

"I see you read the book," Smith said, chuckling.

Not only read it but to some extent lived it many times I was rousted from bed by my father's words, "Get up, son, you're a day late and a dollar short." No less than Lyndon Johnson's father made the same wakeup call. While it eventually led to the White House for him, all I got was a seat in the Aux Box (Auxiliary Press Box) behind the foul pole at the World Series.

Smith not only set the time by which everyone in the program worked, he also tried, in an understated way, to set the message outsiders took away from it. I asked in the telephone interview if he remembered the time in 1981 when the NCAA Final Four was in Philadelphia, and I had come to the campus to do a takeout (long feature story) on the Tar Heels' program. Smith kept a mental dossier on sportswriters around the country. He always tried subtly to control the direction interviews took, often throwing the questioner off-balance early in the dialogue and slipping his viewpoints in amid the confusion he had sown.

"Oh, I remember you. You were pretty complimentary to Carolina," he said, as I smiled, basking in what I thought was justified praise at the other end of the line.

"But I think you've been pretty hard on Bob Knight," Smith, unprompted in any way, said of the former Indiana coach, player choker, and chair thrower. I spluttered and offered a series of fragmented justifications. I was playing defense for the rest of the interview.

Which of course was the point.

In retirement, Smith still followed the game closely. His former players, even greats like Billy Cunningham and Michael Jordan, sought his counsel. Those who followed him into coaching asked him to attend their practices to evaluate their players. Thus did Smith turn up at Team USA's 2004 Olympic practice facility at North Florida University, home of the Ospreys. None other than Carlos Boozer was selected for Team USA, despite some NBA executives' toxic reactions to the way he left the Cavs. One of my first columns from Ponte Vedra, the resort community near Jacksonville where the team stayed in the lap of luxury, had consisted of flurries of disdainful adjectives, describing Paxson's incompetence and Boozer's untrustworthiness. I concluded by dubbing the power forward "Carlocchio," my take on Pinocchio, whose nose grew longer than Cyrano de Bergerac's beak because of lies.

"I see you're going after Boozer now," Smith said, after reading some of the saltier passages from the column that had been excerpted in that morning's *USA Today*. Although Boozer had played at Duke, archrival and usurper of North Carolina's Atlantic Coast Conference supremacy, Smith proclaimed him "a good guy," adding, "But I know enough not to get into arguments with people who buy ink by the barrel [journalists] and who always have the last word."

"In Boozer's case," I said, "the word is 'more.'"

Brown, however, never tried for more from players like James, Dwyane Wade, and Carmelo Anthony, all of whom, in his jaundiced eyes, were victims of their youth and inexperience. Even before exposure to Brown's closed, deadbolted, and barricaded mind, the players were unhappy in the Jacksonville training camp site, of which James said, "There's nothing to do here."

"There's a whole ocean practically in your hotel's backyard," I said.

"Not allowed to swim in the ocean," James said.

"There is a golf course where the Players Championship, a big PGA tournament, is held," I said.

"Don't play golf. Don't do anything I can't do well," said James, who clearly had learned the lesson of the batting cage debacle.

The mix of bored players, inflexible coach, and growing unhappiness by all parties went public in the embarrassment of Brown's benching of James, Anthony, and Amare Stoudemire in the only exhibition game played in the country before the team headed, in a sour mood, for Europe. The young players' absence did not matter against Puerto Rico in a 95–76 victory, in which the visitors apparently were doing more sandbagging—deliberately playing below their capabilities—than workers at a levee during a flood. But the benching revealed the fissures that were becoming cracks, spider-webbing and trapping one player after another in doubt and dislike of Brown, until finally splitting into gaping crevices between the players and their coach. Under Brown, Team USA was less a reflection of the country's values than an embodiment of its stereotypes—Black kids who lacked discipline and were under the thumb of a boss (in this case, a white coach) who was neither liked nor respected, because he blamed the players for almost everything that went wrong while absolving himself of any responsibility.

Brown's analytical mind could visualize the proper position and role in which an underachieving player could thrive. He could quickly classify the strengths and weaknesses of players. But he seemed to believe he had a messianic message to deliver, showing the world how to play America's Game the right way, Coach Smith's way, his own way. To Smith and his coaching disciples, it wasn't merely a tactic in a game. It was a way of life.

It was also a ridiculous presumption. International basketball had improved exponentially since the 1992 Dream Team took the Olympics by storm and awed opponents, who posed for photographs with them before games. Lithuania had a three-point shot in the air at the buzzer in 2000 in the semifinals in Sydney to beat Team USA, but, quicker than you could say Sarunas Jasikevicius, the lithe Lith who took the shot—which, admittedly, is not all that quickly—it fell short, and a flawed American team won, 85–83. Team USA then beat France by 10 points for the gold medal.

The USA followed that close call by finishing an abominable sixth in the 2002 World Championships in Indianapolis.

Moreover, the rules in international basketball were different than those in the NCAA and NBA, which made for a lot to unpack for young players unaccustomed to the international game. Goaltending, in the form of knocking the ball off the rim, was legal. The trapezoidal foul lane widened near the basket. No longer could low-post centers entrench themselves there, because the wider area often meant they were farther from the rim, and the lumbering bigs had to scoot to get outside it within three seconds or it would be a lane violation and loss of possession. The three-point arc was closer to the rim too, which meant double-teams were easier to execute and low post play less effective. This put a premium on shooting threes, but even with the shorter distance, the Brown-out spread to the team's myopic outside shooting. Team USA made just over five outside shots per game, the lowest of any team in the tournament, and shot only 31 percent, the second-worst in its 12-team bracket.

Somewhere along the way, the bottom line was redrawn by the fealty to the game Brown saw in his head rather than to the one Americans had played on the court successfully for so long. The United States' objectives of Olympic basketball, however, are to win the gold medal, popularize the NBA and its merchandise, and not cause an international incident. Bobby Knight did just that in Puerto Rico, at the Pan Am Games, when he punched a cop after being ejected from a game, leading the country's government to try to extradite him and to Knight's surly rejoinder, "F—k 'em. F—k 'em all. All they know how to do is grow bananas."

The objective in Athens often seemed to be to allow a latter-day Norman Dale, the hard-nosed coach of the movie *Hoosiers,* to lug out the folding chairs for the NBA Olympians to dribble around. In the NBA, however, five-man basketball is often an aspiration and not an attainment. Austin Carr, the Cavs' television analyst, remembers watching a Boston Celtics scrimmage, conducted under the stern visage of Red Auerbach, in which the ball did not touch the floor for the scrimmage's 10-minute duration. Perhaps the gauzy veil of selective recall is at work here. But even if it did really happen, it doesn't anymore.

"Give me stars!" I once cried from the depths of my shallow heart, preferring their supernova explosions over systematic regimentation. I meant stars dribbling and prestidigitating with balls that are almost part of their hands, stars who untether us from the common clay and explore the farthest reaches of human possibility. But I had journalistic nuts-and-bolts reasons to say that, too. It is simply easier to tell one story instead of five.

Could Brown have invented a new way to run the three-man weave, however, he would have used that instead of a supernova like James.

In Europe, the change in scenery did little to lift the 2004 team's malaise, as Germany's Dirk Nowitzki nearly led an upset in an 80–77 Team USA exhibition game victory. As the Olympics drew ever nearer, Italy had its way in a 95–76 exhibition blowout.

With the media, Brown used the bullhorn of his position as a forum for personal grievance, criticism of players by name, second-guesses of the roster, while unwittingly putting his intransigence and insecurities in the open for the whole world to see—all of which made Brown the most apocalyptically wrong choice to coach the 2004 Olympic team since Georgetown's John Thompson in 1988. The latter bungled his way to the bronze medal, devising a defense-first team, just as Hank Iba had done as the longtime Olympic coach.

But at least Thompson, like Iba, had the excuse of coaching teams made up of college players. The problem was outside shooting. The lone sharpshooter who could put some points up for the Yanks on the arc, Hersey Hawkins, was lost to injury in 1988.

The 2004 team lacked veterans of the 2002 World Championships, although, with their almost unfathomable sixth-place finish, the omission might be understandable, albeit at the cost of sacrificing the urge for redemption—unless Brown stifled it. Seldom was a Basketball Hall of Fame coach so respected by so many outsiders and, at least after his Olympic performance, so reviled by those on the inside. He had won an NCAA championship at Kansas by hiring as an assistant coach Ed Manning, whose son Danny was one of the nation's most heavily recruited players. The elder Manning accompanied Brown when the coaching vagabond took the San Antonio Spurs job. Ed Manning was such an astute presence on Brown's bench that he was never a college or pro coach for anyone but Brown.

The Detroit championship team Brown had coached in 2004, moreover, was aided by the feud between Kobe Bryant and Shaquille O'Neal, which tore the three-peat Lakers apart.

In Greece, the thin-skinned Brown determined that Stephon Marbury was the player who had told veteran NBA reporter Chris Sheridan after a 78–60 exhibition victory in Belgrade over Serbia that Brown needed to loosen the reins and let Team USA's athletic advantages flourish. Brown obsessed more on Marbury's perceptive remark, demanding, in vain, that he be kicked off the team, than he did in evaluating the talent he had buried on his bench. And no one was more athletic than James.

Assistant Coach Gregg Popovich—who had been an Air Force Academy player in his youth and would coach the 2020 Olympic team in Tokyo to a gold medal—privately believed the young players offered Team USA's only chance to overcome the close-knit European and South American teams, as well as their own coach. "Pop," as he is known throughout basketball, had been a Brown disciple at the University of Kansas, where he was a volunteer assistant coach and graduated to being Brown's top lieutenant soon afterward. After a two-year stint at Golden State, Popovich returned to the Spurs as the general manager, but he soon appointed himself head coach. Enormous success ensued.

When Duke's Mike Krzyzewski, also a control freak who had played at West Point for field marshal Knight, became Team USA's coach after the calamity in Greece, he sensibly freed the players to play a game above the rim, demonstrating athleticism that revived memories of the Dreamers of '92 and their flights of force and fancy. An unbroken period of American Olympic dominance followed after the coaching change, with James being a willing and forceful participant.

Before the opening game in Athens, the NBA's Commissioner David Stern was fretting about a possible no-Olympic-medals-at-all apocalypse. As I pointed out the increasingly likely second iteration of the 2002 fiasco at the Worlds, Stern softly muttered, "Oh, please God. Not on my watch."

Divine intervention, however, was not forthcoming.

Puerto Rico, playing at a much higher pitch of efficiency and emotion than it had in the exhibition game in Jacksonville, gave Team USA its worst-ever Olympics defeat, 92–73, in the opener. Another loss in group play was to the Lithuanians, 94–90. A loss to Spain in the medal-round opener, the tournament's quarterfinals, would mean the birthplace of basketball would win no Olympic medal for the first time ever.

The fortunately uncashiered Marbury scored 31 points in a 102–94 victory over Spain, which looked and felt like an upset. James, now the Reluctantly Chosen One, as far as Brown was concerned, played only seven minutes, missing the two shots he took. He nearly posted "zeroes across," as the scorekeepers call a whole bunch of nothing from a player. It had to be the most humiliating experience of his life on a basketball court.

The Americans' quest for gold ended in the semifinals, when James played all of three minutes, made a three-pointer, and was an inconsequential part of an 89–81 loss to Argentina.

Like the NCAA had in the years before it learned better, the Olympics held a third-place—or bronze medal—game. Such enormous anticlimaxes used to be called consolation games, although they provided little of it. The bronze-medal game ended in a 104–96 victory over Lithuania, avenging the earlier defeat. It was also an emphatic final display of the disarray and incompetence of the entire ramshackle American enterprise. On the court, the Yanks survived a barrage of their opponents' 21 three-pointers made in 37 attempts.

Off the court, the follies had continued. Both Team USA and Lithuania showed up in white uniforms. The game clock, set at 40 for the minutes remaining before tipoff, ticked down to zero as confusion reigned. After being reset at 40, the clock ticked down again, until Team USA reappeared, clad in red. The Americans had made the mistake. Few were surprised.

The uniforms must have matched the shade of Stern's face, for afterward he insisted on a bigger organizational role for the NBA in future Olympics. USA Basketball was most responsible for the 2004 mess and most of those that preceded it. Stern had two clear agendas: make sure people understood he loved the way his players handled themselves and make sure he let them know Brown had disappointed him.

Brown never stopped trying to distance himself from responsibility and blame, to protect his own legacy and reputation.

"Sometimes the historical ways to motivate a team don't necessarily play out quite as well when you're in an international setting," Stern said. "This was a team that was put together, by everyone, including the coaching staff. So, I don't buy the 'well, I'd like to have this, I'd like to have that,'" meaning the griping by Brown.

Stern said, "It's not about who didn't come. You take your team to the gym and you play with what you got and then you either win or lose. This whining and this carping is not fair to those who are representing their country admirably and well."

Overall, James averaged only 11.5 minutes per game, although he got into all eight. He had a 5.4-point scoring average. Even then, he led the team in field goal percentage on bulling, barreling drives, finishing at 59.4 percent. As for points, Iverson at 13.8, Tim Duncan at 12.9, and the outspoken Marbury at 10.5 were the only double-figures scorers.

I thought of the 76ers' ticket campaign in 1976, emphasizing the newly acquired Dr. J and the way his creative play figured to bring spectators out of their seats, screaming in jubilation. "Buy the seat you'll never sit in," the slogan said. LeBron James, a player who was already a household name in provincial Greece, followed wherever there was a basket and a ball, had the seat he'd never sat in. In a way, his unused triple-threat scoring, rebounding, and passing skills showed in their absence how valuable he might have been.

While James might have been slow to adapt to the Smith-Brown emphasis on timeliness, as the 2004–05 NBA schedule was released, he pointedly noted the game scheduled for the night before Thanksgiving, when Brown and the Pistons made their first visit to Cleveland. No thanks would be given, nor any mercy. He buried Brown's team, scoring 43 of the Cavs' 87 points while he was on the floor, outscoring Prince on their individual matchup 43–4, in a 92–76 victory. Gone was the LeBronze nickname. "He was great, not good. Great. We're running out of superlatives for this guy, " said Paul Silas. "Sou to eipa," as a cop in Megara, Greece, could have said: "I told you so."

CHAPTER 8

The Player on the Wall

When the Cleveland Cavaliers charged out in 1970 for the start of their NBA first season, they tripped and fell on their faces. Fifteen straight times.

As bad went to worse and worse to a historic assault on the concept of basketball, coach Bill Fitch was stopped at the entrance door before a road game by an overly officious security guard, who, before granting admittance demanded proof of his identity. "Why would anyone lie about being the Cavs coach?" Fitch's pristine logic earned him quick admittance.

Thirty-five years later, by the dumb luck of a lottery ping-pong ball's bounce, the Cavaliers were possessors of LeBron James, a superstar with global name recognition who only figured to get better in his third NBA season, because he was not even 21. Yet some of the events within the franchise still dumbfounded outsiders, not because of the won-lost record but because of the mood swings of new owner Dan Gilbert, a man who thought a whoopee cushion was comedy gold. Fans believed that Gilbert, a free spender, surely would bolster James with players other than the gang that couldn't shoot straight. If you wanted to add "could pass, rebound, and defend to NBA standards only intermittently," it would have been true too.

James was used to being a big name, but just how big he had become was obvious after a practice early in the 2005–06 season. He pointed out a window of the Cavs' arena and said to Larry Hughes, the latest candidate to be James's wingman, "Take a look at that little picture of me on that building." It was little compared to the pyramids along the Nile, anyway.

It stood 110 feet high and 225 feet wide and covered 24,750 feet in all. Unveiled on November 8, 2005, the huge photo decorated the wall of the Sherwin-Williams paint company's world headquarters. Taken during his rookie season at a home game against Philadelphia, the photo captured James in full MJ mode, all Jordan-aired, wearing the retired icon's No. 23, soaring into the Jump Man's troposphere, throwing a dunk down that would send Thor scurrying to the Valhalla foundry for a bigger hammer.

Beneath the photo, but above the Nike swoosh, were the words *We are all witnesses.* It made James the franchise's one true article of faith. The language, from tent revivals and traveling salvation shows, preaches the gospel according to James in the high church of basketball.

On the flip side was Gilbert, with his huge ego, thin skin, mood swings, and late night Krakatoas of rage. The latter went flaming out at his critics in Comic Sans Serif. Gilbert was big on stage props. He brought a huge clock to the news conference to introduce Mike Brown the first of the two times he hired him as coach. It was a reminder that everyone, particularly Brown, was on the clock as far as turning the sorriest team in the league into the strongest. Brown had better win now. Sooner, if possible.

Brown's boss in his first term with the team was the new general manager, Danny Ferry. A Duke graduate who had starred on Mike Krzyzewski's NCAA 1986 runner-up, Ferry was smart and thoughtful, with strong basketball bloodlines from his father, the former Washington general manager Bob Ferry, one of the NBA scouts at the Akron Central-Hower-St. Vincent-St. Mary game. Unfortunately, Ferry also brought to his front office post a lingering whiff of failure. He was the estimable former general manager Wayne Embry's most colossal draft miss. Ferry was the player who spent a year in Rome on a fat contract rather than test the NBA, the player who would have to fill the colossal void left by the panic trade of Ron Harper on rumors of financing drug deals in his hometown of Dayton, for which he was never indicted. Ferry had been part of the Cavs' gameday rotation on the strong Lenny Wilkens teams of the late '80s and early '90s, but not a key part. Questioned after Ferry's rookie year in 1989–90 about his limited playing time, Wilkens said, tartly, "I gave him all the minutes he could handle, OK?"

One of the biggest physical and emotional boosts to the season was that 7'3", 260-pound Lithuanian center Zydrunas Ilgauskas, for the second straight season, was able to handle all the minutes Mike Brown found prudent to give him. Enormously popular with the fans and his teammates, Ilgauskas had been a member of the 1997 All-Rookie Team. In the NBA draft before that season, he joined Ukraine's Vitaly Potapenko as Cavs' picks while all of Cleveland's Slavic Village presumably celebrated into the night. "Magnum PI," I termed them, which caught on with Gordon Gund, who used it in a news conference once with a glance in my direction.

Those days were past, part of the previous century, but to "Z," as he was usually called, it probably felt a much longer time ago in a place far, far away. He suffered a series of injuries to his left foot. Once, he broke down, weeping, in the locker room, certain his career was over at the age of 25. After one complicated surgical procedure, he joked that he had "more hardware in [his] foot than Home Depot." Eventually, he underwent radical, last-chance surgery, in which the foot was reshaped, and the accompanying rehabilitation exercises were as much torture as therapy.

Z was close to James. He was a critical presence on the court with his shot-blocking, rebounding, and ability as a "stretch [very] big" to make threes. For his career, he made just under one-third of his threes, the same number of points as one half of shots from inside the 23-foot, 9-inch arc. For example, four of 12 threes and six of 12 twos both amount to a dozen points.

In the locker room, Z was a quiet, studious man, often reading at his dressing stall before games. He was a calming influence on the younger players. His ease with his second language surprised everyone. Once, at the team's practice facility in the southern suburb of Independence, Ilgauskas, seated on the edge of the basket support and looking my 5'11" self straight in the eye, discussed his new weapon, the hook shot, a dusty relic last used with great success by Kareem Abdul-Jabbar. Z's hook was not a majestic, skyscraper of a shot like Kareem's. "I know it is not aesthetically pleasing, but it goes in," Z said.

I've never heard any other player use the word "aesthetically," although I did once hear former 76er Eric Money discuss adaptation as the basis of Darwin's theory of evolution—you never knew what currency a man named Money might bring to a discussion.

Unfortunately, there were no other pleasant surprises. The long-awaited wingman for James, free agent signee Larry Hughes, whom James praised with apparent sincerity when he arrived, would prove unhappy in James's shadow. The reaction seemed endemic among those cast as the second banana. Hughes shot only 34.9 percent overall but 43.4 percent from the three-point line. That oddity was offset by how prone he was to injury and how relatively inconsequential were his rebounds and assists.

Later, before Hughes embarked on a vagabond career that saw him play with eight teams, he complained that he wanted clear-outs on one side of the court just as Brown game-planned for James. In terms of exaggerated self-importance, Hughes could have given Edgar Jones, who played 79 games for the Cavs in the 1980s, something to chew on. Unforgettable in appearance because of his missing front teeth, lost to an opposing player's elbow in a college game years earlier, Edgar made a surprise appearance at Jerry Tarkanian's office at Nevada-Reno, rarin' to play basketball although, oops, his scholarship was to Reno. In the NBA, he once observed, "You got to know your limitations . . . and I don't have any."

Better production came from the other free agent signees, Donyell Marshall, a power forward with a three-point touch, and Damon Jones, who was not Steph Curry but carried himself with the assurance of Curry's clone.

Because of the confidence imbued by the winning season the previous year and its effect on the team, because Brown was not Paul Silas, because the big ticking clock gave urgency and focus to his play designs, because Ferry was not Jim Paxson, and because James was for real, the Cavs did not have to sweat out making the playoffs. They finished 50–32, the third-best mark in franchise history, behind only 1988–89's 57–25 and 1993–94's 54–28. Both teams had lost early-round playoff series on closeout baskets by Michael Jordan—at the buzzer in the fifth and final game in 1989's first round and under far less dramatic circumstances in a conference semifinal sweep in 1994. "We were beaten by greatness," said Embry of both shots.

The upcoming series with Washington has not become as big a part of James's lore as it should have. It went six games. Three of the Cavs' four wins were by a single point. The last two games went to overtime. Buzzer-beating drives by James won two of those. The aggregate score was Washington 610, Cavs 609.

Throughout the series, it seemed James played as big as the Sherwin-Williams wall. This time, greatness was in a Cavaliers uniform.

CHAPTER 9

A Prodigy's Wizardry, an Owner's Fart Machinery

The Cavaliers made their first playoff appearance in this century without LeBron James on the team in 2023. They won 51 games, the most since the 2016–17 season. Widely perceived as a team on the rise, viewed by many pundits as the third-best in the NBA East, the Cavs were snapping at the heels of the NBA East's power pair, the Milwaukee Bucks and the Boston Celtics, for much of the season. They boasted two All-Stars from the previous season in point guard Darius Garland and center Jarrett Allen and a member of the NBA's 2023 All-Defensive first team, forward Evan Mobley. They had the 71-Point Man, Donovan Mitchell, one of only seven men ever to score 70 or more points in a game, who twice had been a vivid playoff presence with his former team, the Utah Jazz.

They were the fifth seed, holding home-court advantage in their first-round series against the sixth-seeded New York Knicks. Felicitously, this gave the Cavaliers the perfect platform for their reemergence as a force to be reckoned with. Start spreading the news, along the Great White Way and in Madison Square Garden, the most famous basketball arena in America, tell it to Spike Lee in his Knicks hoodie at courtside and the other glitterati, the Cavs were going to be a part of it in N-e-e-e-w York, N-e-e-e-w York!

Or not.

To say they underperformed is to say one of the hapless Cleveland Browns' biggest draft-day whiffs, Johnny Manziel—of the "This round is on me" Manziels, in his zealous pursuit of a lifestyle that was, to crib a line from the movie *A Thousand Clowns*, "a little to the left of 'Whoopee!'"—was a wee bit disappointing. The Cavs lost in five games. They played the two in New York in a manner reminiscent of a deer in headlights. In the most critical game, the fourth, New York took a 3–1 lead when Mitchell shot 4 for 18 and scored an inconsequential 11 points.

I remembered what 76ers coach Gene Shue said about his team's burgeoning talent, high-strung shooting guard, Doug Collins, before his first-ever playoff game in the 1975–76 season: "I was afraid Doug would go up and up and just jump completely out of the gym."

But there was no fear of opening-night jitters, at least as far as James was concerned.

Nothing speaks as loudly as James's first playoff series against the Washington Wizards in April 2006. He went into it unproven under such pressure. He came out unshakeable in crisis, unflappable before the footlights, unintimidated by the stakes, and unmatched as a prodigy in all basketball history.

For that reason, this book will devote more attention to that series than most of the other first-round series in James's career. Replacements for game-by-game recaps even in later series or NBA Finals will be those games that created lasting impressions of James's greatness and/or his teammates' ordinariness, plus his pursuit of excellence by layering the strata of improved skills on the bedrock of his power and his way of uncluttering the scree of driving lanes and prodigy-intensive defensive schemes with the intangible of his high basketball IQ.

Game 1, at Cleveland, Cavaliers 97, Wizards 86

He scored 32 points in a solid opening game victory at home. "If LeBron James had butterflies before his first-ever playoff game," I wrote, "they were monarchs."

If that was a little over the-top, even for the self-proclaimed King, he would validate the praise. That "godding up" tendency was hard to break around James. Especially in home games at the altar of the High Church of Basketball.

Game 2, at Cleveland, Wizards 89, Cavaliers 84

In an ugly game in which both teams shot below 40 percent from the floor, the difference in Washington's 89–84 victory to wrest home-court advantage away from the Cavs was the trey, an unholy trinity to purists, like the late Celtics coach Tom Heinsohn. Over pregame coffee in Boston years later, the man known in his playing days as "Tommy Gun" confided he longed for the return of the big man and the offenses predicted on getting the best shot available for the biggest player on each team. Washington's 24 points on 8-for-20 shooting on the arc and the Cavs' puny nine points on 3-for-12, showed what threes in near-triplicate could accomplish.

Game 3, at Washington, Cavaliers 97, Washington 96

Tied 1–1 in games and down a point at Washington, James brought the ball down the court from the Cavs' baseline with 23.4 seconds left to play. Gilbert Arenas, whose reign as a superstar was deserved but also very short, made a double-team feint, then slipped back into Washington's zone defense. It wouldn't have mattered. James would have duped him as easily as he lost Antonio Daniels at the free throw line, as razzle met dazzle with his between-the-legs crossover dribble. Occurring in eyeblinks and heartbeats of time, force met flesh as James barged down the lane where 6'8", 248-pound Michael Ruffin confronted him.

In a percussive twist on celebratory chest bumps between joyously leaping teammates, the two collided in midair. Daniels, now standing behind Ruffin's shoulder, flailed his arm vainly, like a semaphore signaling, "Take cover immediately." Rocked by the contact with Ruffin, James tapped a last reserve of strength, slinging the ball like a farmer with a bale of hay into the feedlot. His two-handed shot slapped against the backboard and went in either before or after he landed. Even on video replay it is hard to split the seconds precisely enough for anyone to determine whether James landed before he released the ball or not.

Washington would insist it was the former, which is a traveling violation. Mike Brown would complain about an uncalled foul on Ruffin.

The score would stand, with 41 of the Cleveland points scored by James. They were the most ever in a first-round playoff game at the time.

Game 4, at Washington, Wizards 106, Cavaliers 96

After a spectacular first half, with first-round playoff records for points in the first quarter (18) and first half (25), James overcompensated for occasional double-teaming, turning from dominator to facilitator. He missed the three shots he took in the third quarter and finished with 38, modest after his rip-roaring start. James committed seven turnovers, including four offensive fouls. After one whistle against him in the fourth quarter, he put his palms up and mouthed, "What did I do?"

Wizards coach Eddie Jordan had spent the off-day complaining about the preferential treatment James received from referees. It worked. "I've been called for more offensive fouls in this series than all 82 games combined, probably," James said. James's Washington counterpart, the quirky Gilbert Arenas, made the difference by reversing the sequence of Robert Louis Stevenson's Gothic novella by making a Hyde and Jekyll transformation during the game. After going 1 for 9 with six points in the first half, Arenas changed his shorts. "Bad luck," he said, dismissively, of the first pair. In the second half, he was 7-for-11, 4-for-5 on the arc and scored 28 of his 34 points.

Beware the (under) wear!

Game 5, at Cleveland, Cavaliers 121, Washington 120 (OT)

Michael Reghi, the television play-by-play man Dan Gilbert inherited with the ownership, had been fired in order to hire Fred McLeod, a favorite of Gilbert's from Detroit. Also sacked was the excellent analyst former NBA head coach Matt Guokas, apparently for insufficient homerism, to be replaced by Austin Carr.

A nice man, Carr soon proved to be king of catch phrases but pauper of substantive information. Into disuse fell Reghi's description of James as the "L Train," rumbling to the rim like a Chicago Transit Authority local through the Loop. Game 3 had been decided by that kind of power. Game 5 would be won by the express.

With 3.6 seconds to play and the Cavs trailing by a point, Hughes inbounded in the forecourt to the L Train, whose firebox had already been stoked. James took the pass at full speed on the left side of the court against a defense stretched to the breaking point by the elegant design of Mike Brown's last play. Stationed in the right corner was Flip Murray, on the right-wing was Damon Jones, and at the top of the arc in the middle of the floor, was Donyell Marshall—three-point bombardiers all.

The Wizards had to devote a defender to each, which drew most of the team away from the rim. James wheeled down the left baseline, dribbling with his off hand, his left, past Antawn Jamison, who declined to take a charge although James had scant maneuvering room, staying inbounds by the measure of toenail after a good pedicure. This is called playing matador defense, letting the bull pass with a swirl of the cape while its lethal horns nearly rip the fellow's trousers. Once past Jamison, James was able to swerve into the lane for a right-handed layup, with Ruffin again arriving too late to stop the show.

After the game, Brown settled into his chair at the interview room dais, ready to discuss his strategic masterpiece, James's continuing beat-the-clock brilliance as a result of it, the insanely tight games and—zounds! What were those sounds? Underneath Brown's chair was apparently a leaky methane pipeline, issuing in different keys, what seemed to a perplexed Brown to be terrible, pants-splitting farts. The interview room podium's microphones did not pick up the sounds, although Brown was clearly discomfited by them.

The culprit was none other than the Littlest Tycoon, Dan Gilbert, who stood at the back of the packed room, thumbs twiddling with a remote-controlled fart machine.

Who knew such a device existed? Why would anyone spend time and money—about fifteen bucks, fart noise batteries not included? An age-appropriate notice said that its target audience was "kid."

Gilbert's compulsive meddling and impulsive childish tricks became at first annoying to James, then, later in his career, antithetical to the strict, structured practices and painstaking preparation to which he readily adapted with the Miami Heat. Habitually tardy in his first years in the NBA, James became such a stickler for punctuality that Dean Smith would have approved. In later years, he even decried on Twitter the often-late starts to Cavs practices of David Blatt, a coach who made his name in European basketball.

In a different bit of less ridiculous but still juvenile behavior, Arenas held an impromptu pregame news conference to announce that he was going to be on the cover of the PlayStation videogame NBA Live 08. A second-round draft pick (the 31st pick) in 2001, Arenas seemed to mingle the video fantasy with the hardboard reality. He was a legend in his own mind and had the joystick to prove it.

Game 6, at Washington, Cavaliers 114, Washington 113

The atmosphere at the Verizon Center was charged with cheers and jeers. One sign brandished by a fan cleverly captured the belief in the District that James had traveled on his winning shot in the third game: "LeBron, how was your flight? We know you love to TRAVEL."

The game that unfolded determined who left a lasting imprint on opponents, who was the face of not only of this playoff series but the meetings between the teams in the next two seasons, who lived his dreams for real, and who lived them vicariously through a teenager's videogame.

Arenas scored 36 points, James 32, but the crucial moment came in the last 13 seconds, when the Cavs, trailing by a point, 113–12, seeking to foul anyone but Arenas, fouled the Wiz whiz under the pressure of the clock. Gilbert shot 82 percent, a solid number, which might not put him among the elites at 90 percent and more but was still well above the 75 percent NBA average. He missed the first, leading James to stroll over and murmur, by James's account, "If you miss this one, y'all are goin' home."

Arenas had a different version.

"LeBron said, 'If you miss these, you know who will end the game,'" Arenas said. "It was a running joke about Damon Jones. I kept calling him 'sweet' and forced the Cavs to bench him in Game 5, because anytime he was on the floor, I went iso,"—a one-on-one isolation set with no help available for Jones—"so, he was benched the whole game. So, LeBron was saying if I missed, I know who will finish the game, so they subbed Damon Jones in. LeBron fakes like he was driving left, so I stepped up and he passed the ball to the corner to Damon Jones, and f—king Damon Jones hit the shot like that f—ker said."

Arenas was wrong about the sequence. James, on the right side of the court, swung the ball to Hughes, on the left, who found Jones, who, with every Wizard except Dumbledore of Hogwarts keying on James, was so open that he had time to scrape the floor with his right foot, seeking the three-point line, which was, with apologies to Arenas, his sweet spot.

Jones swished his shot. Caron Butler missed from 26 feet at the buzzer for the Wizards. The Cavs had won.

After hectic minutes of rewriting and filing my column at courtside, I headed to the locker room, knowing I was too late for the comments from both teams' coaches and players in the interview room. Damon Jones, basking in his moment, clearly meaning to stay until the last question from the last reporter, was finishing his answer to a Washington reporter's query. I leaned in, scribbled a couple of his quotes in my notebook, then turned to the only other player in the room, James.

"Your reaction, LeBron?" I said, frantically.

Bending to flick a mote of dust off his shoe, James said, after straightening up and heading for the door, "I'm done, baby."

Oh, but he wasn't!

With only one day off to travel home, then to Detroit, the Palace of Auburn Hills, the Cavs were exultant, but exhausted.

In a way, the coming semifinal series was fitting. The Pistons were the team that had blocked Michael Jordan on his way to his first NBA championship. They were the proudly self-styled "Bad Boys," who defiled basketball by mugging it.

James's only measure would be Jordan, just as Gilbert's was to his fart machine.

CHAPTER 10

The Last, Best Hope of an Underdog

When the Detroit Pistons were across the Michigan state line in Fort Wayne, Indiana, they were called the Zollner Pistons for owner Fred Zollner, whose company made the automotive parts. It had the feel of Chico's Bail Bonds, the sponsor of the Bad News Bears. It was proof of what Jerry West said during his years that the NBA was "a minor league that called itself major league."

It was hard to get to Fort Wayne. Players took a train and got off at the Green Parrot Cafe, which, despite the name, was located in South Whitley, Indiana, and not a pirates' lair. There, they waited for another train to Fort Wayne, 26 miles away. It was like the whistlestop in the 1960s sitcom *Petticoat Junction*, only without the pretty girls and with a parrot.

Zollner moved the team to Detroit in time for the 1957–58 season, hoping, apparently, to get a bump in the (small p) piston business in the (capital P) Pistons' new home. At the time, Ford was on the cusp of the introduction of the Edsel. The Pistons became a flop of almost equal proportions for years. That was then, however. 2005–06 was now.

The Cavs–Wizards series had almost been a dead heat. The term describes the state of the Cavs, who had been through the fires of the franchise's first playoff series since 1998 and were nearly mortally tired and fully mentally fried. With one day before the conference semifinals started in Detroit, the Cavs went through a light practice at their home arena, the Q. The Cavs had no separate practice facility like the one, to his credit, Gilbert built in Independence in the southern suburbs, far closer than downtown Cleveland to James's mansion in Bath Township.

A rock concert was scheduled for that afternoon at the Q, with the music ending as the Cavs were beginning practice. The Q had no elevators reserved for the press or players. I remember excited fans at one stop that day screaming "Zeeeee!" when the doors opened to reveal what resembled a cattle pen filled with reporters, coaches, players, and the unmistakable presence of Zydrunas Ilgauskas at its rear, towering over everyone.

Afterward, the players still had to get to the Palace in Auburn Hills, the Pistons' new home, even farther from downtown Detroit than their previous one in a large domed stadium that looked like a blister, which they had shared with the NFL's Detroit Lions, the Pontiac Silverdome.

2006 EASTERN CONFERENCE SEMIFINALS
Game 1, at Auburn Hills, Pistons 113, Cavaliers 86

The game began only 40 hours after the Cavs closed out Washington. Under the direction of new coach and Cleveland-area native Flip Saunders, the Pistons had eliminated the Milwaukee Bucks in five games and followed that with a day off and two days of practices. Physically, they were the polar opposite of the drained Cavs. The Pistons oozed confidence. The callow Cavs were still fighting the satisfaction of getting out of the first round.

The Pistons had won the NBA championship in 2003–04 under the direction of the Olympian Maestro of Missteps, Larry Brown. They reached the finals the next season, losing in seven games to San Antonio. The team was understandably distracted by rumors that Brown was, in a tone-deaf move even for Gilbert, under consideration to be the Cavaliers' president of basketball operations. Brown had been released from his Detroit contract because he would not disavow his interest in the job. Why Gilbert thought Brown's Olympic debacle and estrangement from James was just the tonic for his LeBron-centric team requires almost an unimaginable leap of illogical thought.

The opener went as predicted. "It was up to us to jump out early after the [difficult] first round they had," the Pistons' forward and defensive stopper Tayshaun Prince said. "I think they had some tired legs."

"They're going to sweep the rest of the playoffs if they play like this," said James, whose team shot 50 percent in the first half, committed a usually absorbable six turnovers, and trailed by 22 points in what became a rout. James scored all of his points in the first half, when the Cavs seemed helpless to stop the flares and blares of the noise explosion from the stands as the Pistons cannonaded them with 10-for-11 shooting in the half from the three-point arc.

"They made 15 threes. What chance did we have?" said power forward Donyell Marshall, who also credited Detroit's vastly greater edge in playoff experience: "Detroit has the knowledge from winning a championship two years ago and going to the championship last year. I think their knowledge is going to overtake our youth right now." Marshall was furious when his comments were taken as a concession speech by many. It was not an unreasonable assumption, because his words were the rhetorical equivalent of raising a white flag.

For his part, Mike Brown looked at the result with the proper touch of wry humor. "I'm glad cumulative points have nothing to do with deciding this series," he said. Of course, Brown was right. On network television, analyst Hubie Brown was trying to keep the audience interested in the final minutes. "The Cavaliers have to understand that they have only lost one game," he said.

Game 2, at Auburn Hills, Pistons 97, Cavaliers 91

It would soon be two. Significantly, the margin of defeat for the Cavs was far smaller.

Long, rangy, wiry, and strong, Tayshaun Prince guarded James with, as the Pistons forward said, "zone principles behind me." In the less esoteric world of amateur basketball, there is a defense called the box-and-one, the box being four defenders in a rectangular spread, playing a zone and covering nearby areas of the court, the one being the team's best defender with his mission being the sticker on the bumper, the stamp on the letter, the shadow on James's smile. Adding to Prince's deterrence was his 7'2" wingspan on a spindly, stringy 6'9" frame, which made his arms seem even longer and more intimidating.

Frankly, he needed a *schtick*, a Yiddish word that meant a characteristic trait, a gimmick. Shot-blocker Marvin Webster had the great nickname:

"The Human Eraser." Shot-blocker Dikembe Mutombo had the finger-wagging, chiding refrain, "No, no, no," by which he reprimanded players who had foolishly challenged him, to their regret.

Prince's chasedown block on the Pacers' Reggie Miller, the best player in Indiana's franchise history, in the final minute of Game 2 of the 2004 Eastern Conference Finals simultaneously kept the game from being tied, the Pistons from potentially falling into a 0–2 hole, Detroit's dream alive of the NBA championship they won that season, and the Pacers from reaching their first NBA Finals since 2000. Because of James, the Pacers are still waiting to reach another Finals. Prince's block would not have happened had Miller not, first, taken a couple of short, choppy steps to align himself for perfect layup position and, second, tried a layup instead of a dunk.

After contemplation of that swat, I was in favor of lifting the nickname of an excellent defensive infielder in the formative days of baseball, Bob Ferguson, aka "Death to Flying Things," and applying it to Prince. It, however, didn't catch on.

In addition to his strong defense for most of the second game, Prince made James work on defense, as the Pacer scored 20 points. The Pistons' leading scorer, with 29, was Rasheed Wallace, soon to be known for his oratorical flourishes as much as his play.

The Cavs surrendered 13 straight points in the first quarter, and Mike Brown showed his desperation by using the "Hack-a-Shaq" intentional fouling strategy, named for the free throw line incompetence of Shaquille O'Neal, on Detroit center Ben Wallace. It seemed an admission that the Cavs could only stop Detroit with gimmicks. Another rout seemed unavoidable, until the Pistons decided three quarters of exertion were enough to polish off the playoff newcomers. "We got lax. We came away from our defensive scheme, and LeBron started to hurt us," said Chauncey Billups, the Detroit guard whose stature on the team was reflected in his nickname, "Mr. Big Shot."

James scored 23 of his 30 points in the second half, 15 in the fourth quarter. The Cavs got as close as a 92–87 deficit in the final 1 minute, 14 seconds of play but got no closer, falling, 97–91, in the game and 0–2 in the series.

Going into the 2022 playoffs, 435 teams had held 2–0 leads in a best-of-seven series. Their record was 404–31, a 92.9 percent success rate.

An old NBA adage in an enormously important game, however, is to beware the underdog if the best player on the floor is on its side.

Game 3, at Cleveland, Cavaliers 86, Pistons 77

Cleveland was down, effectively, to a one-game season because, dismal as was the 7.1 percent success rate for teams trailing 0–2, there was literally no percentage in it for teams trailing 0–3. Such comebacks had been rarely made in hockey and baseball, perhaps due to the outsized importance of a hot goaltender in the former and a stellar pitching rotation in the latter. But no NBA team had ever done it.

James, who had finished second to Dallas point guard Steve Nash in the voting for the regular season Most Valuable Player award, played the third game in a way that validated the Pistons' fears. It was the inevitable consequence of having his back to the wall and of the emotional setting. The game began with a moment of silence for the death of Larry Hughes's younger brother, Justin. Born with a heart defect, recipient of a heart transplant in 1997, Justin Hughes had died suddenly and unexpectedly. Hughes left the team to join his grieving family in St. Louis. Out of respect for his teammate, James wore around his bicep a headband with Hughes's number, 32, on it and a similar one around his calf.

Thus inspired, James delivered another triple-double with 21 points, 10, assists and 10 rebounds, admitting afterward that he did not look to score as much as distribute the ball to teammates in their shooting sweet spots and also help man the defensive boards.

In the fourth quarter, however, James carried the Cavs, scoring two of his 15 points by spinning an 11-foot finger roll into the basket, a shot that had not been done so deftly at such distance since the heyday of George Gervin. In the last 1:32, with a 78–74 Cleveland lead, James hit nothing but net on a step-back three-pointer as Cavaliers fans went over the cuckoo's nest. *Pured* is a term PGA Tour pros use for a ball hit with a perfect clarity of swing, speed, torque, and positioning. James's purity in his mechanics, focus, and purpose made victory undeniable.

As the game ended, James joyously grabbed his one-year-old son Bronny (LeBron Jr.), who was being cuddled by his mother, James's longtime girlfriend, Savannah Brinson, at courtside, then carried him off the court in his arms. It was almost a passion play—new life under the shadow of death, hope resurrected after loss.

Game 4, at Cleveland, Cavaliers 74, Pistons 72

Everyone learned that just because something is, in Rasheed Wallace's term, "Guaran-Sheed," does not mean it is worth the breath it is presented on. Rasheed had pledged after the Cavs' first series win that it would be their last one and that Game 4 would be their last before their home fans. He had been undefeated in such predictions, which resulted in the Cavs' fans erupting in boos on his first appearance two hours before tipoff and then throughout the game.

Behind James's 22 points, which accounted for nearly 30 percent of the Cavs' meager total, and his near-miss of a third playoff triple-double with nine assists and eight rebounds, the Cavs won the kind of defensive struggle that had been the impetus behind Detroit's rise to elite NBA status. Possessions per game were lower, so each one meant more. Conversely, the defensive emphasis was higher on making them empty possessions. The almighty trey of the future was still incubating in places like Davidson College, where Steph Curry was a freshman.

With the score tied, 72–72, broadswords could have been clanging on armor while archers shot arrows from yew bows and quarrels whistled from crossbows. Even at its highest level, basketball was still Kansas in *The Wizard of Oz*. Until the three-pointer dramatically increased offensive potential, technicolor Oz was only a dream.

James won the fierce defensive struggle by splitting four free throws in the last 1:02. On the first pair, Billups approached James at the line and tried to get into his head, as James had done to Gilbert Arenas in the closeout game against Washington. Mike Brown leaped off the bench to protest the illegal tactic James had gotten away with.

James—5-for-10 in the game at the line, a weakness that would recur occasionally throughout his career—did not quite rebuff Billups at the hairline. But he did split the pair and give his team a follicle-thin lead. Fouled again in the final 1.3 seconds, James missed and then again made the second shot. The Pistons threw the ball away on the last play, and James grabbed it, then punted it into the second deck. Ohio is on a small fault line, with occasional earthquakes of a comparatively inconsequential magnitude on the Richter scale. In terms of decibels, anyway, after James jumped atop the scorer's table amid the fans' roaring, the Q was Cleveland's own little San Andreas.

"Everybody was counting us out," James said. "Even people in our own backyard were counting us out. That's extra motivation for us. We don't listen to nobody. We're not feeling pressure. They are."

Not a bit of it, disagreed Wallace. "I ain't worried about these cats," he said. "There's no way in hell they beat us in a series. They played well. I give them credit. We lost. We shot 30 percent, and they had to play their best to beat us."

It was hardly the Cavs' best except in floor burns and bruises. No one knew it at the time, but the series was about to go Full Washington, with its tight games and competitive gamesmanship.

Game 5, at Auburn Hills, Cavaliers 86, Pistons 84

The game began with the Cavs under a pall of sorrow. The entire team attended Justin Hughes's funeral in St. Louis on Tuesday, the morning after winning Game 4, then flew to an airport in Pontiac, in suburban Detroit, without a practice between games. Perhaps, mused *Detroit Free Press* sports columnist Mitch Albom, "the team that grieves together plays together."

James invoked a fairy tale to predict the Cavs' chances. "It's just basketball," he said. "They're not the Big Bad Wolf, and we're not the three little pigs."

In Game 5, the best player on the floor again had the effect of widening the underdogs' bite radius. James led the Cavs to another 10-penny nails-tough defensive victory before a hushed and stricken Detroit crowd. This was not basketball as muscular ballet. It was a scrum at the line of scrimmage, with blocks sublimated to screens and tackles to hard fouls. James scored 32 points but required 30 shots to get them. Detroit's Ben Wallace, 0-for-7 in the game at the line and one of the poorest free throw shooters in the league, missed two foul shots with 40 seconds remaining, in a tie at 82.

With 27 seconds to go, Drew Gooden scored in the low post against the multiple resistance of the Pistons' Hydra, with defenders flailing at him, for the game's final points.

The Cavs had to survive a last flurry on Marshall's block of Prince, James's tip of Lindsey Hunter's errant shot to Eric Snow, and Snow's cagey toss of the ball too far downcourt for the Pistons to have a viable shot when they finally chased it down with 1.9 seconds left.

"I took a picture of the basket," Gooden said. "That's what my freshman coach in high school used to tell me, take my time and make the shot." The Cavaliers headed home as the very picture of conviction and self-belief.

"I'm still not worried," said Billups. "I know what's possible." So did the Cavs, however.

Game 6, at Cleveland, Pistons 84, Cavaliers 82

In 2018, a dozen years after the epic Detroit series, when all of the participants except LeBron had retired, while he did such things as score 56 and then 50 points in the same week at age 37, I saw a suspenseful documentary about mountain climber Alex Honnold. The movie *Free Solo* followed Honnold as he became the first ever to climb, alone, without ropes, pitons, or other aids, the 3,000-foot face of El Capitan in Yosemite National Park. He did it by balancing between life and the Ultimate Elimination with one toe on an eroded nub of rock, scratching and clawing at cracks split in the stone by snowstorms and ice melt, defying the percentages, inching ever upward toward the summit of his sport.

Hell yeah, with basketball skills, Honnold could've been a Piston! They, too, liked living on the edge. Between 1988 and 2006, when Detroit won three NBA championships, lost twice in the Finals, and set the bruising, battering tone of NBA basketball for much too long, they beat the odds time and again. In 2005, the Pistons were down 3–2 in the conference finals before rallying to beat Miami in seven games. In 2004, they won Game 6 at New Jersey and then ousted the Nets in Game 7. A year earlier, Detroit won a Game 6 at Orlando and then ended the Magic's season in the next game.

Their victories against the odds were almost as remarkable as former Cavs owner Ted Stepien's idea of halftime entertainment. This was epitomized by one Don "Boot" Buttrey, who stuffed lighted firecrackers in his pie hole, surviving the blasts without need of a mouth transplant. Before you could say, "Don't try this at home, kids," he could also rip open and crush beer cans with his teeth. He belonged in Ripley's Believe it or Not Museum. (So, for that matter, did Stepien.)

"We know what it takes," said Ben Wallace. "We've been together a while. We don't panic."

James, bulling to the basket at every chance, hit six straight free throws in the late going, with the first pair giving the Cavs a 77–76 lead. The Cleveland crowd reacted by going to an insane pitch of sound. but the Pistons surged back behind a three-point play by Wallace and Billups' jumper as the shot clock expired.

As big as those shots were, the hustle plays meant every bit as much. First Tayshaun Prince, then Rip Hamilton, and last Chauncey Billups all corralled misses that kept possession with the Pistons and kept the Cavs in extremis in relation to the game clock.

Trailing by three and at the line with 1.3 seconds to play, James sank his first shot to cut the lead to 84–82, then deliberately missed his second. I had seen the desperate play, the basketball equivalent of pulling the goalie in hockey, work once. Julius Erving, positioned on the three-point wing and not along the foul lane, wheeled through the free throw circle and dunked Doug Collins's deliberate miss to force overtime in Atlanta, in a game the Sixers went on to win. There is no playbook diagram for the wings that propelled Erving to the rim, however.

In the era of analytics, the scenario has been found to work only 5 percent of the time. Yet it almost happened again. The 7'3" Ilgauskas, shielded from the rim by the leaping Billups, reached over the Detroit guard's head and shoulders to get enough of his hand on the ball, aided by Billups, who also struck it unintentionally, to flick it off the backboard just inside the top corner on the nearest side, barely missing a tip-in.

James was undaunted. "Nobody thought we would be here. Nobody thought we'd be in a Game 7 against the Pistons. We proved the doubters wrong. We have to prove some more wrong. I thought it was in. Z is a good tipper," said James, who on the basketball court recognized one, even if he did not early in his career play the part well at all.

Game 7, at Auburn Hills, Michigan, Pistons 79, Cavaliers 61

Until Game 6, the Cavs had won five straight playoff games by two or fewer points.

But the Palace was the toughest arena in the league for visiting teams after the ramshackle Boston Garden finally went under the wrecking ball. The PA man's fire-engine scream on every possession change forced by the Pistons' ferocious defense—"DEEEEEE-TROIT BASKETBALL!—

could have almost been heard by Yoopers (Upper Peninsula Michiganders) deep in the North Woods. The arena was huge and loud. The noise, along with the pride that the din embodied in a city that had seen its share of economic problems, had nothing to do but rocket back off the roof and sing in the blood and minds of the players it inspired.

So, imagine what it was like in the exponentially greater stakes of a seventh game. "In a pressure situation, you do what you do best, and for us, that's defending," Detroit coach Flip Saunders said. "We locked down." It was a lockdown that was the sporting equivalent of walls with razor wire, searchlights, guard dogs, sharpshooters in towers and gun bulls on horseback.

"They trapped me, they went under screens, they went over screens," said James, who was held to one second-half field goal. The Cavs' 61 points were the lowest in a Game 7 in NBA history. Their 23 points in the second half were the fewest in a playoff game since the NBA adopted the 24-second clock a half-century earlier.

"I've seen almost every defense that I could possibly see for the rest of my career in this series. That's why they're Eastern Conference champions, and that's why they keep winning," James said.

James had carried the Cavs in the first half, outpacing the rest of his team with 21 points. He shot 10-of-15 while his teammates totaled 17 points and missed 19 of 24 shots. The Cavs trailed then by only two points. The problem was that the other Cavs collectively didn't overtake James until Drew Gooden's two free throws cut the Detroit lead to 46–45 in the third quarter.

Overall, James was 11-for-24, for 27 points with eight rebounds and only two assists, because his teammates couldn't shoot well enough to exploit the obsessive attention Detroit gave James. Larry Hughes, playing for the first time since taking bereavement leave 10 days earlier, was the only other Cavalier in double figures, with 10 points.

"There's nobody on his level that can get his teammates involved like he does," Tayshaun Prince said of James. "He sees the plays before they even happen, and no one else does that. That's the reason this went seven games."

It was a strange ending for a series that began and ended in blowouts by Detroit, but in between was as tense and close as almost any series.

Only Boston and Philadelphia in the 1981 Eastern Conference finals also played three straight games decided by only two points. "They took it up to another level in the second half," Ilgauskas said. "We got real stagnant on offense, and they showed us a level we hadn't seen in these playoffs.

So did James, of course, by exceeding every expectation. The season ended with everything seemingly in place for fans to enjoy more of what James had shown.

CHAPTER 11

Hexing the Wiz, Vexing the Nets

No one realized it at the time, but Washington's playoff experience had already peaked.

James had put the Wizards at death's door with his two game-winners in 2006. The next season, he made sure Harry Potter's quidditch games at Hogwarts were livelier than another first-round series with the District's Dumbledores, as the Cavs advanced, 4–0.

It probably would never have been a sweep but for an injury to the doyen of videogame box covers, Gilbert Arenas, the pure-shooting Wizard, who had been having a season worthy of the sorcerer in the Who's song "Pinball Wizard."

Typically, he had a chip on his shoulder the size of a bag heavy with eyes of newts and toes of frogs. He had voluntarily withdrawn from tryouts for the FIBA World Championship, charging that the coaches, Nate McMillan of Portland and Mike D'Antoni of Phoenix, had already determined the roster. In the subsequent NBA season, in which Arenas was chosen as an All-Star Game starter for the first time, it was obvious Team USA, which took home the bronze medal, could have used him.

Arenas's cauldron of fury boiled and bubbled. He had 54 against Phoenix in a 94–73 Trail Blazers victory.

Then he went for his career high of 60 in a 147–41 overtime win over the Lakers, setting a record for 16 points in the overtime period. He hit a 32-footer to beat the buzzer and the Milwaukee Bucks, a late three to thump the Utah Jazz, and a layup to take the Seattle SuperSonics, all barely beating the buzzer.

But on April 4, in a collision with Charlotte's Gerald Wallace, Arenas tore the meniscus in his left knee, necessitating surgery. A second surgery would be needed to fix it when he tore it again in overly rigorous rehabilitation workouts.

By 2009, Arenas would be suspended by the NBA's Commissioner David Stern for a locker room dispute over a gambling debt, in which teammate Jarvaris Crittenton was also suspended. Stern really had little choice in what had become a Clantons vs. Earps case, escalating when the players almost went Full OK Corral, both pulling guns. Agent Zero, as Arenas was called because of his uniform number and his last-second shots, lost his chance to play with Kobe Bryant in Los Angeles when negotiations broke down after the incident.

Like most journalists, I missed him. The series' flair went out like a police flare at an accident scene.

Although the series was a sweep, James paid the Wizards a compliment afterward. "We're not playing a high school team. We're not playing an NCAA team. This is the NBA," he said, after his best game of the series, 30–9–6 across in the triple-double categories proved just enough to win the third game 98–92.

It was James's passing that stood out most. In Game 3, as a 17-point halftime lead dwindled, with the Cavs leading by only a three-pointer with 25.4 left, James whipped a pass to Sasha Pavlovic, who was 4-of-11 with five turnovers, yet who ripped the net cords with a three changed the playoffs to a death watch.

Shaking his head in the locker room afterward, Ferry said, "Can you believe that kid?"

I was pretty sure he meant Pavlovic, who shook off an entire afternoon of negative reinforcement to step up and nail the decisive shot.

But he could just as well have been speaking of James and his trust in even his most embattled of teammates.

No team has ever come back from a 3–0 deficit. The decimated Wizards had no chance.

While James struggled, Ilgauskas, with 20 points and 19 rebounds, and Hughes, with 19 points, scored 18 of Cleveland's final 20 points.

Cleveland was a franchise that considered a candle in the wind the equivalent of a new dawn because it was still flickering. This marked the first time in the Cavs' modest history that they had won back-to-back playoff games on the road.

"We can't win if these guys don't play well, Z and Larry," James said. "Simple as that. I need them every game to be a factor."

Next, the Cavaliers had to deal with the New Jersey Nets—and their prototypical point guard, Jason Kidd—in the semifinals.

To casual fans, basketball's mystique most depends on the players who can trip the flight fantastic with, as David Foster Wallace wrote in "How Tracy Austin Broke My Heart" (included in his collection of essays *Consider the Lobster*), "Jordan hanging the air like a Chagall bride." Continuing the nuptial theme, great athletes, argued Wallace, marry physical superiority to the hard data of analytics.

Until at least Oscar Robertson in the 1960s, if not all the way until Magic Johnson in the 1980s, point guards played low to the floor and were gravity bound. Nevertheless, they had their own prestige almost from the NBA's inception. Red Auerbach derided Bob Cousy as a "local yokel" from Holy Cross in Worcester, Massachusetts, 50 miles from Boston. Cousy's name was literally picked out of a hat in a dispersal draft of players from the defunct Chicago Stags. Before Earvin Johnson reinvented the position through his natural flair and the size and strength that allowed him to double as a power forward, Cousy's name became synonymous with flashy behind-the-back passes and sleight of hand showtime.

James, like Magic, actually could play every position, even center for short stints. His versatility let him see the game as a panorama of possibilities and led to comparisons to a Swiss Army knife, although the "knife" was machete-sized. Not even Magic, though, fired James's imagination the way Kidd did.

The point guard of the New Jersey Nets, Kidd was bigger than John Stockton, the perfect trigger man for Karl Malone on the pick-and-roll; big enough, at 6'4", to be a better facilitator than Oscar Robertson, who monopolized the ball while backing in and still became the season-long triple-doubles king long before Russell Westbrook was born; and every bit as clever as Steve Nash, the point guard who beat James out for MVP honors the previous season, or Chris Paul, the friend who became godfather to James's first son.

James sometimes would receive criticism for excessive dribbling, but he seldom backed in, Big O–like, in the manner of a boat maneuvering down the launch ramp when hitched to a pickup truck. James instead scanned the defense from the top of the key while dribbling, seeming to have more eyes on more spots on the court than a peacock has tail feathers.

Like Bill Bradley, the New York Knicks' Basketball Hall of Famer, Rhodes Scholar, and US senator, Kidd had a wider range of peripheral vision than normal. Thus was born the idea for the archetypal point guard's commercial, starring the archetypal point guard in James's view, Kidd. In the American Express ad, Kidd aces an eye examination while looking in the opposite direction from the chart on the optometrist's wall. As he settles his account at the office secretary's desk, he alerts teammate Richard Jefferson, seated in the waiting room behind him, that Jefferson's car is being towed on the street outside the window. Kidd was the new Cousy, who it was said to look due east and still enjoy a sunset in the west.

Kidd would finish his career second on the all-time assists list. The Nets guard had averaged a triple-double in New Jersey's opening series victory over Toronto.

The Cavs won in six games, the first of which was a defensive struggle that featured a "chasedown" block, although the term had not yet been coined for what years later would become the most famous play in James's career. The usually defensively indifferent Sasha Pavlovic made it on Kidd's layup attempt after a steal in the final minute. Call me a skeptic, but as Pavlovic closed on Kidd like a heat-seeking missile, an impartial observer might be moved to question the truthfulness of Kidd's eye test and tow zone alert in the commercial.

With 21 points, James continued his assault on the record book. He scored 20 or more points in each of the first 20 playoff games of his career.

The Cavs took a 2–0 series lead into Brendan Byrne Arena in the "Meadowlands," a term that surely needs the brackets of sarcastic quotation marks, is located in a swamp suitable for *The Godfather*'s "leave the gun, take the cannoli" scene.

The Cavs' perfect postseason ended, as did their streak of 10 straight victories going back to the regular season, as did James's string of 20-point playoff game scoring—when he had only 18 points while guarded part the fourth game. of the time by Kidd.

The next three games brought back memories of the *Philadelphia Inquirer*'s late, acerbic Ron Reid, who blurted during a blooper reel Eagles–Browns game, "Pro football's just not the word for it!"

The Nets made only three field goals in the fourth quarter of the fourth game.

Six was the number in the fifth game, when the Cavs failed to clinch at home. The Nets scored six points in the fourth quarter. It was the lowest total in any quarter by any winning team in the shot-clock era. New Jersey was 1-of-15 from the field then, .067 percent, yet won.

The Cavs shot a dismal 3-for-17 (.176) in the final quarter, 1-for-7 on three-pointers, and scored only 13 points. Fans sarcastically cheered Larry Hughes (3-for-17 in the game) after a late basket. "I laid an egg," said Hughes. James led the Cavs with 20 points. In the final minutes, however, he cut and bruised his knee after diving into the Cavaliers' bench in pursuit of a loose ball.

It fit the bizarreness of the Cavs in the playoffs, beginning with the 61-point record low in Game 7 at Detroit the previous season.

Incredibly, back in the New Jersey swamp, the series in Game 6 ended with egg on far more faces than just Hughes's. The Cavs closed out the Nets, but not without long, barren stretches when nothing much went right. The Cavs managed only eight points in the third quarter, just missing the coveted (and imaginary) golden raspberry, which the Nets' six-point fourth quarter in the previous game surely deserved. "I think it was tough on every Cavs fan to watch that third quarter," James said.

The difference was Mike Brown got 18 points from Donyell Marshall and 8 from rookie Daniel aka (honest!) "Boobie" Gibson. Between them, they had totaled 26 points in the first five games. Marshall's improvement was so drastic as to require proof of identity. In the first five games, he scored 10 points, shot 3-for-15 and was 0-for-5 on the arc. In Game 6, the figures were 18, 6-for-11, and 6-for-10.

I set the Wayback Machine my head for a long, long time ago in the opening game's last seconds—1984, to be exact, and a place far, far away, the Seattle Kingdome, the site of that year's Final Four. It was there that I covered Kentucky, a 53–40 loser to Georgetown, scoring 11 points in the second half in a loss to Georgetown, 53–40. University of Kentucky coach Joe B. Hall said, "It was like an extraterrestrial force was knocking the ball away from the basket."

After Hall finished his dazed trip through Malaprop Land, Kentuckian and sports columnist Billy Reed said, "Somebody should have told him, 'You're not making a lick of sense.'"

When the Eastern Conference Finals began in Detroit, evidence aplenty was produced to indict Brown for his substitutions, which, frankly, didn't make a lick of sense. Nor did the storm of criticism that roared around James in the final seconds of the opening game.

CHAPTER 12

Transcendence

"You were blessed last night," Philadelphia 76ers assistant coach Jack McMahon said in 1976, the morning after I covered the triple-overtime fifth game of the NBA Finals in Boston. I had hurriedly called him for a reaction before jumping on a plane to Phoenix for Game 6. McMahon was a man who had seen it all in the NBA, from the Green Parrot Cafe days of the Fort Wayne Zollner Pistons to the bicentennial.

Decades ahead of his time, he was the first NBA player ever to sport a tattoo—an anchor on his bicep, acquired during his time in the navy. But not even he, had he lived long enough, ever saw anything like LeBron James in hostile Detroit on May 31, 2007.

No one ever had. Maybe no one ever will again.

It would live on as the only plausible equal to Michael Jordan's flu-ravaged 38 points in Game 5 of the 1997 Finals at Utah. Jordan was sick, so sick he couldn't even spare the energy to trash-talk, which was one of his trademarks. Yet he still hit the winning three-pointer.

But Jordan had Scottie Pippen, close to the greatest wingman ever, and the eccentric but effective defender Dennis Rodman, who could dominate the entry to the offensive and defensive boards the way a hungry boardinghouse diner dominates the access to the roast beef platter, mashed potatoes bowl, and gravy boat.

Although he was healthy, James had no such support.

2007 EASTERN CONFERENCE FINALS
Game 1, at Auburn Hills, Michigan, Pistons 79, Cavaliers 76

An old complaint about James, known mostly to Ohio high school basketball junkies, took on new life before an exponentially larger audience in Game 1 of the Eastern Conference Finals at Detroit's Thunderdome. The play planted the seed that became the poisonous fruit of that sportswriters' favorite, the contrarian column. (Trust me on this; I should know.)

Driving from the top of the foul circle, he burst to the rim with what was becoming the most famous first step since Neil Armstrong's. With the advantage given him by fast-twitch muscle fibers, he bolted past Tayshaun Prince, then, just before two other Pistons could swarm him, he passed up a layup to tie the game in the last seconds. Unbelievably, at least to many fans and writers, he lasered the ball to Donyell Marshall, open in the corner for a possible game-winning three-pointer.

After Marshall missed with 5.9 seconds to play, Chauncey Billups chased down the long rebound and then split a pair of free throws, clinching a 79–76 Detroit victory.

Suddenly, Marshall was Chad Mraz, the unlikely recipient of James's pass in high school, who had missed a crucial three-pointer way back in the Roger Bacon upset of St. Vincent-St. Mary in the state high school championship game of James's junior season. Mraz did not take the last shot of the game, but he took the most important one.

Atlas had shrugged. James had put the weight of victory or defeat not on himself but on Mraz, then on Marshall.

Marshall said, "You're going to make some, and you're going to miss some. Unfortunately, that one was to win the game. I'd take that 100 times out of 100."

"I thought [James] was going for the shot," Rasheed Wallace said. "But Tay was all over him"—not an accurate comment, by the way—"and he got that pass off somehow."

After some quick search-engine sleuthing, critics turned up Michael Jordan's quote about perseverance: "I've missed more than 9,000 shots in my career. I've lost almost 300 games, 26 times I've been trusted to take the game-winning shot and missed. I've failed over and over and over again in my life. And that is why I succeed." Not as well-known but nevertheless as apt was Julius Erving's mantra, "Dare to be great."

James had no such mantra, although the embattled soldier's saying "Praise the Lord and pass the ammunition" was something of a fit. A problem with that, though, was that James often *was* the ammunition.

Critics ascribed the play to a tragic flaw, one that became the uncrowning moment for a member of the sporting royalty. The media beast's favorite meat, you see, is scapegoat. The *deferral* to Marshall, a word with connotations of buck-passing, slammed the brakes on the growing chorus of national adulation. The game as a whole, however, accelerated the Cavs' growth simply by the narrowness of Detroit's victory. It purged them of their memories of the opening and closing routs there in the previous season. Still, James took just three shots in the fourth quarter, making only one. Even a defender of the pass to Marshall, as I was then and am now, could not justify such meager totals as those.

"We had three guys in his face everywhere he went. We have to keep that up," said Prince, making the same argument James would make for himself.

"You just have to take what's there," said James, who was averaging 26 points in the playoffs on an average of 19 shots. "It's not about taking a high volume of shots; it's about trying to win the basketball game. We had an opportunity to win."

"If he makes the pass and they score, we'll live with it," Piston guard Rip Hamilton said.

I took the point of view that the pass was worth the gamble. Overtime is a struggle in any hostile arena, but it was particularly so with the Pistons' raucous fans. Moreover, Marshall had made six of his 10 three-point tries in the closeout game against the Nets three days earlier. He would take the shot with confidence. The play was the right one, but the execution was lacking.

On some of his penetrations, Rasheed Wallace was leaning toward James like the rickety tower in Pisa. He was, however, afraid to make the swarm of Piston defenders a mob, because James could crisp him with another pass to Marshall, whom Wallace was supposed to be guarding.

A jab must also go to Mike Brown, who had an amnesiac episode or something, forgetting all about Marshall's difference-making spree in the Game 6 against the Nets. He used Marshall for 23 seconds in the first quarter, 2:53 in the second quarter, 2:01 in the third, and 4:41 in the fourth.

Billups scored 10 of his 13 points in the final quarter, making all three of his shots from the floor. It was a big moment for Mr. Big Shot. Later in the series, everyone would learn who was Mr. Bigger Shot.

Game 2, at Auburn Hills, Michigan, Pistons 79, Cavaliers 76

It was not only the very same 79–76 score and the very same margin of victory for the Pistons that led to the overwhelming sense of déjà vu. It was also another last-gasp frustration for James, who spun and missed a hook shot from seven feet away with the Cavs trailing by a point, 7.9 seconds remaining, Hamilton covering him like a tarpaulin, and Larry Hughes, to scant surprise, missing the follow up.

It was a perverse twist on the "one if by land, two if by sea" signal to Paul Revere. For James, the two defeats were "one if by three, two if by own hand."

Mike Brown got a technical foul because he thought referees had ignored the contact the Pistons' defenders had meted out on James's shot. This, too, echoed the Roger Bacon loss, when teammate Dru Joyce drew a technical foul as the time drained away.

James finished with a rambling stat line of 7-for-19 from the field for 19 points with seven turnovers, six assists and six rebounds. Hughes, Zydrunas Ilgauskas, and Drew Gooden combined for only 11 points. The teams headed to Cleveland with Detroit holding the same 2–0 advantage it had in 2006.

Game 3, at Cleveland, Cavaliers 88, Pistons 82

"I've got to be ready," said James, who wore a black "Witness" T-shirt to a workout on the Quicken Loans Arena's main floor three hours before tipoff. "This is probably the biggest game of my life, and probably one of the biggest games in Cavaliers history. I've got to recognize that. I have to be prepared to go out there. It's all out," he said.

It was also 2006 all over again. The Cavs held serve at home and got back in the series. With a 32-9-9 stat line in points, rebounds and assists, James's near triple-double was impressive in its own right and also expressive of a concern that had lingered for years, the hot-and-cold nature of his jump shooting.

A powerful dunk over a rival's arm-extended barricade, bullwhipped or windmilled down, a Thor ball hammered home, smoking and hot, is the literal stuff of legends. It's called a posterizing dunk because it achieves iconic status in posters on bedroom and den walls. He did just that to Cavs fans' favorite villain, Rasheed "(Not so) Guaran–Sheed" Wallace, to break a 68–68 tie.

"That was sick," said the rookie, Gibson, who, foreshadowing, chipped in with nine points. In this context, *sick* actually meant hale, hearty, and awesome. "Jawsome-dropping," were it a real word, would perfectly describe the reaction on the court and in the Q.

The contributions of Gibson, whose nickname, "Boobie," invariably caused bawdy snickers, would have to grow even more. Hughes tore the plantar fascia in his left foot in the first quarter while making a layup and played only 22 minutes.

Yet the difference in Game 3 was James's jump shots. They were not the nothing-but-net dead-eyes that gave Golden State's Steph Curry and Klay Thompson their Splash Brothers nickname, but they were suitable enough.

"James picked us apart driving to the basket. But that's how it is if his jump shot is on," said Prince.

"LeBron stepped up and put us on his shoulders. He said, 'Come along for the ride.' And we all hopped on," said Mike Brown.

Game 4, at Cleveland, Cavaliers 91, Pistons 87

"Get me to the fourth and close in the fourth quarter, and I'll do my best to win it," James had told his teammates before the start of the fourth game. He then proceeded to do just that.

James scored 13 of his 25 points in the fourth quarter, shooting 4-for-6 from the field, 5-for-5 at the line, adding four rebounds and three assists. In the last four seconds, he drained two free throws to make it a two-possession game. He proved as unimpressed by copycat hex whisperer Hamilton, as he had been when Billups had tried in the previous year—without satisfactory result—the ploy James used with such success against Gilbert Arenas.

"I invented that," said James. A student of the game's history, he quickly added, "Scottie Pippen actually invented that with Karl Malone. Rip tried to mess with me, and I had to stay focused."

Moments earlier, Wallace, enraged by a call against Hamilton, was called for a technical foul—his fifth of the playoffs—for throwing his headband in frustration as Cleveland fans sensed a change in momentum.

Among those who gave the Cavs a lift was Hughes, who played 10 minutes with an injury he described "as painful as anything I've dealt with." But he wanted to play, and Cavs doctors cleared him an hour before tipoff. He started and played 10 minutes in the first quarter.

"Him being on the court and saying, 'Who cares about the injury. It's about this team,'" James said, lauding Hughes for his grit and commitment to the team.

Game 5, at Auburn Hills, Michigan, Cavaliers 109, Pistons 107 (2 OT)

Psychologists speak of moments of self-actualization, the realization of potentials reached and goals surpassed. Actually, factually, James had just such a moment in his greatest game ever.

The term for it has changed. Psychologists call it *flow state. Flow*, however, connotes the smooth ripples of a river. It was more like a cataract or cascade state, so powerful was it. This was not just being in the zone, as players without degrees in psychology call it. It was being in the tropics, with musical complement by Nelly of "Hot in Herre" of top of the music charts fame. It is when limits stretch and self-doubt is blinded by a supernova of extraordinary talent.

Despite all that James did later, this game, so early in such a long and storied career, was his chart-topper. He scored 48 points. He also had nine rebounds, seven assists, and two steals. He was the only Cavs player to make a field goal in the last 17:48 of play and the only one to score in the final 12:48. He scored all 18 of Cleveland's overtime points. He scored his team's final 25 points. He scored 29 of their last 30.

It was so incredible that the figure "filberts" at the invaluable research site basketball-reference.com posted next to the game's place in the Cavaliers' regular season and playoff results: "LeBron's 48 Special." If it had been an opera, only Maria Callas could have handled the high notes. His stupendous effort reflected not only his own greatness but also the poverty of performance in his teammates. Throughout the game, he drove from his observation post at the top of the foul circle, once taking an Ilgauskas pass for an assist on his dunk; otherwise doing his own solo, going around Billups as if he were a mulberry bush; dunking, absorbing contact; going to the free throw line; one vs. five.

He dunked as regulation play was ending in a way that no one had dunked in a long, long time. It was a Dr. J / Darryl Dawkins retro/hybrid with enough throw-weight to send Prince scurrying out of the lane, lest he be forever posterized, ducking and covering his head like a kid hiding under his school desk in A-bomb survival drills in the 1950s. Basketball guru Bill Simmons called the game LeLeap: a quantum jump into the air up there, where ruled the Jump Man, Jordan himself. Except James was bigger and stronger, with a body that could have belonged on a tight end. Simmons wrote that Prince was "ducking for cover like someone reacting to a fly-by from a fighter jet."

Simmons also offered a football tight-end comparison for James. The same analogy was made in Philadelphia to George McGinnis. But McGinnis was a dainty finesse player inside a superhero's physique, a non-shot-blocker, unlike teammate and rival for crowd favor Dr. J. McGinnis would never really reclaim the reputation he list in his struggles in the 1977 NBA finals after Maurice Lucas dominated him; the bitter joke was that "Big Mac" was nothing but a sandwich. James had never been dominated that way.

James's field goals were all snapshots that would flash in the memory for years—two dunks; two layups; three longish two-pointers of 20, 19, and 18 feet, the last with three Pistons running at him on the right wing as he nothing-but-netted it. He crossed over on his dribble and tangle-footed defenders. He could go left, go right, go through places where a rabbit couldn't go because he simply ripped a swath through the underbrush, root and branch. The barrage of baskets went on and on.

I recalled a brief time when the 1976–77 Sixers, in a brainstorm concocted by sixth man Steve Mix, aided and abetted by bombardier Lloyd Free (aka "World B. Free"), had a team within a team, the self-labeled "Bomb Squad." The 1812 Overture's salvos of cannon fire serenaded them as they bounced off the bench and made shots.

Except with the Cavs, James was his own gun captain and crew. He fired and reloaded, rammed dunks home, sighted and shot again and again. All the blessings of what can only be called an athletic state of grace were his.

The second three-pointer, with 1:14 to play in the second overtime, almost had to go in, because the bedlam in the stands was at its peak as the fans knew another stop might finally allow the Pistons to take more than a one-possession, three-point lead. This had not happened since the Pistons led, 88–84, with 2:49 to play way back in the fourth quarter.

James lofted an in-your-face 26-foot demoralizer to the Pistons players, bench, coach and fans. He drove hard to his left without picks to assist him, let fly mere feet from the Pistons' bench, where coach Flip Saunders watched, bent over, hands on his knees, and winced as the ball clattered through the rim. Unfazed by most of James's barrage, the Pistons were staggered enough to call timeout after that one.

Why the Pistons did not double-team him is a lasting blot on Saunders's reputation. Indeed, he coached only one more season in Detroit. In letters as big as the LeBron banner in downtown Cleveland, fans in the arena, in bars, and in front of the TV sets had to be asking: Why? Why would you let him have the ball? Why wouldn't you make someone else, anyone else, try to beat you?

And, on cue, here came Sasha Pavlovic.

As Shakespeare introduced the bumbling night porter just after the homicidal Macbeth couple offed Duncan, so the Cavs brought the comedic stylings of Donyell Marshall and his foil, Pavlovic, on stage during the timeout to release the mounting tension. Pavlovic was 2 for 10 in the game and worse, 0 for 4 in the second overtime with James so hot he might have self-combusted. As the pair walked past the press table during the timeout, Marshall turned to Pavlovic and asked, "What the hell are you doing?"

Getting out of James's way was the order of business on the final possession for the Cavs.

James stormed past Billups, nearly as immobile as Larry Hughes when compared to James, and went crashing down the lane for a right-handed layup for a 109–107 lead as Jason Maxiell yanked his left arm like a wishbone. James grabbed his left arm with his right, gesticulating to the referees as if to say, "Do you miss the *E* on an eyechart too?" No foul was called. There were 2.9 seconds left when Billups's—you should pardon the expression—big shot missed from the lane and time ran out.

Mike Brown tenderly kissed James on the top of his head before LeBron headed to the locker room for an IV. Finally, utterly spent, he dragged himself on to the interviewee room dais. "I feel terrible," he said, in a soft mumble.

On TNT's *Inside the NBA* postgame show, Charles Barkley said, "Cleveland is running downhill. This series is not going back to Detroit this time."

Game 6, at Cleveland, Cavaliers 88, Pistons 72

"Get ready. Get that gun out," James had told Gibson before the Game 6 opening tip, clearly indicating his intention to involve his teammates more, because he knew all Pistons' eyes would be on him.

For all the transports of joy it produced, this closeout game can be summarized with a statistic so astounding basketball purists had to look twice, thrice, and whatever "numerical-ice" comes after that to believe it:

Daniel Gibson took nine shots from the field and scored 31 points.

You will never see such an anomaly again, but it was testament to the Pistons' James obsession. Gibson shot 7-for-9, 5-for-5 on three-pointers and was 12-for-15 at the line. The game squeaked along tightly for three quarters, with the score tied after the first and second quarters and the Cavs leading by single point after the third. At winning time, James so monopolized the Pistons' defensive attention that Gibson was as open as an unkept secret, knocking down three triples, from 25, 25, and 24 feet, all in the first 2:16 of the telltale final quarter.

He moved either slightly up on the arc or slightly back, like a human pendulum, ceaselessly reminding the desperate Pistons of both the diminishing clock and their own shriveling chances. When defenders contested his shot, Gibson dribbled past their headlong rushes, going inside to draw fouls often enough to shoot nine free throws in the final quarter alone and sink an inside-the-arc jumper. Adding to the home crowd's joy, Wallace fouled out with 7:44 to play and then was ejected for two technical fouls. Just over a minute later, Gibson hit another trey from 24 feet.

James flung the ball into the stands as time ran out, then made a cross-court beeline for Ilgauskas, who stood near the Cavs' bench, jumping into the arms of the man who had persevered through so many foot injuries to return and share in the championship chase.

Only one of the other fresh-from-high-school phenoms had so quickly done anything like this. Not Kevin Garnett, not Tracy McGrady, not Moses

Malone—and, let it be said, not the young Jordan, who reached (and won) the NBA Finals for the first time in his seventh season 1990–91, even though he received collegiate tutoring from Dean Smith at North Carolina. Kobe Bryant was the exception, becoming an NBA finalist in his fourth season, the same as James, and winning the championship.

"This is the best thing that ever happened to me, man," James said, addressing the 20,562 delirious fans. "But look here, look here. It doesn't stop."

But it did.

"If I'm dreaming, don't wake me up," said Gibson.

But they did.

Driving home through the citywide block party that had broken out in celebration, I smiled as fans piled out of their cars at red lights and danced together.

Starlit, aglow in their headlights' beams, they didn't know it, but they were doing the last, biggest tango in Cleveland for a long time.

In a newspaper photograph taped to an inner wall of LeBron James's dressing stall in the Q for at least a year, the Cavaliers' forward's right arm is cocked, he holds the ball high above his head in his hand, and he is soaring in proof positive that a man can so fly. He is frozen in time above a defender who is no more able to stop thunder from clapping than James from dunking.

In the photo, it is always November 3, 2007, in San Antonio, Texas. James is eternally flirting with the edge of incredulity as he cups the ball above the 11½-foot-high white outlined square on the backboard. This is the really rare air up there. This is where Gus "Honeycomb" Johnson made his hive. This is where Michael Jordan became a legend.

An instant later came James's lightning strike of a dunk.

The victim, his arms upraised to try to obstruct the flight of the ball, has made a gesture that resembles the universal hands-up posture of battlefield surrender. The player getting posterized is not gangly, spindly Detroit forward Tayshaun Prince, who, as he tried to guard James in the Eastern Conference Finals, could've used the protection of a helmet. The victim is Spurs power forward Tim Duncan, at 6'11", two inches taller than Prince, at 250 pounds, 38 heavier, and at his position, the best ever. Yet, Duncan had no chance on the play. James's chest bump as he completed the dunk sent him reeling backward, almost spilling Duncan on the floor behind the baseline.

The Cavs won the game, 88–81. It was the second of the season for both teams. The Cavs won again, 82–78, in Cleveland on the second day of 2007, but it was not commemorated in either the locker or lore of LeBron.

The dunk was as good as it ever got for James and the Cavaliers against a loaded Spurs team. The Spurs' 4–0 sweep in the 2007 NBA Finals was only a small surprise. The Immaculate Perception of James's greatness in every corner of the basketball universe after Game 5 in Detroit was really his loudest and close to a last playoff hurrah that year.

After filing my column on the "48 Special," I walked to my car with my friend Fran Blinebury, formerly a competitor on the 76ers beat for the defunct *Philadelphia Journal,* then a *Houston Chronicle* sports columnist. Blinebury had been particularly outspoken about some of the LeBron wannabes. Tracy McGrady, a heralded addition to the Houston Rockets, had never gotten past the first round, for example, as Fran, in his understated, face-red-with-anger, veins-bulging way, had pointed out from time to time to time.

"And you look at LeBron, and he's going to take this piece of s—t team to the Finals," said Blinebury. I thought he was a bit harsh. I believed the Cavaliers could get one victory, maybe two, at home and then, holy déjà vu, the Detroit series would ride again. It was a pipedream, ephemeral as the smoke from Sherlock Holmes's pipe as he contemplates the game that is afoot. So thoroughly had James dominated the Pistons and Flip Saunders in the "48 Special" that they never even thought to double-team him. James got on one of his streaky shooting nights in the epic game, but overall he was consistently inconsistent from long range. In the Finals, San Antonio and coach Gregg Popovich would force him to rely on his jumper, the most unreliable part of his game.

For James in those Finals and for years afterward, the struggle to make outside shooting as an effective counter to defenders sagging off and daring him to try one partially defined him. The Spurs gave James four painful lessons in the truth whispered to victorious generals by the slave sharing his chariot in triumphal processions through the streets of Rome—that all glory is fleeting.

James's hot streaks, his threes in sprees, came and went with his fickle touch. At the very fundament of greatness, a multidimensional talent like James in his power drives and laser passing checked more boxes than did pure shooters. But he had to discourage defenses stacked to prevent his drives, which often led to his pass—his *kick*, in basketball vernacular—to shooters for corner threes.

What James had to develop was a three-point shot that was replicable under pressure. Painful setbacks occurred until he finally became an archangel whose "trumpet" shook the defenders' walls down as Joshua had at Jericho.

Afterward, the 2007 Cavs were almost universally called "the worst team in the history of the Finals." The runner-up was Allen Iverson's 2001 Sixers, who won a game against the Shaq-Kobe Lakers. "At least Iverson's team could play defense," said the critics nationwide.

The only happy people at the Q were gamblers who had won their bets. Drew Carey, comedian, Clevelander, and local icon after his years on his eponymous hit television sitcom, explained it this way in *The Great Book of Cleveland Sports Lists* (which I coauthored): "The Cavs got three points in the spread. There was a guy in my section who had a $50,000 bet on the Cavs plus three. The deficit is four, then five, then four, then five all the way to the end. The horn is sounding, the Spurs are celebrating, and just before all that, the Cavs' Damon Jones hits a junk 3-pointer to make it a one-point loss. Our whole section started high-fiving."

The civic mood in most of Cleveland was somber but proud. Some tears undoubtedly were shed. But bettors who cover the spread are happy everywhere forevermore.

CHAPTER 13

Return of the Celtics

The Celtics were back. Twenty-nine other NBA franchises liked it when they were far back.

Their rise was as sudden as a sneeze. Twenty-nine other NBA franchises, slimed by Kelly-green mucus for years, cried in unison, "Cover your mouth when you do that, you snotmonger!" The 2006–07 season was one during which the NBA's most successful franchise had won the second-fewest games in its history: 24. It was a total lower than only the 15–67 season of 1996–97 and the 19–31 record in the strike-shortened 1998–99 season. Their winning percentage, .293, was lower only than the .183 in the '96–'97 season.

Worse for their longtime hostile and highly spoiled fans, the Celtics had not won a championship since Larry Bird, Kevin McHale, and Robert Parish, their last triumphant triumvirate, in 1986. At the time, the NBA had been on a merry-go-round, usually with only three riders. From 1980 to 1987, the Sixers, Celtics, and Lakers shuffled Finals appearances and championships among themselves, a streak broken only by two Houston losses in the Finals.

This made the NBA something of a chalk-pick league, in betting parlance. And with that cue, heeeeere's LeBronny and the Cavs, treating a canister of chalk dust as if it were a powder keg, flinging cumulus clouds of the particulate matter in the air at the scorer's table, where it fell like bee pollen in the springtime into reporters' coffee cups. The callow Cavs would go sneaker toe to toe with the Celtics for supremacy of pro basketball.

The newly threatening, bulked-up reputation of the Cavaliers was only in keeping with the huge mural of James in downtown Cleveland on the side of the Sherwin-Williams building with the legend *We Are All Witnesses*, as the white stuff drifted over James's head like a pinch of angel's feathers. I attended a wedding in Cleveland in which the bride, groom, and the entire wedding party flung talcum powder in the air as a prelude to the bridal bouquet toss.

In two breathtaking strikes going into the 2007–08 season, the previously dormant Celtics made dramatic moves to reclaim their proud heritage. In doing so, they changed the NBA's power equation, metaphorically cleaning the blackboards and clapping the erasers clean by creating the first "Super Team," despite all the credit/blame that mistakenly goes to James as the team stacker-in-chief.

On June 28, 2007, the Celtics traded for star shooting guard Ray Allen, sending a package of point guard Delonte West, small forward Wally Szczerbiak and forward Jeff Green to the Seattle SuperSonics in exchange for Allen and center Glen "Big Baby" Davis.

On August 31, barely more than a month later, they acquired Kevin Garnett in the largest NBA trade ever for a single player. Minnesota received Al Jefferson, Ryan Gomes, Sebastian Telfair, Gerald Green, Theo Ratliff, two first-round draft picks, and probably a bag of magic beans, knowing how Boston operated in fleecing the NBA's rubes.

Allen was a must-have. Trading for Allen was as essential a move as when Roman Republic plotters decided Julius Caesar had to die on the Ides of March. Thrusting a shiv into Caesar's ribs was supposed to prevent him from declaring himself an emperor. Getting Allen enabled a one-season Celtic imperium, for Garnett had believed he and holdover top draft pick Paul Pierce—who was coming off one of his worst seasons—would not be enough to challenge for a title without a third major contributor.

Importantly, all three were veterans who had served long and well and had yet gone unfulfilled. Pierce had been with the Celtics for eight seasons and never gone past the Eastern Conference semifinals, which he reached only twice. Garnett had played 14 long seasons in Minnesota, as a LeBron forerunner, a preps-to-pros jumper. He had reached the conference finals only once and then lost. Allen had been in the NBA for 12 years, seven in Milwaukee and five in Seattle. He had reached one Eastern Conference final and lost.

These experiences made the "Big Three" in reality a "Big One." They all "bought in," as the expression goes, willingly sacrificing self for team. Two of the three had suffered enough elsewhere to leave for greener pastures. James would do the same eventually, and he would do so five years sooner into his career than Allen and nine sooner than Garnett. In all their maneuvering, the Celtics avoided the charge of team-stacking because the transformation was accomplished through the usual mechanisms of the draft and front-office horse-trading, not players colluding to do so.

That would become James's controversial contribution to fan estrangement and competitive disparity.

The Celtics, however, were not through. On August 1, 2007, they signed Eddie House from the Nets as a free agent. They also signed free agent P. J. Brown from Chicago. Each would play a huge part in the seven-game war the second-round Cavaliers–Celtics series became. So would newly acquired Celtic Glen Davis two years later in another unhappy outcome for the Cavs against Boston.

These were all ominous developments. It wasn't only what Boston gained that immediately put retention of Cleveland's Eastern Conference championship in jeopardy, it was what the Celtics gave up and the Cavs later collected.

On February 21, 2008, in trying to match or at least put some checks on the Celtics' stunning rebuild, the Cavs wound up with nearly a whole new team. As part of a three-team deal, they traded Donyell Marshall and Ira Newble to Seattle and then Shannon Brown, Drew Gooden, Larry Hughes and Cedric Simmons to Chicago—whereupon the Bulls traded to the Cavs Joe Smith, Ben Wallace, and a 2009 second-round draft pick (they later selected Danny Green), after which—whew!—the Bulls traded Adrian Griffin to Seattle, which then sent Wally Szczerbiak and (sinister music playing in the background) Delonte West to Cleveland.

Szczerbiak, a Miami (Ohio) player who had had a huge NCAA Tournament in his final collegiate season, was the most recognizable newcomer to fans. He also turned out to be a significant disappointment.

Delonte West was a disturbed and disturbing player. His effect on the team was at the least disruptive and at the most destructive enough to play a part in convincing James to leave Cleveland.

The interstate chess game between the Celtics and the 76ers and the Celtics and the Cavaliers teams I covered, the former as a beat man, the latter as a columnist, was very familiar to me. It was hardwired into the teams, from Wilt vs. Russell and Havlicek stealing the ball to Bird vs. Erving.

I remembered driving home after covering a Sixers game and picking up, on WEEI out of Boston, play-by-play man Johnny Most's voice, like "phlegm-coated gravel," in the accurate but unpleasant description of *Boston Globe* beat man John Powers. Describing Bird's driving layup and its butterfly kiss high off the backboard for a basket on the night of my eavesdropping on the Celtics' game, Most growled, "I know you're listening down there in Philadelphia. I don't want any hate mail from Philadelphia. But I gotta say: 'Block that one, Dr. J!'"

Most's voice had been cured like a ham by the cigarettes he chain-smoked during games in an era of a laissez-faire approach to carcinogens. Before, during, and after games, he smoked only when he was living and wheezing. In the mid-1980s, wrote the *Boston Globe*'s Dan Shaughnessy, he accidentally flicked burning ashes on his pants and set them on fire during a broadcast. Rumpled, smoke-wreathed, Most was a human chimney with a death mask for a face and a Homeric approach bigger than any blind Greek poet.

By the first decade of the new millennium, the Sixers were in decline. The Celtics were on the climb. They were not the fly in the ointment to James. Called in Boston newspaper headlines the *C*s, they were really a swarm of killer *B*s; his playoff roadblock; they stamped his exit visa from Cleveland; they would be the crucible through whose fire James had to pass with Miami; they exploited James's supporting cast after his return to Cleveland; and finally, they replaced Washington as his favorite foils.

CHAPTER 14

Celtics at the Summit

In the NBA playoffs, the legends grow as the games go on.

As Julius Erving said of seventh games, "That's when the respect is highest."

So is the romance. Usually, romance has reality for lunch in the big games. You don't find a lot of that in the first game. Sometimes, this is because one or both teams must deal with fatigue. The Cavs had to travel, and the Celtics played with one fewer day of rest.

Often, a series opener is an exercise in basketball chess, trial and error, "feeling each other out," as the saying goes, using past tendencies that will inevitably get twisted like the plot of a mystery novel as the series goes on. It was mostly error in the unsightly, ugly, nearly unimaginably poorly played opener of the 2008 Eastern Conference semifinals in Boston.

The fact also was that the Cavaliers would have immediately broken through on the Celtics' floor, had James not had the worst performance in a playoff game thus far in his career.

There are three themes to this epic series—James's terrible start, which lasted through the first three games; his fourth game dunk, which the crew of a B-52 would have admired; and a seventh game whose brilliance, edginess, and high stakes rivaled any of the Celtics' epic games against the 76ers and Lakers.

From the start, the Celtics treated James with something approaching disdain, as *Grantland*'s impresario Bill Simmons called it:

"That's why Rajon Rondo, the Celtics' point guard, angrily yelped, 'Let's go!' before defending LeBron's final drive of regulation in Game 1. LeBron ended up settling for a 25-footer against someone seven inches shorter than him, followed by Rondo strutting back to the huddle and probably telling his teammates, 'I knew he didn't have the balls to come at me.' They spent that whole series challenging his manhood."

Eventually, James had to internalize that and nullify it. It took two more seasons of defeat and disappointment for the message to sink in.

James's incredibly off-key series start reminded me of my 76ers beat man years, when Bill Veeck admirer, showman, and team general manager Pat Williams sprang one "Pepper, the Singing Pig" on unsuspecting fans as a halftime act. Alas, Pepper could not carry a tune in a lard bucket and was so vehemently derided that the *Inquirer*'s headline the next day read, "Sixers Win; Pig Booed."

The problem was the Celtics were playing Philly's role and the Cavs Pepper's.

"He's got to be frustrated. He's such a good player He puts so much on his shoulders," said Wally Szczerbiak. It was wasted sympathy at best. Given the chance to shoulder some of the burden in the seventh game, "Wally Wonder"—his nickname in the mid-major Mid-American Conference—had, like novelist Ayn Rand's Atlas, shrugged.

However, the fat lady had not sung to indicate that the opera was over, nor had Pepper squealed to indicate that bacon could be in the offing.

In the third game at the Q in Cleveland, James brought 40 minutes and 15 seconds more of dismal play. He shot only 5-for-16, which pushed his three-game aggregate to a ghastly 13-for-58, 22.4 percent. With James playing so badly, the Cavs couldn't have beaten the Providence Steamrollers, a charter team in the Basketball Association of America, a 1948–49 NBA precursor, who bowed out in the league's final year with a 6–42 record.

Amazingly, the Cavs won anyway, led by Delonte West, who scored 21 points. James's teammates shot a giddy 59 percent (32-for-54).

James never participated in the NBA Slam Dunk Contest. In game 4, he showed the Celtics and others why he never needed to.

Once the greatest show of NBA All-Star Weekend, the contest, born in 1976, was the last gasp of the American Basketball Association.

The inaugural Slam Contest winner was Julius Erving, Afroed, goateed, the very model of 1976 chic. Although a dunk was never worth more than two points on the scoreboard, after the first Slam Dunk Contest, it earned immeasurable street cred. Years later, the dunk contest's winner received the Julius Erving trophy for his efforts.

The Slam Dunk Contest was instrumental in the Jordan legend, after he won a ballyhooed big-air battle against Atlanta's Dominique Wilkins. Kobe Bryant won it fresh out of high school, switching the ball from one hand to the other in midair with a handoff between his legs, then finishing with a dunk that was pure slam-bang theater.

Unlike Bryant, James needed no cloud-hopping cachet. The *Sports Illustrated* cover gave it to him in his junior year in high school. Unlike Erving, he had no league to save—Erving, followed by Larry Bird and Magic Johnson had already done that. Already, James had nothing to prove. Since he first stepped onto an NBA court, he had been dunking on big men who were usually cleared only by objects flight control had okayed for takeoff.

Golfer Lee Trevino once called Jack Nicklaus, multitasking with his course design company while winning 18 major championships, "a legend in his spare time." For his part, James posterized great players like Tim Duncan in his spare time between passing and rebounding and shooting threes. He kept the dunkin' on Duncan photo, but it was only a souvenir. It wasn't who James was.

James again struggled with his shot, taking 20 of them to score 21 points. His seven baskets boosted his shooting percentage through four games to 25.6. Early in the game, Pierce and James became entangled and tumbled into the crowd near the seat occupied by Gloria James, who rushed to her son's defense.

Later, Pierce grabbed James from behind on a breakaway, and the pair spilled into the crowd again, with Gloria bolting from her seat and getting in Pierce's face. James later apologized, admitting he said "words I shouldn't have used in front of my mother." What James said, ear witnesses later related, was, "Sit yo' ass back down in that chair!"

In the fourth quarter, James clinched the victory in the last 8 minutes, 45 seconds, with a three-pointer, four assists, and a dunk over Garnett, the reigning NBA Defensive Player of the Year, that went 'round the world of televised highlights and into headlines and photo captions in newspapers from the *Boston Globe* to the *Cleveland Plain Dealer* and points west.

On the play, Joe Smith's screen in the foul circle slowed Pierce, who had been dogging James but could only rake a flailing, futile hand at the Cavaliers' star. A head fake made the Celtics' James Posey take a single, irredeemable step the wrong way, and suddenly, James was down the lane on two lickety-split steps, with Garnett coming over from the weak side, too late, too low, and squarely in James's bomb sight.

James launched himself with his right hand cocked behind his shoulder and dunked as quick as the crack of a lash. All Garnett could do was decide insult beat the hell out of injury, intact fingers were an easy choice over jammed or taped together ones, and what's a little posterizing for posterity when posthumous rites were the option?

"We needed that. The team needed it. Our crowd needed it. I needed it. I hadn't had a play like that yet in the series, and it kind of built up in me," said James.

The dunk filled the hearts of Celtic coach Doc Rivers, and network play-by-play man Kevin Harlan with thoughts of regret and inspiration, respectively. Rivers said, "He can dunk. Especially if you give him a running start at the basket. It's probably going to be a pretty good dunk, and he's so darn powerful that once he gets up there, there's not a lot you can do."

The Q quaked with the fans' roars. James's throwdown seemed more like an act of nature than anything else. It belonged outside, among the elements of storm and wind, to be paired with lightning flashing from a bruised sky, blasting and burning anything that got in the way.

All Garnett could do was get out of the way and let the atoms smash.

Harlan screamed, "LEBRON JAMES! WITH NO REGARD FOR HUMAN LIFE!!"

The legend of LeBron James had become fact without the myth-making of *The Man Who Shot Liberty Valance*, the deceptions of the Fox News anchor creatures, or the folklore surrounding Paul Bunyan, Pecos Bill, or Joe Magarac.

The Celtics were winless on the road but undefeated at TD Garden in the playoffs. To me, it was a much purer record than anything from the Boston Garden days, with the win-at-all-costs cheap tricks of Auerbach;

the slovenly discomfort of restrooms with more amenities than an outdoor privy but not much else; the strong smell of urine in lobby corners that seemed to have been mistaken for urinals; the electrical wiring that could have dated from Ben Franklin's experiment with his kite in a thunderstorm; the basket, rope, and pulley system of delivering reporters' copy in the typewriter days to the balcony press room to be sent by Western Union to the newspapers of the land; the beggar with his tin can of pencils for sale and seemingly eternal squatter's right to the space he occupied against a wall; and the dungeon feel of the entrance in the dark at the top of the stairs.

Still, the new Garden was watered by visitors' tears, and it grew only home team victories when it counted most.

The fifth game in a series tied 2–2 is always described as pivotal. The reason is obvious. The team that wins Game 5 wins playoff series in the NBA 82 percent of the time. Everything that pivots, however, is not guaranteed to decide everything.

With West supplying some improbable heroics, a surprise because he had been troubled by eye irritation, even seeing a doctor in Boston, the Cavs kept Game 5 close, but Boston won.

"It's hard to play this game with just one eye, unless you're a pirate," he said.

Playing with an eyepatch would be tough. Playing without pants, not so much. Rondo, as they say on the middle school playgrounds, got pantsed by his own zeal, elevating to block a shot by West, while his baggy shorts headed south, puddling around his sneakers.

James's totals in the sixth game victory—32 points, 12 assists, and nine rebounds—looked robust. But he was only 9-for-23 from the field, as the Ghost of Missed Shots Past made an encore appearance.

Fans who expected consistent dominance instead saw inconsistency.

Back went the frayed series to Boston.

Despite the interregnum that had lasted 22 long years, the new arena's address was grandly called Legends Way. James had done little inside its doors burnish his own legend.

Few things can exert more hold on a team, people or nation, for that matter, than a dream of empire, and even sharper is the desire to regain one that has been lost.

The Celtics' sudden ascent after nearly hitting bottom brought that familiar ache to Boston fans, as well as rueful recollections of failed saviors.

The most notable was Rick Pitino, the celebrity college coach who became head of all things basketball with the Celtics. He dismissed unrealistic hopes for an immediate restoration of greatness: "Larry Bird, Kevin McHale, and Robert Parish are not coming through that door."

It was true, however, as both fans and media members in Boston were fully aware, that LeBron was coming through that door for the seventh game, on Sunday, May 18, with all the grim possibilities he might present.

It had all the trappings needed for a prominent place in history, a shootout between Pierce and James, who had body-and-soul-deep loathing for each other that began in 2003, when a jealous Pierce, upset at the national attention James was getting in his rookie season, spat at the Cavs' bench and James.

It was the greatest shootout of top of the marquee names playing at the top of their games in the 20 years since Larry Bird and the Celtics squeaked past Dominique Wilkins and the Hawks in an epic seventh game in 1988.

The Celtics won that one, 118–116. Wilkins scored 47 points on a surreal 19-for-23 shooting effort. Bird scored 34, 20 in the fourth quarter, including a left-handed three-pointer, which sounds like something out of a book of tall tales.

Introduced to the roaring crowd as "The Truth," Pierce was known less for what he did not do than for what he actually did. He had the open contempt for James he had exhibited with his "great expectoration," while James had overtopped most of the great expectations that were held for him.

"Not Today, LeBron," read a sign a fan brandished in the stands.

It certainly started that way, with the Celtics roaring out to a 16–4 lead. The replay board showed again and again the highlights of the 1988 game, one in which Celtics general manager Danny Ainge and their coach Rivers both played.

Rivers, then a guard with Atlanta, remembered the circumstances of the near-citywide effort to help the Celtics, when he and other Atlanta players never received the room service breakfasts they had ordered hours earlier.

"I bought a candy bar in a hotel shop on the way to the team bus," said Rivers. "That's what I played Game 7 on—a candy bar."

Not many points were available for other players in the 2007 game, in which neither team scored 100 points and both players scored close to 50.

Even with Allen—mired in the type of funk James had been in the opening games—scoring only four points, the Celtics still got 13 from Garnett, despite his deferral to Pierce, and 10 from former free agent P. J. Brown, whom Garnett and Pierce had recruited at the All-Star Game in New Orleans.

Brown retrieved one miss on the bounce in the lane, all the Cavs having so diligently boxed out Celtics that no one was available to snag the rebound, which Brown promptly deposited in the basket by flipping in a short jump shot.

Representing LeBron's Cleveland posse, West had 15 points, and after that, exactly zero other Cavs were in double figures. Crucially, trailing 89–88, in game in which they had never led and last were tied at 4–4, James—rather than storm to the rim for a basket with a possible and-one attached, with the Cavs trailing, with 1:41 to play—settled a for a three-pointer, 29 feet out. It went long, but the Cavs' season did not, in a 95–92 loss.

James played 46 minutes and 48 seconds. Probably because of that, the Celtics made all the hustle plays with more sweat and scrap. They had nine offensive rebounds and capitalized on each for nine crucial points in a game they won by five.

Like Dominique Wilkins, James won the head-to-head battle, 45 points to 41, but he and his team lost the war. James's points came on 14-for-29 from the field and 14-for-19 at the line. Pierce was 13-for-23 and 11-for-12. Shooting less than 50 percent in every single game of the series, James finished at a dismal 35.9 percent, missing nearly 100 more shots than he made—153 to 55.

"He was well overdue for a breakout game; he played really well—and that's why he's going to the next round and we're not," James said of Pierce afterward.

The lack of self-awareness is stunning, for, at least in this series, he could have been speaking of himself. It was not only the two alpha males putting up numbers like Bird and Wilkins, "the Human Highlight Reel," but it was also—excepting only the example of the third game, in which his teammates carried James to victory—the same plot line of LeBron vs. the world.

During timeouts, the replay board showed the generation-old high-lights of the epic 1988 game. Flashes of it even popped up when play resumed, as if by subliminal suggestion the double helixes of victory in the Celtics' DNA could do their stuff for the current generation in green.

Another free-agent pickup by the Celtics, Eddie House, led me to write in a retrospective in the *Cleveland Plain Dealer*: "Every Cavaliers player walks past the words as he nears the court and hears the screaming crowds at The Q. Last season, they were the handwriting on the wall for the Cavs."

The words are from Al Pacino's speech in the football movie *Any Given Sunday*. They are about inches, about how the inches of extra effort translate to victory. On the Sunday they were given, before a wild, roaring crowd in Boston, the Cavs lost because the Celtics simply clawed and scratched for more of the vital inches.

In the movie, Pacino's character deconstructs victory, breaking it down into its smallest increments. The inches are all around the players, he says. All they have to do is extend their grasp.

In a raspy voice, he bellows: "It's the guy who's willing to die that will win that inch. On this team, we fight for that inch. On this team, we tear ourselves and everyone else around us to pieces for that inch. We *claw!!* with our *fingernails* for that inch."

In the second quarter, he could have been screaming in the ear of Boston's Eddie House, a summer pickup playing for his eighth team in eight seasons, as House ran down the court.

First, James Posey knocked the ball away from Sasha Pavlovic. Wally Szczerbiak was six feet ahead of House as both chased the ball, which was rolling toward the Cavs' basket. Szczerbiak seemed to be running in mud. As the pair neared the baseline, Szczerbiak tried to shield House, who was closing fast on him.

Szczerbiak did not dive for the ball. But House did. He flung himself under Szczerbiak, grabbing the ball as he rolled along the floor and sling-ing it to Posey, whom Szczerbiak then fouled on a layup attempt. Posey made both free throws.

Then and now, I wondered why Szczerbiak didn't dive. Afraid of a floor burn? Poison oak allergy because of the red oak boards beneath his feet? Szczerbiak played 15 minutes, 12 seconds, missed all three shots, and was the only player who saw action on either team who did not score.

The last decisive inches came with 60 seconds to play. Ilgauskas, at 7–3, figured easily to win a jump ball near the Boston basket against 6–8 James Posey. Except, like Havlicek so long ago, against the Sixers, Pierce stole the ball, jumping in front of James to claim the tip.

One more memory was revived when Pierce clinched the victory in the last seconds with a free throw that went full (Don) Nelson, bouncing off the back of the rim straight up—boinnnng—dropping straight down into the basket in Game 7 of the 1969 NBA Finals.

"The ghost of Red [Auerbach of the 1969 NBA Finals] was just looking over us," Pierce said of the founding father of the old Celtic dynasty, who died at 89 in 2006. "I think he kind of tapped it in the right direction. It sort of put a smile on my face."

While Pierce basked in the cheers, James beelined to the locker room.

The Celtics went on to win their 17th championship, beating the Lakers in six games, including their only road victory of the postseason in the fourth game after overcoming a 24-point deficit.

For his part, James went to the interview room in Boston and unburdened himself.

"Boston got better," he said of the Garnett and [despite his lame series] Allen deals. The Lakers [who acquired Pao Gasol and thus dissuaded Kobe Bryant from leaving] got better."

The implication was clear. The Cavs had two years before he became a free agent to give James teammates who could carry their own weight.

The Celtics' instant success compared to the Cavs' regression in regular season and playoff victories was a determining factor in James's assumption of a de facto general manager's role.

He did, however, seem sincere in the honor he felt as part of the game he had just played in and lost. "This will go down in history," he said—not simply for the two big names but for the little things, measured in inches, summoned from sweat, drawing the line of demarcation between playoff life and death. After finishing his remarks, LeBron went out the door that closed on his season.

Two years later, he would walk out of the same door in the same arena in defeat again and then out of Cleveland.

CHAPTER 15

The Magical Misery Tour

Do you believe in Magic?

That was my lede for the Philadelphia Inquirer on May 18, 1980. The *lede* is the first sentence or paragraph (*graf*, in journalese) of a story or column. It should be an attention-getter, the literary "hook" that readers can't resist. Journalists always spell it *lede* because, if you buried the *lead*, you indicated an unfamiliarity with journalistic principles (and we do have some). Besides, *burying the lead* reads like the denouement of the unfortunate events at the OK Corral.

Earvin "Magic" Johnson had his abracadabra night in the sixth game of the 1980 NBA Finals, accomplishing something that would live in memories forever and be revived by other players' tours de force in games to come. Without injured Kareem Abdul-Jabbar, who remained behind in Los Angeles, getting treated for a severe ankle sprain, Johnson and the Lakers broke the spirit of the 76ers behind his stunning 42-point, 15-assist, 7-rebounds spree. The Lakers won, 123–107, closing out the Sixers, 4–2, in the NBA Finals before a shocked crowd at the old Spectrum in South Philadelphia.

Even after an 8–0 blitz in the first two playoff rounds in 2009, the Cavs were worried about Magic, the team, and Magic, the kingdom. The latter was used in the sense not of the amusement park but of the NBA championship, which the Orlando team, after the promise of a Finals run in their infancy in 1995, had never won. But this edition of the team appeared capable of doing it, closing out the defending champion Celtics in a 101–82 rout in Game 7 at previously impregnable Boston.

Sometimes, an NBA season has much in common with the lyrics of the Broadway musical *Rent,* which enumerates the 525,600 minutes in a year. In the 2008–09 regular season, the Cavs could count 3,956 minutes (counting four overtime games); 237,360 seconds; over 40,000 miles in the air, much of that time spent crisscrossing four time zones; with the players' body clocks as broken as the Mad Hatter's watch in *Alice in Wonderland;* with little of it spent with their families or in the same place very long, all of it to play one more game at home at the end a playoff series.

The problem was that the Cavs learned the wrong lesson from their loss to the Celtics, which was not wholly decided by Boston's home-court advantage. The argument was as specious then as in 1981 when Bill Fitch's cheating denied the Sixers home-court in what became a bitter seventh game loss in the Eastern Conference Finals. A very good columnist, the *Philadelphia Daily News's* Tom Cushman, wrote a very silly column, claiming the biggest game was the last of the regular season on the occasion of Fitch's spying. Most players play better at home than on the road, but great players usually have fewer fluctuations in performance.

I disagreed forcefully. The biggest game is an elimination game in the playoffs. As Dr. J argued, "the sweetest sound on the road is silence." He saw such games as a clash of opposites, a sonic squall line in which the crescendo of the partisan crowd's cheers could be satisfyingly reduced to a diminuendo in their team's defeat. In that regard, the Cavs lost to Boston because James, even considering the slam-bang theatrics of his dunk in Game 4 and his heroic shortfall in Game 7, clanged the ball off enough rims to be his very own anvil chorus.

The all-time record for regular season home court dominance was set by the 1985–86 Celtics at 40–1. They finished with a 67–15 record. The 2008–09 Cavs made a serious run at that record. They lost to the Lakers in Cleveland on February 8, 2009, 101–91, and did not lose again at home until the meaningless final game of the season, a 111–10 overtime loss to Philadelphia in which James did not even dress. A distraught Delonte West obviously did not agree with the front office's decision to pass on tying the record and rest its meal ticket, LeBron. "I never won anything in my whole life," said West, who would lose almost everything but the life he lived, on the streets as an indigent, profoundly distressed homeless person.

It is always a balancing act between the seemingly endless regular season and the home-court advantage a good season brings, on the one hand, versus the imperatives of rest and good health for the playoffs, on the other.

Travel is far easier now than when I became a beat reporter in 1975. Franchises have their own corporate planes. Back in the day, travel through America's four time zones was by commercial jet. NBA-sized men were stuffed, knees nearly at their chins, into cramped coach-section seats. Only players with NBA seniority were in the first-class cabins. Three games in three cities in three nights were sometimes on the schedule, a regimen not allowed now. Each of those games could come at the end of a day that began with a 5:00 A.M. hotel wake-up call in a different city, a 5:30 bus to the airport, and a 7:00 flight. This was how room service operators in the destination city sometimes took breakfast orders from players and reporters in rooms with the nonexistent numbers of their previous hotel rooms. The NBA assessed a $10,000 fine—big money in those days—on teams that did not take the morning's first available flights and then could not get to scheduled games in time. Even with the improved amenities and the razing of pits like Boston Garden, the NBA gives its players an exhausting, though well-paid life. In recent years, the NBA had to fine players who skipped interconference games, thus stiffing fans in faraway cities in their only chance to see them.

There is no obvious solution to trying to win 'em all and gain a piece of forever in fans' memories and concentrating most on winning the big one, which brings remembrance enough. The 2009 Indianapolis Colts, unbeaten through 14 games with Peyton Manning at quarterback, prudently took him out with five minutes left in the third quarter of a game on December 17, with the Colts holding a 15–10 lead. Back-up Curtis Painter immediately committed two turnovers quicker than you could say, "Why is Curtis Painter in the game, and what the hell is he doing?" The Colts lost, 29–15, to the New York Jets, surrendering 19 straight points and scoring none with Painter at the helm. Fans and reporters chided them for being glory-bound all season and then, with a chance to become only the second undefeated team in NFL history after Miami in 1972, at the next-to-last minute saying, "None for us, thanks."

The tribute given during the first round of the series to dying Detroit "Bad Boys" coach Chuck Daly was like a farewell to the brutal style he had countenanced. Rules changes had saved the game from the stranglehold intimidation had taken on it, and without violence, the Pistons lacked enough skill to pose a threat.

In the closing moments of the first half of the Cavs' opening romp vs. Detroit, James sank a 41-foot three-pointer, running to the locker room as the ball banked off the backboard and in, while cheers engulfed him. Asked his range after the game, James replied, "Right now, it's pretty much unlimited."

So was everything else about him in 2008–09, the first season he was named the NBA's Most Valuable Player. In addition to the coveted MVP award, the 2008–09 season also marked James's only First Team All-Defense selection, an unjust exclusion to many, including his more successful Olympic coach Mike Krzyzewski of Duke.

The ESPN SportsCenter Play of the Day entry came when James had a spectacular, breakaway dunk that included whirling the ball in a circle in front of himself and then Richter-scaling the basket.

With the game tied, 53–53, after three quarters, James took over long enough to dissuade Detroit from dreams of grandeur. "He wasn't getting the calls, so he said, 'I'm going to will this team to a victory. It was exciting to see him flip the switch. I got a rush out of it," said Mike Brown.

The Pistons had been in the conference finals six straight years, the longest such streak since the Los Angeles Lakers in the 1980s. That run ended in a sweep at the hands of the Cavs with no game closer than 11 points.

The Cavs waited around for a week to face the Atlanta Hawks, who, by successive margins of 27, 20, 15, and 10 points, were summarily sent to their rooms.

Early in the week, James had been honored with the MVP award in an intimate ceremony at his high school in Akron, one with pep banners and signs that coach Mike Brown likened to a scene from the classic basketball movie *Hoosiers*.

Before the opener of the series in Cleveland, the NBA's Commissioner David Stern presented James with the MVP award, which he won in a landslide. "You led the team by playing team first," said Stern.

The Hawks remained in the visitors' locker room rather than listen to the wall-shaking roared and music during Stern's MVP trophy presentation.

The game was held on the 20th anniversary of "The Shot," Michael Jordan's dagger to the Cavs' heart in Richfield Coliseum at the buzzer of the fifth and final round of a fierce playoff series in 1989. It had been a blight on the Cavs' franchise ever since, with Jordan carrying the Bulls to six championships and the Cavs crumbling in the face of a wave of injuries. But now the Cavs had James, who became almost giddy about the high level of basketball he and his team were playing in another rout. He hit walk-off shots at the end of each of the first two quarters. The second one was a three-pointer as time ran out, creating bedlam for the first minute of the halftime break. "I'm having a ball," he said, calling the Cavs "a great team."

"It's honestly unexplainable," James said. "There's only a few guys in this league that can get into a zone like that, and I'm blessed to have the ability to be one of those guys. You just feel like you can make pretty much every shot you take."

He admitted being inspired in the closeout game by a taunting Hawks fan, dressed in garish green and orange, who sat at courtside Saturday night. "A gentleman over there decided to talk back with me," James said. "It's happened in the past. It usually doesn't work out good for the other team."

The Cavs were jovial in victory. James made only 9 of 22 shots, but West chipped in 21 points. "You saw I had LeBrons on?" said West. "It was the shoes."

"Delonte is our glue. When he gets going, he's almost unguardable," James said.

Everyone (dramatic foreshadowing) would soon learn West was just possibly the exact opposite of a player who glued his teammates together, although the shocking rumors about him were never confirmed.

2009 EASTERN CONFERENCE FINALS

Game 1, at Cleveland, Magic 107, Cavaliers 106

The Cavs lost the home-court advantage in the series for which they had worked so hard in the very first game in Cleveland. Really, it shouldn't have been that astonishing, except for the ease of the Cavs' first two series routs. Orlando won two of the three games between the teams during the regular season, beating Cleveland percussively by 29 points in early April.

Leading big at the half of the opener wasn't enough. A circus shot by Mo Williams wasn't enough. Leading until Orlando took its first lead at 85–84 wasn't enough. James's three-point play that gave the Cavs a 106–4 lead and fouled out Dwight Howard late in the game—with his 30 points, 13 rebounds, and defensive presence that reduced the passageways to the rim to Gibraltar-like straits—weren't enough. Williams's frantic shot to win hit the heel of the heel of the rim.

The Magic had stolen the Cavs' hard-won home-court advantage in an arena silent as a tomb at game's end, except for Magic coach Stan Van Gundy shouting mockingly in the locker room, "We are all witnesses!"

Game 2, at Cleveland, Cavaliers 96, Magic 95

The last second again coincided with the last shot. The Jordan memory, "The Shot" that made up the nightmare of 1989, was like tea leaves whirling in a kettle of roiling, bubbling water, ready to boil over and scald everyone again. A 23-point first-half lead hadn't been enough. James's 32 points hadn't been enough. Now, with 1.0 showing on the game clock, the buzzer was about to sound, the kettle to whistle, the season to go on life support. Williams was inbounding from the 28-foot mark in the forecourt with the Cavs trailing by two points.

Of course, the ball would go to James if he could get open. Gene Shue won 648 NBA games as a head coach and twice was named Coach of the Year. In the sixth and last game of the 1977 NBA Finals, in which, with Julius Erving already having scored 40 points, Shue diagrammed the last play for George McGinnis, who was slumping precipitously. Mac's four-foot jump shot at the buzzer came up short, glancing off the rim, as so often they had all series long. I don't know how many Philadelphians suffered self-inflicted concussions after slapping themselves upside the head and screaming, "Now why in hell wouldn't you get the ball to Dr. J?" But it was a lot. In their press corps too. (Blush.)

Mike Brown was certainly not going to throw himself, or at least his reputation, on a similar funeral pyre. Of course, the ball would go to James. It is almost axiomatic in the playoffs to go to your best player when the stakes are highest. James faked toward the basket to get Hedo Turkoglu, his defender, on his heels. Maybe he even nudged Turkoglu with a bent shoulder, as Jordan had done in the "Goodbye Game" in Utah. Or maybe not. Nothing was called. Reversing course, James, wearing Jordan's No. 23, caught the pass at the top of the foul circle as he was running cross-court toward Williams. He had to catch the ball cleanly, leap, and twist his body so his shoulders were lined up with the rim 25 feet from the basket, and, as Turkoglu leapt toward him, he had to fade away, much as the crowd's hopes were doing, and loft a high-arching shot. Time had run out by the time the ball settled into the net, like a bird feathering its nest.

English Romantic poet Samuel Taylor Coleridge once wrote that watching the English actor Edmund Kean on the stage was "like reading Shakespeare by lightning flashes." Watching James play basketball had the same kinetic effect. It was the old "poetry in motion" idea. The last flash of James's brilliance brought a roar from the crowd that not even Kean playing King Lear going mad in the thunder on the heath could match.

The Q quaked with the tumult of triumph, as if an SST—a supersonic transport of joy—had taken off on a runway from the arc to the rim. The building reverberated from its floor to its rafters as it never had resounded when it was called Gund Arena, nor as it had been shaken all its preceding years as "the Q" and James was hitting a Jordanesque stride in dramatic finishes. It was louder than the Dunk of Death over Garnett because of the circumstances; the Cavs led by seven points when James strafed the basket and the Boston center. They won by 11.

The rumble from the stands for the do-or-die shot against Orlando was like a landslide coming down. The Cavs were back—back from the brink of a very bad outlook. The three comebacks from 0–2 deficits that took Detroit to seven games, then beat Detroit in six, and finally extended Boston to seven, had all occurred after two losses on the road, not at home.

"You couldn't hear anything but a roar. It was the biggest shot I've hit in my career," said James, who, as usual, led the Cavs with 35 points.

Williams, witness to a transfiguration of defeat into victory, fell to his knees as if in a revival tent and pounded his hand on the floor. "I was punch drunk. I couldn't move. I was stuck," he said.

Van Gundy, witness to a coaching move he openly second-guessed, chided himself because he neither sent a second defender at James as soon as Williams threw the pass nor had his players cheat toward the three-point arc and take away the long ball and the defeat it could bring. "I wish I had the last play back from a coaching standpoint," he said.

But James's shot was only reprieve, not deliverance.

Game 3, at Orlando, Magic 114, Cavaliers 106

Like everyone else from Florida in Amway Arena, the Magic players and coaches, the Magic's fans, and possibly Mickey and Minnie over at the Magic Kingdom, too, were sick and tired of seeing James's three-pointer on TV and even on the arena's replay screen. During the game, the players emphatically registered their unhappiness with shoves, pushes, face-to-face altercations, and Anthony Johnson's elbow to the face that split Williams's eyebrow open, earning a Flagrant 1 foul and necessitating four stitches in Williams's face.

Fifty-eight fouls were called. Three players fouled out. Two drew technicals. A total of 86 free throws were attempted. The game started Sunday night and threatened to run over into the Monday morning rush hour.

The alarming part, and it would stay alarming throughout the series, was Howard's free throw shooting. Of his 30 points, 14 came at the line in 19 tries. A notoriously poor foul shooter, through the 2022 season Howard averaged 56.7 percent. He shot 59.4 percent in the 2008–09 regular season. Against the Cavs in the playoffs, he drained 47 of 67, a stunning 70.1 percent.

After James's three-point play closed the deficit to 90–86 in the final 3 minutes, the Cavs played "Hack-a-Howard," bear-hugging him near the basket. He made both free throws. It was the Magic's sixth victory in the last seven meetings with the Cavs.

The Magic really didn't have a spell over their opponents. But they had matchup advantages in Howard, the surprising Hedo Turkoglu and Rashard Lewis, both of whom would be convicted as drug cheaters in the future.

The next season, Lewis was nailed for testing abnormally high for testosterone, a dead giveaway for anabolic steroid use. He had the series of his life against the Cavs because of a Mike Brown–out of a defensive scheme. Brown had James defend Rafer Alston, fearing his three-point ability, instead of Rashard Lewis. Lewis shot 15-for-31, nearly 50 percent, and averaged 18.3 points. Alston shot 14-of-37 on the arc, 38.3 percent, for a 12.5-point average in the series. It was a stupid idea that got stupider with Brown's refusal to adjust to the realities of the two players in the series.

Turkoglu, whom Toronto acquired the next season as a possible incentive to keep pending free agent Chris Bosh there, was caught in 2013 for using methenolone, a fat-cutting agent classified as a steroid. That substance disqualified Belarus's Nadzeya Ostopchuk, the 2012 Olympics women's shot-put gold medalist. Turkoglu said he was unaware of the illegal substance when he was treated in the off-season in Turkey for a shoulder injury. Well, of course he was. None of these athletes are ever aware of what they put into their bodies (heavy sarcasm), which just happen to be the means by which they make the money to live such luxurious lives.

Turkoglu, presumably playing clean, had the worst season of his career in Toronto, being dismissed in a bitterly funny and frankly un-Canadian column by sportswriter Bruce Arthur in the *National Post* as "6-feet-10 inches of Turkish noodle soup," or, alternatively, "nearly seven feet of oatmeal." One speculation on Turkoglu's nosedive: it's hard to smuggle illegal drugs through Canadian customs.

Game 4, at Orlando, Magic 116, Cavaliers 114 (OT)

Michael Jordan, Cleveland's top basketball villain, was third overall behind former Denver quarterback John Elway and the perennial leaders, the Pittsburgh Steelers. Had James sunk buzzer-beating game-winners twice in four games, he would have had a chance to take his place in Orlando infamy along with Force 5 hurricanes and an invasion of alligators. James's deadly double was not to be, however. Should they hold a narrow lead in the last second, Van Gundy and his players had a no-encores game plan. James scored 44 points. Williams, who had guaranteed Game 4 and series wins, backed it up through three quarters with 18 points, then backslid with none in the fourth period.

West again had a strong game, with 21 points. The memory remains of the moment in the late going, when West, diving, barely missed a long rebound and then pounded his hand on the floor in frustration. The inches that the franchise so emphasized and for which he was all but tearing himself apart still would not allow him to reach the ball he had to grasp. And yet, as long as it is a one-possession game and LeBron James is on the floor it can still turn into a show-stopping number from Broadway, the Street of Dreams. Call the number "Some Enchanted Evening," "Anything Goes," or, more to the point, "Anything You Can Do I Can Do Better."

With the Cavs taking the ball out of bounds near midcourt and 3.2 seconds to play, everyone in Amway Arena, everyone watching at home on TV, and all the sailors on all the ships at sea knew who was going to get the ball and take the last shot. It had to be a three-pointer.

"With LeBron James on the court, doesn't 3.2 seconds seem like two minutes?" Van Gundy asked. "We had two guys on him, and he made a move like a tight end, caught the ball and still got off a reasonable shot. This guy is unbelievable."

The ball seemed to track straight and true from 38 feet away after James had swerved around some defenders and sped past others. In the still of the night, the Orlando fans held their breath in the arena until the ball hit the rim and bounced harmlessly amid roars pealing like thunder.

As the Cavs headed for effectively a make-or-break game, I remembered what Cleveland Indians manager Pat Corrales used to say of Nogales in the Mexican state of Sonora, just across the border from Arizona where the team then conducted spring training. "It's not the end of the world," said the skipper, "but you can see it from there."

A 3–1 series deficit isn't the end of the world for the trailing team, but you don't need binoculars to see it.

Game 5, at Cleveland, Cavaliers 112, Magic 102

Everything was on display that validated James as a virtuoso, his opponents as valiant, and the Cavs as indefensibly complacent with big leads. The Cavs wasted their advantages like Art Modell, the liar who moved the Cleveland Browns, wasted his reputation. This time it was a 22-point lead that vanished as if someone said, "Hocus-pocus."

Often, Cleveland fans simply would not let the Cavs lose when they played at home. It was a bone-deep attachment to the savior from just down the road, and it was heightened by the Indians' agonizing extra-innings loss in the 1997 World Series after blowing a ninth-inning lead against Miami and by the pre-perfidy Browns' near-misses in reaching the Super Bowl.

James was at his unstoppable best with a box-score-stuffing triple double of 37 points, 14 rebounds, and 12 assists. It was the first time since Oscar Robertson in 1963, 46 years earlier, that anyone had posted such a huge triple-double in a playoff game. James scored 21 in the second half, 17 in the fourth quarter, and had a say by shooting, passing or offensive rebounding in his team's first 29 points in the last quarter.

On the white board in the locker room after the game were the words "Flight 1 A.M."

Game 6, at Orlando, Magic 103, Cavaliers 90

The Cavs were going back to where the mouse roared. The special season still lived. I recalled that when soon-to-be-NBA-champion Washington sprang an unfathomable upset on the 76ers, the Sixer players' boomboxes—it was 1978—were playing, almost unimaginably, Roy Orbison's "It's Over" in their locker room before the game. Joe Bryant, Kobe's father, argued for the less morbid "Keep the Ball Rollin'," by Jay and the Techniques. As a true-blue and bluesy Rolling Stones fan, I thought of "Not Fade Away."

To answer the questions and the songs in order:

It was indeed over.

The ball stopped rolling.

Despite their fans' "bigger than a Cadillac" love back in Cleveland, the Cavs did indeed fade away,

The Magic made Tomorrowland vanish.

So did Nike's sales campaign that had assumed a Lakers–Cavs NBA Finals by airing a series of commercials in which puppet LeBron and mannequin Kobe Bryant traded insults. James had often praised Bryant as the league's best player and had dreamed of facing him in the Finals.

This would have recreated the great superstar matchups of the past, such as Wilt Chamberlain vs. Bill Russell and Magic Johnson vs. Larry Bird.

Baseball is a trinity of sorts, with three strikes and you're out and three outs per inning. So was basketball, and not only because of the three-point shot. James thought in terms of the Bible's three kings. Instead of

Garnett, Pierce, and Allen or Howard, Lewis and Turkoglu, he had had Hughes (physically fragile and jealous of James), Williams (often a playoff cipher) and Szczerbiak (overrated and, in the footrace for the crucial loosed ball, undermotivated). As for Delonte West, his head was full of enough demons to daunt an exorcist.

After sweeping Atlanta, James had called West the team's glue. It was not true. In an almost unfathomable way, he was a divisive force that tor the season and the team apart.

"The Magical Mystery Tour," sang the Beatles, was "waiting to take you away, waiting take you away."

The Magical Misery Tour took James away from Ohio and the Cavs to Florida and Miami, where he joined the Heat, where Dwayne Wade and Chris Bosh joined him as the Three Kings of the NBA.

When he returned to Cleveland after four seasons away, it was to create a triumvirate that was triumphant at last.

CHAPTER 16

The Mystery of Delonte West and Gloria James

On September 28, 2009, Delonte West was arrested for being an arsenal on motorcycle wheels, specifically a Can-Am "Trike" Spyder, a three-wheeled cycle. He was carrying a pistol and, as the showstopper in the story, a rifle in a guitar case slung across his back in the manner of a traveling troubadour of trauma.

It brought thoughts of Don Vito Corleone's capo Clemenza, who blasted away at a rival Mafioso with a shotgun pulled from a similar instrument case in *The Godfather*. Although West had been the closest thing to a reliable wingman for James, he suddenly seemed more suited to supervision by Nurse Ratched than by coach Mike Brown.

The wingman for the 2004 National College Player of the Year, Jameer Nelson at St. Joseph's University in Philadelphia, West would become an unproven villain, one of the most controversial figures in Cavaliers history. Burdened by bipolar disorder and subject to perversely unpredictable mood swings, West, an accomplished amateur artist, went so far down the black hole of depression that he seemed doomed to an early, sordid death in squalid circumstances until saved, on September 20, 2020, by television celebrity and Dallas Mavericks billionaire owner Mark Cuban for whom West had briefly played. Alas, he was recidivist in his inclinations and hit the bottom again, leaving a rehab facility and begging on a roadside in July 2022.

Delonte West, in sum, was a very leaky vessel into which to pour Cleveland's hopes.

If only the limitations of the Cavaliers' roster, despite its repeated makeovers, had clearly been responsible for the wreckage of the 2009–10 season . . .

. . . or the pad protecting James's injured right elbow, which forced him to make a lefthanded free throw in an opening series closeout game, had been the clear culprit . . .

. . . or Glenn "Big Baby" Davis of—where else, Boston—had not knocked Shaquille O'Neal, of the Superman, Shaq Daddy, Big Diesel O'Neals, out of a meaningful playoff role with a damaged thumb after the Cavs had traded for him to bulk up James's supporting cast . . .

. . . or superb play in the Game 5 rout by Boston, the Cavaliers' great nemesis during the LeBron 1.0 Cleveland version, were simply the reason . . .

. . . or the salacious rumor could have been indisputably proven false or true . . .

. . . or the hype, like so many sensational stories about celebrities, whether true or false, had not sent a frisson of prurient thrill through many fans . . .

. . . or the Cavs' purported scandal about a rumored but never proven affair between James's mother and his teammate Delonte West had not made the case of the Los Angeles Lakers' strife between Karl Malone and Kobe Bryant over Bryant's wife, Vanessa, seem, by comparison, just more of the usual shameless goings-on in Hollywood . . .

. . . then the broken person who became Delonte West would still have his reputation intact and would not have fallen all the way to homelessness on what amounted to Skid Row in Dallas, Texas, cursing venomously at passersby and looking, in the lens of a television camera, like so many other homeless and destitute Americans who might as well be left at the curb for trash pickup . . .

. . . and if the ever-louder whispers had not besmirched the true and tender love between mother and son or had not cast a sad pall over the end of James's first stint with the Cavaliers . . .

. . . then this would be a different book.

The truth was that in the category of taboos allegedly broken, the leading nominees for the 2010 Creepy Story of the Year Award in sports were Gloria James and Delonte West.

For guilty role models in history and legend, the leading creeps were King Arthur and Guinevere, Oedipus Rex of Thebes and his literal mother, Jocasta. And the winners are . . . in basketball terms, anyway, the Boston Celtics. After brushing off the Chicago Bulls in five games, the Cavs faced the Celtics as a hurricane of gossip raged inside the walls of the Cavs' locker rooms, home and road. It is doubtful any team could have survived, although, as is true to this day, no one knows enough with absolute certainty to say yea or nay to the maybe-or-maybe not scandal.

In 2010, James was a rare back-to-back winner of the NBA Most Valuable Player award. He was the holder of age-group records for milestones reached in almost every positive statistical category and the likely owner in the not-all-that-distant future of all the records worth having.

The stories of mankind's sexual caprices go back at least 2,600 years, to Sophocles's tragedy about King Oedipus. Blind to the predicted consequences of his own rashness, he unknowingly murdered his father and married his mother, thus fulfilling an oracle that warned that King Laius would be murdered by his son, who would marry his mother and become both brother and father to their children.

Oedipus disregarded the oracle, but had he not quarreled with an older man or married an older woman, he would have avoided the shame and exile that were the price for his heedlessness.

I spent my nearly half-century as a newspaperman covering most of the major sports events under the sun but in love with only one, basketball. When I wrote about Dr. J in Philadelphia or LeBron in Cleveland, it was not only my job but my pleasure to do so. There is no pleasure in writing or commenting about the destructive triangle of sin or maybe "only" slander, of truth or maybe lies, of incrimination or maybe exculpation, in the gossip that rocked the Cavs after they arrived in Boston.

One member of the Cavaliers' press corps spoke of the rumor using street slang, "bumping uglies," for sexual intercourse but shrugged when asked if it was absolutely true.

"Nobody knows," he said. And to this day, nobody does.

West and James's mother vehemently denied their rumored affair.

One who was not afraid to express an opinion was Calvin Murphy, a stellar guard in his time who was known as "Little Muhammad" (Ali) for his lightning-fast fists. However, he was hardly a good character witness.

Murphy's career included a trail of sexual molestation allegations almost as long as the 5'7" Murphy was high. Confirmed to have fathered 14 children by nine different women and sued for sexual molestation on behalf of five of his daughters, who ranged in age from six to 16, Murphy was acquitted in an eight-month-long trial.

But a month after he was awarded the more than $52,000 at stake in the pension of his deceased wife, he was arrested on charges of indecency and public molestation. This was a man who knew his way around sexual irresponsibility. This was hardly a credible witness.

In a radio interview, Murphy said, "Unfortunately, my sources in the NBA tell me, and they're legit, that the only people who didn't know it was happening was LeBron and me."

There is just the chance, of course, that Murphy was a liar whose pants, like Johnny Most's, were on fire.

Actually, the basketball problems were hard enough for the team to overcome, the rumors aside. Other teams were drafting players who would become franchise cornerstones. On Saturday, March 28, 2009, during a home stand, after a victory Friday night over Minnesota and before a victory Sunday afternoon over Dallas, LeBron James, basketball junkie, went to Ford Field in Detroit, home of the NFL's Lions, and saw Davidson's Steph Curry play in person for the first time. In an NCAA Tournament Sweet 16 game against Wisconsin, Curry scored 33 points on 11-of-22 shooting overall and 6-of-11 on the arc, respectively. Wisconsin had allowed an average of only 53 points per game before Davidson's 74–70 upset.

James, who had his share of misses on player acquisitions—see Larry Hughes—was adamant that not only could Curry, the son of former Cavalier Del Curry, play in the league despite worries that he was too spindly but also that he would be a great success. "I saw a guy playing free and easy, the way you want to play," James said.

In the NBA draft, the Golden State Warriors selected Curry as the ninth pick of the first round. The greatest shooter in NBA history would alter the game with his shooting range and accuracy, nuking up the impact of the three-pointer.

Yet, as James was celebrating free and easy, the Cavaliers were signing the original Dwight Howard / Superman / T-Rex in Shaquille O'Neal, trading Ben Wallace and Sasha Pavlovic for a player who, along with LeBron, surely ranks in the all-time Top 10 of NBA players. It was yet another less-than-optimal move by Danny Ferry, who, in his fourth season as the Cavaliers' general manager, still had done nothing to make fans forgive and forget when he, a bust in the NBA, was acquired by trade at the enormous cost of Ron Harper early in the last decade of the previous century.

Shaq was not quite over the hill, but if you followed his enormous size-22 footprints, at the age of 38 he was certainly heading there. In the low post, he could stop a game in its tracks unlike anything other than a LaBrea tar pit. He was incredibly strong: case in point, a putback dunk in 1993, in his rookie season with Orlando, on which he clung to the rim briefly but long enough to make the hydraulics of the apparatus go kablooey. The basket, backboard, and stanchion all slowly collapsed, descending in a manner that oddly suggested a formal bow by someone meeting royalty.

He was signed specifically to negate hulking Dwight Howard, the man most responsible for the previous year's upset, yet the Cavs would not even face Orlando, which had been eliminated by Boston.

The Cavs made acquisitions beyond Shaq. In July, they threw free agent Anthony Parker, the brother of Olympic and WNBA star Candace Parker, against the wall and hoped he stuck. Pacers' sharpshooter Reggie Miller, the brother of the women's basketball pioneer Cheryl Miller, said, "The only thing Anthony Parker and I have in common is our sisters were better than us."

Next, in February 2010 the Cavs traded for Antawn "Ole!" Jamison. The only difference between Jamison's matador defense and an open door was that you could put a lock on the door. Defense was not his thing. Jamison had almost ushered James to the bucket for his last-second wining layup in Game 5 of the first Cavs–Wizards series.

Those players aside, it became clear that the O'Neal the Cavs signed was not likely to open any doors to riches and rings. He suffered a sprained right thumb on Thursday in March in a game at Boston, in which Glen "Big Baby" Davis hit his hand while he was shooting. Television replays later showed Davis pulling on the thumb while defending O'Neal.

My column afterward was angry, an indication of how fed up I was by the Celtics' scurrilous tendencies being excused as "physicality" and their chicanery dismissed as "gamesmanship." I let former Cavalier Austin Carr make the case for me:

"When I played, you wouldn't go after a guy on purpose," said Cavaliers television analyst Austin Carr, who played from 1971 to '81. All but one of those seasons were with the Cavs.

Carr said Boston's Davis bent the unwritten rules the same way he tried to twist Shaquille O'Neal's already injured thumb: "I thought what 'Big Baby' did showed the kind of character, or lack of it, that he has."

Like most viewers of the TNT telecast, including me, Carr had no problem with the original injury, when Davis's flailing hand cracked Shaq's thumb as O'Neal readied to shoot a layup. Davis was making a play on the ball. Given the size and strength of NBA players, it is surprising more serious hand injuries don't occur when defenders are swinging their arms around near the rim. Shaq tried to stay in the game, and that's when Davis defended the Cavs center as he posted up by grabbing the tender thumb.

Apparently, Davis mistook it for a wishbone, viciously yanking on it because he was intent on knocking Shaq out of the game.

"He crossed the line," Carr said. "When I played, if a guy had a hand injury, I would go aggressively after the ball and try to knock it away. If I got his hand, too, it happens. I would not purposely try to hit his hand."

The NBA has tried to legislate dirty play out of the game with the flagrant foul rule and fines. As the money got better, a bond grew between opposing players, who realized they all needed jobs, and many had families. But even today, when opposing players film commercials together and text each other constantly, it is no surprise to Carr that the Celtics resorted to a deliberate attempt to injure.

"They try to win at all costs," he said. "That's the way they function as a franchise.'"

To barroom brawls, rock fights, and gang warfare add games against Boston Celtics as without rules or limits.

Even with O'Neal out for five weeks after thumb surgery, the Cavs again had home-court advantage for the playoffs, with a 61–21 record, a scant two games ahead of their conquerors from the year before, Orlando, but 11 ahead of the Celtics.

In the first round, the Cavs played the Chicago Bulls, a team that seemed the definition of mediocrity, with a near-.500 record that was 20 games worse than the Cavs'. The Cavs brushed them aside in five games.

2010 EASTERN CONFERENCE SEMIFINALS
Game 1, at Cleveland, Cavaliers 101, Celtics 93

It started well, at least, on the shocking updraft off Mo Williams's dunk, which loomed large in the victory. Listed at 6'1" and thus brushing the boundaries of incredulity, Williams dunked in the third quarter over 6'8" Paul Pierce to begin the run that rescued the Cavs.

"I told Mo if he ever dunked in a game, it would spark us like we've never been sparked before," said James. Williams's dunk occurred with the Cavs trailing, 69–58, and the Celtics, supposedly as washed up as driftwood on the Lake Erie shoreline, showing no signs of competitive senility. In the quarter, Williams, who had frequently seemed overwhelmed by the task of guarding Celtics' point guard Rajon Rondo, scored 14 of his 20 points.

"He sparked himself too," said James, who had his usual—or so it seemed at the time—active and rarely resisted impact on the game with 35 points and a matched set of seven rebounds and seven assists.

After twisting in midair to get open, shooting while falling, and seeing the ball hit the net as he hit the floor, James gave the Cavs their first lead since 7–6 at 79–78. Because of an injured elbow, he had tried only two long shots in the first half, but he said it loosened up as the game wore on. He added a dozen points in the fourth quarter, validating Boston coach Doc Rivers's fears that just such an assault was coming as the first half ended and James's shooting motion became more fluid.

The rambunctious Shaq of the playoff opening series against the Bulls remained a mirage. Looking every tick-tock of his 38 years, he contributed a two-foot follow-up in the late going and little else.

Without exposing James to possible foul trouble, only Anthony Parker, at 6'6", had size and quickness enough to at least contain Rondo's damage. The Celtics' guard had often been the best player on the floor in the epic seven-game series between Boston and the Cavs.

I thought not only of Red Auerbach's premium on quickness but also of Bobby Knight, the volatile Indiana University coach, who at an NCAA

Final Four said, "If you have a quickness advantage, you have about 30 other advantages."

With help from friend and basketball sage Tim Corbett, I came up with a list of ways spot-to-spot quickness is an asset in basketball, as opposed to sheer speed as in track. Our combined list included fast breaks, secondary breaks, transition defense, the one or two steps conceded by defenders on jump shots to guard against drives to the basket, loose ball retrieval, step-back jumpers, crossover dribbles, pump fakes, rebounding position, rebounding in a crowd, outlet passing, drive-and-dish penetration, chase-down blocks, intercepted passes, ball deflections, steals, beating double teams, executing traps, full-court pressing, jump balls, backdoor cuts, rolls after screens, defensive hedging on screens, beating the shot clock, counters to the pick and pop, defensive rotations, and getting into proper defensive position to take offensive charges. That is 27 advantages, 28 if you count stepping lively to avoid chairs hurled by Knight.

In sum, quickness is the battery that drives much of basketball.

Astonishing quickness and a ruthless desire to win were Michael Jordan's biggest physical attributes. Remarkable quickness for his size, yoked to overwhelming power, filled the bill for LeBron.

Boston kept punching, but they could not overcome the lead the Cavs, flashing and sparking like a downed power line, had built after Williams dunked.

The confetti fell in a blizzard of gold, like doubloons, and wine, like cabernets. It would be the last time for a long time that they fell in homage to LeBron and celebration of his team.

Game 2, at Cleveland, Celtics 104, Cavaliers 88

The game proved why the old saying is "once in a blue moon." Wingman Mo Williams, surprise best supporting player in Game 1, scored four points in 1-of-9 shooting. Shaq, after seeming to become an afterthought in Brown's plans, popped up with 17 points as the second-leading Cavs scorer.

Rondo embarrassed whomever the Cavs chose to guard him. Williams in particular played the role of the statue and Rondo that of the pigeon.

The Celtics, who had dominated much of the opener but lost, won handily, despite James's 24 points and nine rebounds. They shillelagh-ed the Cavs in the third quarter, 31–12, building a 25-point lead in the fourth quarter.

After the Cavs mustered a belated challenge, I was not disposed to make too much of the comeback. Any self-respecting NBA team, playing at home in a playoff game, can man up and make an unsuccessful run when friendly fans are imploring them to do just that.

On the road, particularly on the road in Boston, not so much.

Game 3, at Boston, Cavaliers 124, Celtics 95

So much for the theory advanced in the preceding sentence. James scored 21 of his 38 points in the first quarter. He shot 8-for-10 from the field, all on medium- to long-range jumpers, in the Cavs' rout.

"I think he's healthy," said Rivers. "So enough about the elbow, and let's concentrate on basketball."

James set a team record for playoff scoring in the quarter. The Celtics set a team record for their biggest margin of defeat in the playoffs. The Cavs led by as much as 30 in the third quarter and never by less than 24 in the entire second half.

"He was playing H-O-R-S-E," Rivers said. "We were awful. We just didn't play with the same intensity they did. They played with a Game 7 mentality."

Game 3 was an outlier, just as was James's occasionally torrid jump shooting.

The Cavs shot 59.5 percent from the field, 41.7 percent on three-pointers (40 percent is excellent), and 91.2 percent on 34 free throws. As a team, the Cavs had qualified for the 50–40–90 Club, the sharpshooter's rare season-long marks in overall percentage in field goals, treys, and free throws. Even the Big Diesel seemed to have been refueled. Shaq scored 12 points, missed only two of his seven shots, and was a strong deterrent near the rim.

The truth was that the Cavs had simply made their shots. Nothing would be that simple for them again.

Game 4, at Boston, Celtics 97, Cavaliers 87

The "MVP! MVP!" chants broke out. Boston fans were cheering not for James but for one of their own: Rondo.

The Cavs had nobody who could guard him. He played ring-around-the-"Mo-sie" with Williams, accumulating numbers not seen in nearly a half-century—29 points, 18 rebounds, and 13 assists, totals that sent researchers reaching back to the Wilt and Big O Era to find comparisons. The Celtics evened the series at 2–2.

Ominously, after taking a charge from Rondo early in the game, James clearly babied the troublesome elbow and showed little of the aggression with which he had played in the third game.

The Cavs returned to Cleveland with the Delonte and Gloria rumor mills creating whole cloth out of speculation; spinning wicked possibilities like spiders with their webs, turning bundles of whispered accusation into tapestries of lies or truth, depending on whom and what you believed.

Game 5, at Cleveland, Celtics 120, Cavaliers 88

Amid troubles off the court, the Cavs found no end of them on it. Rondo scored 16 points in the second half. The Cavs couldn't stop him.

Moreover, the Celtics didn't have to worry about James for a change. He stopped himself. He shot 3-for-14, scored 15 points, and played as if waiting for the next plane out of town.

With James becoming eligible for free agency on July 1, his body language spoke broadly of a planned getaway. In the final minutes, James left the game to a scattering of boos, slapping hands with teammates, especially O'Neal, who contributed 21 points to the worst playoff loss in Cleveland history.

It was Shaq's last hurrah, although he had an inconsequential stay with Boston the next season. He had come to Cleveland seeking "to win a ring for the King." But the thumb injury changed everything.

Said O'Neal, "We were in first place. Big Baby breaks my hand. I had to sit out five weeks late in the year. . . . I know for a fact if I was healthy, we would have gotten it done that year and won a ring. I knew my role: just to back LeBron up. If he looks to me, I score. If not, I set picks, get him open, rebound, knock other players on their ass. We were playing against Boston, and Big Baby [Glen Davis], who could never stop me, did a Hack-a-Shaq. As soon as I grabbed the ball, I couldn't feel my thumb. I knew it was broke. I did everything I could do. Did cardio, I ate right, I went to the gym. I was there every night, running the treadmill. I was in 'people' shape, but not in 'basketball' shape."

It reminded me of the bitter comment the Cavs' superb former television analyst Matt Guokas told me when he did Cavs' games, about Rick Barry, the star of the soon-to-be-champion 1974–75 Golden State Warriors. Guokas was then a reserve on the Chicago Bulls, who, geography aside, were lumped in with the Left Coast teams. Barry was the high scorer in the seventh game, which the Warriors won, with 23 points.

"He quit twice in the game," said Guokas. Such occurrences are rarer than a Mo Williams dunk over Paul Pierce, but they do happen.

Most interesting is how the national Internet and TV talkers avoided the Denali-sized rumors. James was troubled by his elbow, some said. The Cavs tried to pound the ball inside to O'Neal too much, others claimed. It was an off-game, pure and simple, still others diagnosed.

It was eerie. The basketball world blew up, and nobody could say why. The Cavs needed the younger Shaq and the off-the-Trike West, but they needed a traveling therapist even more.

In his take, Mike Malone, a Cavs assistant coach in 2009–10 and the Denver Nuggets' head coach in their 2023 NBA championship season, praised the Celtics.

"It's a great question," he said. "LeBron made us look like pretty good coaches in Cleveland. We owe him a lot. Boston was our nemesis. We could never get past Boston. But that series, in 2010, I don't know if it was an injury. A lot of people said he quit, mentally. Look, we won Game 3, took back home-court advantage, and went home for Game 5. We're down six at halftime. I remember this so clearly. They come down, miss, offensive rebound, kickout three for Ray Allen. We're down nine. They come down again, miss, offensive rebound, kick out, another Ray Allen three. We're down 12, series over. We never recovered."

My own belief was that something was going on between James's ears. Henry Abbott of the *TrueHoop* website said it best: "'I don't hang my head low or make excuses about anything that may be going on,' James said after Game 5. Honorable and all that. And telling. You'd say that, I suggest, only if something was going on. And something—whether his dog died, he's injured, he's exhausted or something else . . . —was most definitely going on, even though he swore to TNT's David Aldridge at halftime that he was physically fine. Until he spills the beans on that, all we can do is guess. But LeBron James has a big ol' track record, and that was not him, so I believe something is up."

The respected Michael Wilbon of the *Washington Post*, later an ESPN studio analyst on NBA games, said cryptically and possibly tellingly, "There are things about his family that LeBron doesn't want to get out."

Game 6, at Boston, Celtics 94, Cavaliers 85

In the game that ended an era in Cleveland, James's box score numbers looked great—27 points on 8-for-21 from the floor, 19 rebounds, 13 assists—but none affected the outcome in any measurable way. "An empty triple-double," many called it.

That was because James also committed a shocking nine turnovers. His mind seemed disengaged from his body. Whether true or not, the gossips might have been wagging their many tongues, like the spectral creature Rumor, as depicted in literature and art, poisoning James's thoughts, then speeding on to infect others.

James would stand on the weak side, the side away from the ball, like an uninterested bystander, waiting to hail a cab or an occasional teammate's pass. His errant passes had previously resulted from excessive ambition and confidence, trying to squeeze through defenses built to obstruct them. This time they were off target and ill timed.

He bit his fingernails, an old habit he had taken up again. He gazed over the heads of teammates and coaches at the crowd in timeouts, a pattern he would petulantly allow to recur later in his career, all but ignoring Brown's instructions.

A sample of Mike Breen's play-by-play on ABC describes James's difficulties: "The ball is knocked away! He lost the ball, and [Boston's] Cody Allen picks it up! . . . [He dribbles] off his foot! Rajon Rondo picks it up for a layup! . . . Another turnover by LeBron James! That's eight! . . . James lost it again! Unbelievable! His ninth of the night!"

Nor did James help himself in the final minute. Brown popped off the bench, screaming, "Foul 'em! Foul 'em!" as a last-ditch tactic.

It almost certainly would not have worked in the madhouse that was TD Garden, which would have become church-mouse quiet with a Celtics player at the line for crucial free throws. But you play out the hand you're dealt. You hope for the crazy, mad fluke of a royal flush. Miracles do happen. The obligation is to play hard in a closeout game to the end. Period.

Instead, waving one hand disgustedly, James motioned for Brown in a gesture that meant—sort of as he had once said to his irate mother during a game against Boston—"Get yo' ass back on that bench."

I knew a coach or two would have erupted if a player did that to him. Jerry Sloan had to be restrained from doing his worst to Ricky Davis in "The Case of the Revoked and Fraudulent Triple-Double." Air Force Academy graduate and San Antonio coach Gregg Popovich would not have taken that lightly either.

Mike Brown, however, sat down.

Walking through the tunnel to the locker room afterward, James peeled off his Cavs jersey and slung it into a corner, never bothering to look back. In the interview room, as if the just finished game had never been played, James chose as his defense the comment, "I spoil people."

He seemed to be blissfully ignorant of the fact that he had bombed as badly as the 76ers' George McGinnis in the 1977 Finals against Portland.

After the loss to Boston, James would take three seasons and an epic performance on the road to shed another, more current comparison. Magic Johnson's errors in clock management in the clutch in the 1984 NBA Finals led to the sarcastic rhyming nickname "Tragic" Johnson. LeBron's flop was more spectacular than either McGinnis's or Johnson's.

McGinnis did try and even came out of his funk when it was too late in the sixth and final game. Magic's glitch began in a moment of indecision during which the passing window to Kareem Abdul-Jabbar closed on a crucial play.

LeBronze had been a clever coinage for the third-place Team USA in James's Olympic debut. LeBacle, a creation of Cleveland's Associated Press sports reporter Tom Withers, was worse by several orders of magnitude.

To many, James had become a false savior who couldn't salvage his team or the reputation of his mother and himself.

In the wake of the colossal collapse, the Cavs shuffled West and O'Neal off to Boston's Home for Broken Careers and Bent Thumbs. James was widely thought to have demanded West's removal from the roster.

All this is understandable to me only because the rumor must have spread through the team like a fever. It unmoored James from the safe harbor he had found in team sports after his chaotic, haphazard childhood.

James had always given words such as *promise, prodigy,* and *greatness* deep meaning and perspective. Some 26 million Americans play basketball at some level. But among that horde, James was sui generis, one of a kind. Game 5 not only regulated him, so to speak, it also degraded him.

The words *Family* and *Loyalty* are tattooed on the right side of James's rib cage. Yet, in the staggering, surprising twist to the end of the season, these terms soon proved to be only skin-deep.

The second Boston series was an inflection moment, in which the vulnerability was born in a King whose realm consisted of a basketball court's 4,700 square feet. Unfortunately, life is not conducted inside the lines, and referees do not exist outside those lines to blow the whistle on flagrantly foul behavior. Game 5 of the 2010 Boston series would be the signature game of James's first seven years with the Cavs—not Game 7 at Boston in 2008 or Game 5 at Detroit in 2007, or any of his last-second miracles against Washington in 2006. James had had bad numbers in playoff games before and would have them again. But his lassitude and lack of commitment in that game against the Celtics was unmistakable. It would be widely interpreted as tanking so he could get out of town and join a team that was on the cusp of greatness so he could take it to the finish line.

James had spent his career swaddled in praise. His previous failures had been heroic ones, inviting comparisons to Jerry West and Julius Erving, who for so many years could not overcome either the frailties of their teammates or the Celtics. Throughout James's many successes, he had been wrapped in light like a great actor on the Broadway stage. But the curtain and the darkness were descending.

James had vowed to be with his surrogate family, his teammates, in the 2007 playoffs, even if it meant missing the birth of his second child, Bryce Maximus, whose middle name was for Russell Crowe's character, Maximus Decimus Medius, in the hit movie *Gladiator*.

Two years and a second crushing loss to Boston later, the kid's daddy threw down his sword and shield.

CHAPTER 17

"The Decision"

James had said before free agency began on July 1 that the Cavs "had the edge" in signing him. After the loss to Boston, however, he said, "Me and my team will sit down and see what's best for me."

The "team" was not the Cavs. It was the "Four Horsemen" of the LRMR Ventures, the company of sports advisers James had founded with long-time friends at the dawn of his NBA career. James seemed to delight in his contrarian choices that flew in the face of public sentiment. First he spurned Akron Buchtel, the Black community's choice, for St. Vincent-St. Mary; then he flouted Ohio High School Athletic Association rules on illegal benefits and flaunted his disdain by bringing a remote-controlled miniature version of his gas-guzzling automotive beast Hummer to a game and letting it skitter hither and yon on the court before a game.

Among Clevelanders, his most egregious sin was wearing the cap of his beloved New York Yankees to a Cleveland Indians playoff game against the Bronx Bombers. His choice of lid so annoyed octogenarian Cleveland legend and Hall of Fame pitcher Bob Feller that the "Heater from Van Meter [Iowa]" vowed to sit in the front row of a Cavs game with a cap of the team's arch nemesis at the time, the Detroit Pistons, jammed on his head.

James also rooted for the Dallas Cowboys, whose Lone Star helmet logo he had doodled as a child, not the Cleveland Browns. Finally, he had confessed that as a youth in Akron, he had always hated Cleveland, with its NBA, NFL, and MLB teams overshadowing Akron's sports.

The first 10 days of July 2010 provided a strange reversal, in which NBA team owners and executives, most of them as rich as Croesus, waited their turn to bow, scrape, and court the King on bended knee. Perhaps some got hurt in their pride as well as their knees.

As Cleveland mobilized, Governor Ted Strickland and US senator Sherrod Brown dedicated a music video to James. But when it came time for the Cavs to try to match the wooing of the Nets, Knicks, Bulls, Clippers, and Heat, the hometown team dived headfirst into an empty pool. Equal parts high school pep rally, NBA show biz, and puerile exhibition, it missed the competitive mark entirely. It included a fan tunnel of Clevelanders holding black-lettered signs beseeching James to stay, all provided by the Cavs. They lined the approach to the arena and its entrance, and threw cumulus clouds of chalk dust in the air. Finally, James was viewed a cartoon, based on *Family Guy*, a James TV favorite, with characters based on the mannerisms of James and his teammates.

Maybe it's just me, but I suspected the hand of a sophomoric remote-controlled fart-machine manipulator in the choice of a cartoon character to champion the home front cause.

Next up were the Heat. Team president Pat Riley threw a bag on the table. In it were Riley's seven championship rings. (He was to win two more with LeBron.)

"If you want one of these, come to Miami and let's go to work," Riley said.

No nonsense. No contest.

Although some would hail James, along with free agency coconspirators Dwyane Wade and Chris Bosh, for their self-sacrifice in each leaving $15 million on the table to form the super team and for exiting with the blessing of the NBA's collective bargaining agreement as free agents and not demanding trades, nobody in Cleveland, and only a distinct minority anywhere, felt that way.

This was because of the ghastly misstep of James's ESPN interview with reporter Jim Gray, which was called "the Decision," but really should have been dubbed "the Disaster."

Importantly, James had never been recruited. He was a Cavalier because of a jet of air at the bottom of a standard lottery machine. After whirling around with those of the other 13 other teams that missed the playoffs, a gust of destiny propelled a ping pong ball out of the hopper that had the Cavs' number on it, delivering James to the NBA city most eager to embrace a savior, particularly one considered a native son.

Cleopatra arriving in Rome on her golden barge might have been more ecstatically greeted, but just barely. Austin Carr, known as "Mr. Cavalier," for his sterling career spent in a Richfield pasture and his loyalty to Cleveland, wept on live local television. As for the ordinary citizens, cue Mama Cass of the Mamas & the Papas, singing the lead vocals on "Dancing in the Streets."

But even that was topped, or perhaps bottomed, if you have a taste for obsequiousness and a fondness for watching powerful figures kowtow, bow, and truckle to a 25-year-old who was finally legally able to rent a car, by the courtship of the King.

Gray said, "We've seen 30-foot billboards. We've seen teams clear out all kinds of cap space. We've seen cartoons made about you and for you in part of their pitch. President Obama, for crying out loud, seven times has commented that he'd like to see you go to Chicago. What did you expect from this process?"

James, perhaps properly, considered it his due. The seven years he had played for the Cavs had made him one of the greatest athletes in the city's sports history. He was clearly behind only Jesse Owens, because he drove his spikes into the track surface in Berlin at the 1936 Olympics and punctured Hitler's master race theory, and possibly behind running back Jim Brown of the Cleveland Browns, the irresistible ground-gaining force on the city's most popular team. Bob Feller would be fourth on a theoretical Mount Rushmore of Cleveland sports figures, because he never won a World Series game, while the other three reached the summits of their individual and team sports largely on the basis of their personal efforts.

On July 9, 2010, one day before free agency signings began, before the many witnesses and a national television audience, James blasphemed the high church of hoops and jilted the Cavs at its altar.

Gray jokingly asked whether James had his powder ready to throw. "Left it at home," said James.

Gray: "Do you want to sleep on it?"

James: "I've slept enough. Or the lack of sleep."

Gray, inanely: "Do you still bite your nails?

James: "A little. Not a lot."

Pursuing the manicure issue, Gray said, "You've had everybody else biting their nails. So I guess it's time for them to stop chewing. The answer to the question everybody wants to know: LeBron, what's your decision?"

James: "In this fall, this is very tough, in this fall, I'm going to take my talents to South Beach and play for the Miami Heat."

Near the huge photo of James on the Sherwin-Williams building, outrage, not paint, erupted, covering if not the earth, almost every place in the old Lake Erie port city, most of Ohio, much of the nation, and possibly many ships at sea.

On the front page of the next morning's *Cleveland Plain Dealer* was a huge photograph of James in his Cavs' uniform, with the Jordanesque number 23 on his back, as he was walking with his back to the camera. Above his right shoulder in large, but not apocalyptic type, was the word *Gone.*

Surrounding the single four-letter word and the unobtrusive but all-important punctuation mark of a period was white space. The period ended the discussion. The emptiness on the page reflected that in the hearts of many Clevelanders.

A thin diagonal line with a V-shaped tip, like an arrow's, pointed to James's bare right hand. Accompanying it were the words, in small type, like that reserved for rec league results and summer softball scores: "Seven years in Cleveland. No rings."

Plainly spoken. Plainly dealt.

A thrilling time in Cleveland sports had ended not with a bang but a whimper.

The only analogy was to the Browns' 1993 decision to cut another beloved hometown-ish hero, quarterback Bernie Kosar, from the Youngstown suburb of Boardman, and a lifelong Browns fan, and replace him with one Todd Philcox. When two-faced owner Art Modell asked PR man Kevin Byrne what the *Plain Dealer* coverage looked like, because Modell lacked the guts to find out for himself, Byrne replied, "Art, it's Pearl Harbor."

On an impulse that Sunday when the Browns played their first game without Kosar at Seattle, I took a stroll around my suburban neighborhood, listening to the game, the coverage of which was blaring out of television sets and radios on a 51-degree afternoon. On the very first play from scrim-mage, 14 seconds into the game, the new quarterback fumbled, Seattle recovered and ran the ball in for a touchdown. Cheering for a score against the formerly most beloved team in town rang out from house after house.

The James decision was worse. Kosar had not chosen to go. Modell decided for him. James had wanted out.

Some fans took to the downtown streets and ostentatiously set fire to the LeBron jerseys they had bought at the Cavs' merchandise store and at sporting goods shops around town. They were never more than a small, publicity-seeking minority, but they were savvy enough to know the jersey burning was the photo-op of TV and newspaper dreams.

The sense of betrayal and the explosion of hate that followed rocked James, although he did not admit it at first.

"My first seven years, I could be the light," James said. He seemed to mean something greater than the spotlight or the limelight, something closer to the incandescence of skill and talent, or to the color-streaked light pouring through the stained glass of the cathedrals of basketball, or perhaps something as simple as a midmorning blaze filling a basketball goal like a blessing from above.

"Then to be on the other side, the dark side, to be the villain, some-thing I had never been called . . . it took long time to deal with that. When I made the Decision, I was living in Ohio. You could feel the hate. You didn't have to hear it. It was unfortunate. It was challenging. It was a situation I had never been in before."

James's introductory news conference in Miami was another public-ity backfire. James, Wade, and Bosh danced across a stage at their intro-ductory news conference, as special effects machines spewed a vaporous fog over the trio while Terpsichore, the Greek Muse of dance, wept.

In the trio's welcome party in July, James made his instantly infamous "Not one, not two, not three, not four, not five, not six, not seven . . ." half-joking prediction of championships for the Heat.

Dan Gilbert responded with a late-night "Open Letter to Cavaliers Fans" that was the equivalent of a hissy fit. Spittle all but flew from the oddball Comic Sans typeface.

Gilbert went fully mad dog in his letter in the wake of the royal abdica-tion, calling "the Decision" "unlike anything ever 'witnessed' in the history of sports and probably the history of entertainment, and decrying the "several day, narcissistic, self-promotional build-up" of "our former hero, who grew up in the very region that he deserted this evening." He lambasted James's "cowardly betrayal" and added that the "shameful display of self-ishness and betrayal by one of our very own" has "shifted our 'motivation' to previously unknown and previously never experienced levels." In Comic Sans type, he promised:

"I PERSONALLY GUARANTEE THAT THE CLEVELAND CAVALIERS WILL WIN AN NBA CHAMPIONSHIP BEFORE THE SELF-TITLED FORMER 'KING' WINS ONE.' You can take it to the bank."

Banks must not be what they used to be.

The Cavs did not remotely threaten to win a championship or even reach the playoffs, but they did lose 26 games in a row, enabling lottery bonanzas, in the years before James's contrition and atonement. This inspired conspiracy theories in other NBA cities, particularly since those picks became Kyrie Irving, Anthony Bennett, and Andrew Wiggins. Bennett was a bust, but Irving for a time was the ultimate wingman, much as Ted Williams had been for John Glenn when they flew combat aircraft in the Korean War. Wiggins was later traded for the Cavs' third future musketeer, Kevin Love.

My reaction, with an eye to the failed LeBron and Kobe puppets in the ill-fated Nike ad campaign, was to pen a poem—a nursery rhyme, actually:

The little king sat on a tuffet,
Wet with fake fog spray.
Along came a Laker, to sit by the faker
And say, "You're no king. Go away!"

CHAPTER 18

The Pros and the Prose

My troubles with team owners and other NBA poohbahs started early and stayed late. It is part of the give-and-take in a country with a free press. Somebody has to speak truth to power. Often, the voice is that of a mainstream media member.

This leads to a scrum between the media and the moguls. It's a sporty little takeoff on the US and Soviet nuclear arsenals during the Cold War, in which an uneasy peace was created by the apocalyptic consequences of nuclear war in a doctrine called MAD, for mutually assured destruction. In journalism, it was more like mutually assured dislike.

I sometimes thought of the example of the oyster and the pearl, in which an irritant such as a parasite or food bit inside the mollusk's shell attacks the invertebrate. The oyster secretes a liquid containing carbonate material and protein, which form protective nacre, mother of pearl. It was our words that we sportswriters sometimes considered pearls and our stories that team owners and league commissioners often thought of as slimy (in keeping with the oyster motif) and that hurt their feelings.

I was upbraided in person and over the phone and on radio and television by NBA players George McGinnis, his index finger jabbing me in the chest with each angry word; Doug Collins, his voice climbing up an impressive range of octaves, his arms waving like a berserk human semaphore; Cavaliers general manager Jim Paxson and coach Paul Silas; the Sixers' owner Fitz Eugene Dixon and Cavs' owner Ted Stepien; Indians manager Mike Hargrove; Browns coaches Marty Schottenheimer, Bill Belichick and Pat Shurmur; NBA commissioner David Stern; and the ever whiny, repetitively lying Art Modell, this last in a phone call to former NFL commissioner Pete Rozelle that was carried live in Cleveland.

The only one I regretted was former Cleveland relief pitcher Ernie Camacho, whose ERA as the closer brought the same sensory reaction to spectators as Robert Duvall experienced in *Apocalypse Now*, savoring the smell of napalm in the morning because "it smells like victory." But Camacho's "Molotov fastballs" bore the stench of defeat. This led me to conflate his last name with fireballs, flaming debris, and raging infernos. The baseball world was ablaze with objects such as "Fourth of July Camachoworks," the movie *Chariots of Camacho*, and the "ubiquitous presence of a Dalmatian at the Camacho house." The day the column ran, Camacho charged toward me in the clubhouse but was restrained by two other players. The column was over the top. His rage was justified.

Back in the tweedy precincts of owners and commissioners, Dixon, a Main Line blueblood and heir to the Widener fortune, put up some impressive numbers in his snubbing of and distaste for newspapermen. But Dixon didn't do his own fighting. He let his peeps do it for him. "Boot 'em out!" he once ordered a hulking Philly cop when the *Philadelphia Bulletin*'s Mark Heisler and I, the *Inquirer*'s doughty man of the moment, tried to question him before a game as he sat in his seat near the baseline. With the cop grasping us rudely by an elbow each, we were escorted out of His Radiance's glow.

Dixon also gave me a giftwrapped book at a team Christmas party in the one year he ever made the mistake of inviting those inquisitive, rumpled newshounds with their edgy questions. When I unwrapped it, I read the title: *Everything I Know About Good, Honest Sports Writing*, by Bill Livingston. Every page of the sporty little tome was blank. I had to chuckle. It really was funny.

No one else got a book, so there was that. It's the thought that counts, as they say. Ted Stepien, reeking of class, once invited *Akron Beacon Journal* beat man Sheldon Ocker to his house to "drink some beers and watch some porno." Ocker declined.

Stepien became so agitated at my daily references to the Cavs recovery after "the black night of the Ted Stepien era" that he called me at the

Plain Dealer told me if I continued he would "come down there and kick your ass!"

I indicated my doubt that he was able to find the building but noted that if he were, "I would kick his ass," addressing him with a 12-letter expletive popular around Thebes in Oedipus Rex's day. My outburst astonished a Boy Scout troop, which was touring the newsroom in that more innocent era.

Stepien first made his name a Cleveland codeword for *stupid* by volunteering to recreate an ill-fated 1938 Indians stunt to honor downtown's Terminal Tower, a commuter rail hub, on the structure's 50th anniversary. Stepien ordered deployment on the pavement below of outfielders from his American Professional Slo-Pitch Softball League team. They circled warily under the softballs Stepien insouciantly flipped off the top of the 771-foot-high building. While an estimated 5,000 spectators looked on, the spheroids, reaching top speeds of 144 mph, smashed up a few cars badly enough to put them on the wrecker's hook, broke a women's wrist, and injured another spectator. Finally, one of the bombs was caught and the carnage stopped. I could not resist calling Stepien Teddy No Game, after slugger Ted Williams's nickname, Teddy Ballgame.

Stepping up in class, I next got on Stern's bad side. I did a takeout (long feature) on him in his Manhattan office in 1984, shortly before leaving the *Inquirer* for the *Plain Dealer*. He had just gotten the job and joked, "That story was so flattering that my mother could have written it."

Things did not stay so jolly between us.

He came to town to check out the hoopla the day before LeBron's first game in Sacramento. The seven days of special sections leading up to the big day were on display in a *Plain Dealer* meeting room for Stern's perusal. The franchise had been in the wilderness since the days of Mark Price and Brad Daugherty in the early 1990s. I had not been nice about the years of revolving-door coaches, bungled drafts, and lackluster-to-ludicrous records. In front of the assembled top editors and the publisher, Stern asked if I had written any of them. I had not. He was told that the coverage was the work of beat writers and feature writers. "Good. Livingston is far too negative," Stern said.

I made no reply, stifling an impulse to say, "Well, I hear your mama likes me."

And finally, we have arrived at the most vindictive and the most du-plicitous—except for Modell—of them all, the little trickster Dan Gilbert, Loki with a fart machine, remotely dialing the blasts of flatulence up to terrible, pants-splitting volume.

In the wake of the Decision, I was doing an interview on ESPN sports talker Tony Kornheiser's podcast. The topic of Gilbert's slavering, mad-dog letter to the fans came up. "I could understand playing to his base," I said. "But this is not the first time that he had released statements like this that weren't pretty. They were sent out late at night, and draw some connotations from that if you will."

Nothing could stop me. I was on a roll, headed for Angry Billionaire Land.

"He can have a bit of a hair trigger," I continued. "He can become in-fluenced by all the things that a late night would engender. I think prob-ably alcohol probably [sic] played a part of it, just to come out with it. It's just suppositional on my part, but he's sent out messages like this before, to Plain Dealer people on the casino issue, that were over the top."

Eighteen days after I made the comments, the Cleveland Scene, the city's alternative paper picked up the story. My inference from the fortnight-and-more that passed until the delayed reaction was that I had only said what most people believed true. What sensible man would burn his bridges to the greatest player of the era?

Gilbert went straight to my bosses at the Plain Dealer with his com-plaints. He was lashing out in frustration, trying to get me reprimanded, suspended, or fired by going over my head. And this was, literally, quite a stretch since I'm almost 6 feet tall, and Gilbert is listed as standing 5'6".

About the same time, in a bit of unsolicited corroboration of my char-acterization of Gilbert's LeBron letter, the Northeast Ohio Media Group, the Plain Dealer's digital arm, ran a screed by political columnist Brent Larkin. In a September 2014 piece, Larkin called out Gilbert's failure to live up to the jobs he had said, in his push for approval of his proposed casino on a citywide vote, would bring 34,000 jobs.

The reality: 10,600 temporary jobs and 4,844 full time.

"Just days before hoodwinking voters in 2009," Larkin wrote," Gilbert sent vile emails to top Plain Dealer executives after the newspaper ran a legitimate story reporting Gilbert had been arrested on gambling charges while a student at Michigan State University."

There was more from Larkin: "In May 2013, [Gilbert] tweeted that I [Larkin] was a yellow journalist for having the audacity to suggest he hadn't kept his word to voters, adding 'more to be revealed in the months ahead' about the new casino."

As for me, my *Plain Dealer* bosses twice postponed my hearing with them and my Newspaper Guild representative. It's an old management trick, giving me time to think about what I had done. It loses its effectiveness, however, if the alleged miscreant thinks he has done little wrong.

When we finally met, I was presented with an already written letter of apology to sign. This was not as high-handed a move as it seems. As I told my guild rep, the estimable firebrand Rachel Dissell, they had to do something, because Gilbert was petty enough to reduce access to the players for our beat writers. They did not suspend me or dock my pay. They had done the least they could do.

The letter asserted that I had made "statements that were speculative, unprofessional and unfair." I didn't like it, and Rachel, a terrific reporter who, in my opinion, should have won a Pulitzer Prize for her coverage of the gang rape of a student by football players at Ohio's Steubenville High School, advised that I refuse to sign it.

But I did, wanting to put the whole thing behind me.

The *Plain Dealer* never wrote a word about it, although the inquisitive *Scene* was on the scent, calling L'Affaire Gilbert "a sanctioned snipping of one of the few who dare call Gilbert to the carpet." The sports blog *Deadspin* picked the story up and gave it national exposure.

"You know, Livy, that story did nothing but make you look good and the *Plain Dealer* and Gilbert look bad," said one of my journalism mentors, the late Bill Millsaps of the *Richmond Times-Dispatch*.

"I know," I said. "That's why I leaked it."

CHAPTER 19

Fall and Rise of the Heat

For some of us baby boomers, the best Christmas gift was neither a bicycle nor Ralphie's Red Ryder BB gun in *A Christmas Story,* but a basketball. Mine was a J. C. Higgins model, the Sears & Roebuck brand.

The sharpshooters of our dreams had nicknames like Seattle's "Downtown" Fred Brown, sinking jump shots from the inner-ring suburbs, or the Lakers' Jamaal "Silk" Wilkes, with a shot Coach Paul Westhead memorably described as "like snow falling off a bamboo leaf." Our reveries were not of dunks that exploded backboards the way Ella Fitzgerald's recorded voice shattered fine crystal in old Memorex audiotape commercials. We dreamt instead of shots Silk would appreciate, rustling the net with their passage as softly as snowfall on the silent, sleighride countryside in Currier & Ives lithographs.

We shot baskets at all hours and in all weathers, developing cats' eyes in the dark when parents balked at bringing a bedroom lamp outside to the driveway, connected by several umbilicals of extension cords to an electrical outlet just inside the backdoor. (I had read that the great Bob Pettit did that as a boy.)

We took passes from compliant phantom teammates, their parts played by the bounce of the ball off the picket fence alongside the driveway. We got off spectacular buzzer-beaters as the imaginary play-by-play men in our heads went full Russ Hodges on the day the Giants won the pennant. A swish sent sibilants whispering doom through the net cords.

We were all Jimmy Chitwood, and Shooter was running the picket-fence play in *Hoosiers* just for us.

When the three-pointer arrived in the NBA in the 1979–80 season, followed in 1986 by a shorter college triple, itself preceded by a chump-change three that didn't even extend past the foul circle in the Atlantic Coast Conference, we cursed our fate at being born too soon to enjoy the canonizing of outside shooters.

When I became a sportswriter, I found all games of H-O-R-S-E among journalists were games of range. In June 1971, I knew personally no one who could dunk a basketball, although Bob Asher, a 6′5″, 250-pound, NFL football player I had known in college at Vanderbilt, could dunk a golf ball. (So could PGA pros in, for example, places like Rae's Creek on the 12th hole of Augusta National, and nobody made a big deal out of that.)

We shot in the city parks, at baskets with chain nets whose links jangled and clashed. Sometimes there was no net at all, and we developed cats' eyes to cope with the parks' dim night lights, It was this concentration— wait, call it by its right name—this *obsession* with shooting to which James committed himself. He would turn himself into a *puddle jumper,* not a commuter plane but a player practicing his shot until the sweat pooled at his feet.

He curtailed his taunts at writers or opponents when he was hot because cold snaps inevitably followed. He sought a simple, replicable shooting motion, created by muscle memory. Muscles don't have actual memories, but enough repetitive movements allow the brain to organize neural impulses with such efficiency and power that the end product of a ball and a flicked wrist can electrify a crowd like a thrown switch brought a blaze of light into the arenas where they sat.

But before that . . .

"Not two, not three, not four, not five, not six, not seven. I'm not just up here blowing smoke at none of these fans, because that's not what I'm about. I'm about business. And we believe we can win multiple championships if we take care of business and do it the right way," explained LeBron James, would-be octuple NBA champion in Miami at his introductory news conference.

And after that . . .

James returned to what most Clevelanders saw as the scene of the crime on December 2, 2010, his first trip to Cleveland in a Heat uniform. That night, he dropped shot after shot, figuratively emptying scores of coal scuttles in his former fans' Christmas stockings.

The hatred was almost palpable because, while Philadelphia might be unmatched for public displays of civic dissatisfaction with local teams, Clevelanders' sense of betrayal by one of their own might have been even sharper than their antipathy for the feckless team-moving NFL owner Modell, a native New Yorker. Modell had reduced a Browns dynasty to an also-ran. James, hailed as a savior, had proven false. The closer was a quitter. The least fans expect is effort. A tumbril would have conveyed King James to the guillotine in a burst of revolutionary Gallic regicide, if locals had their way.

Boos bellowed from every corner of the arena whenever James appeared on the "Humongotron." This—like the remote-controlled fart machine—was a Dan Gilbert concept, in which the enormous replay screen was flanked on each end by a pair of the Cavalier mascot's emblematic swords. During the caterwauling introduction of Cavs players, the blades swung away from their adjacent pyro tubes in unison, almost as if being drawn from their scabbards. In the darkened arena, flame suddenly erupted from all four corners of the scoreboard, accompanied by jets blazing atop the backboards. In the firelight, the crowd roared. It was quite a sight, but so, one supposes, was Vesuvius when it got mad at Pompeii. It always made me worry I'd be covering a game on Accidental Fan Incineration Night.

Before the game began, five fans stood bare-chested, each torso painted with a letter that together spelled out *LeBum*.

"Play it like it's Game 5," others shouted, referring to James's disengagement / distraction / possible "DeLonte-fication" in 2008. It was a twist on Prince's song "1999," with the lyrics "Party like it's 1999," as if it were the end of an era. Certainly, James's departure seemed to mark just that.

Cleveland native and game-show host Drew Carey, Browns icon Bernie Kosar, Indians slugger Travis Hafner, and most of the current Browns were cheered wildly when they made their way to courtside seats. The biggest cheer went to "Dan the Ripper" when owner Gilbert appeared on the replay screen. Had I known what would be in store in my contentious relationship with the thin-skinned, meddlesome billionaire owner, I would have muttered, "Forgive them, Lord. They know not whom to boo."

"So many things went through my mind," James said. "I have nothing bad to say about these fans at all. We grew from the year before I got here, a 17-win season to the last two years I was here, we had the best team in the league in the regular season. I understand their frustration. I was frustrated also because we didn't accomplish what we wanted to. I wish this organization and these fans, who are great, the best."

"It felt like a playoff game to us," said Heat coach Erik Spoelstra.

New Cavs coach Byron Scott muttered of his players' timid defense on James, "I can't believe we were so scared of another man."

That night, I flashed back to Albert Belle's belligerent, malign effect on the 1990s Indians. Before a stint in a rehab center for alcoholism, Belle made his drink of choice a "Gorilla Fart." It had the same effect on sobriety as a Molotov cocktail did on Nazi barracks. The ingredients were half Bacardi 151-proof rum and half Everclear pure grain alcohol. It seemed capable of blowing your face off. Added to this was Belle's volatile personality, probably made of one-half bully and one-half trinitrotoluene.

I stood on the left field Home Run Porch on the night of his return to what was then called Jacobs Field. I leaned on the railing above left field, as fans chanted obscenities and threw soda-cup ice and full cups of beer at Belle. They littered the warning track with Monopoly money because he had signed a record contract with the Chicago White Sox, ripping Cleveland as he stomped out the door.

Fans called Belle the same 12-letter name the boyz in the 'hood would have called Oedipus. I noticed a screaming fan nearby, holding his young son atop his shoulders as the invective spewed. "I wanted him to see," he shouted over the venomous din.

I'm still working on processing that.

It did not go well for Indians supporters that night. Chicago won, 9–5. Belle doubled twice, hit a three-run homer, and had three RBIs in his five at-bats. He also gave the fans who stood jeering him the middle finger as he hid his throwing hand behind his back, for which he was fined. David Justice, the new Tribe left fielder, committed two errors.

As for James's aforementioned boast about rings enough to satisfy an octopus, he would settle for two with the Heat. He had many gifts, among them fast-twitch muscle fibers, prodigious strength, the speed and power of a one-man stampede, court vision, and a basketball IQ that made him the smartest player in the league. It remained a mystery why such an intelligent person would so long neglect to shore up such an obvious weakness as his outside shooting.

In middle school, a geometry teacher drummed into his dimmer students, of whom I was certainly one, a famous quote from Euclid, the father of the discipline. When Euclid's royal sponsor, Ptolemy I, the pharaoh of Egypt after the death of Alexander the Great, asked if there were an easy way to learn geometry, Euclid replied, "There is no royal road to geometry."

Nor to shooting the three, even for a King. You're not born with touch. It's refined under heat, purified under pressure, and anointed with puddle-jump sweat.

In the 2011 NBA Finals, Dallas assistant coach Dwane Casey put a searchlight on the hole in LeBron's game and unsparingly exploited it. Casey and coach Rick Carlisle devised a zone that took advantage of James's unreliable jump shot. James had seen every trick defense there was—the "church altar"; the Bruce Bowen ankle buster, named for the Spurs' villain; the double teams; the pterodactyls in sneakers like defenders Tayshaun Prince, Shawn Marion, and DeShawn Stevenson; the overplays and crowded lanes; the hard fouls; the clutching and grabbing. Every bit of it was designed to force James to take long field goal attempts in which he had little faith, try to bang through defenses stacked to stop his drives, or pass to less dangerous teammates. After his futility in the NBA Finals against Dallas, four years after his impotence against the Spurs in his first Finals, James finally committed to filling the hole in his game.

James credited Casey after he scored 43 points in the Cavs' rout of the Toronto Raptors in Game 2 of a 2018 first-round sweep. "I wasn't a complete basketball player," he said. "Dwane Casey drew up a game plan against me in that '11 series in the Finals when I played Dallas to take away things I was very good at and try to make me do things I wasn't very good at. He's part of the reason why I am who I am today."

James repaid the pain of 2011 in triplicate, leading the Cavs to swift dismissals of Toronto in 2016–18, the first a 4–2 decision, the others a pair of 4–0 sweeps. The NBA's only Canadian team decided Casey was, to use the hockey word, a *hoser*, a term born of siphoning gas from farm equipment, perhaps in Manitoba or Saskatchewan, in the wheat fields. The term became synonymous with *loser*, an unfair characterization of Casey, a good man and coach.

The biggest crisis for James's development unfolded during Dallas's stunning upset of Miami in six games the 2011 Finals. I wondered how James would react when faced with a menu of his own words. All those championships he predicted were turning out to be a hard eight, as they say at the craps tables.

Because this book's primary focus is on James's 11 seasons in Cleveland and his high school career in Akron before that, the attention on the time between the abdication and restoration of the "King" will be mainly on the four straight NBA Finals Miami reached during his years there, with a few exceptions for other games instrumental in shaping his career.

2011 NBA FINALS

Not until Miami's stacked team fell apart, like Jenga blocks, did James confront the shaky foundation of his shooting. James had always been able to refute criticism with what everyone in basketball knew was his threadbare supporting cast. "And now he's taking this piece of s—t team to the Finals," as Fran Blinebury said in 2007.

Game 2, at Miami, Mavericks 95, Heat 93

After the Mavericks lost the opener, 7-foot German-born Dirk Nowitzki overcame a torn tendon in the middle finger of his left hand and scored the final nine points in a 22–5 surge. The right-handed Nowitzki, who would become the first European player named NBA MVP, had a soft three-point touch and was almost unstoppable on a step-back jumper he took off one leg, with the knee of the other crooked like a shepherd's staff. He also had plenty of Teutonic blood and iron in his game. Nowitzki made two left-handed baskets of his final three, despite the mangled finger. The last, on a driving layup, won the game with three seconds left to play. "Just battle it out. This is the Finals. You have to go out there and compete and try to do your best for your team," said Nowitzki, while sniffing frequently, in the postgame interview room, his warm-up jacket zipped to his chin.

Game 4, at Dallas, Mavericks 86, Heat 83

James had a mini-LeBacle, looking confused, passing up open shots, missing eight of the 11 he took, deferring so often to Wade that he should have switched his shorts and jersey for a butler's livery. It so angered Wade that he got in James's face during a play stoppage and delivered a tongue-lashing. The Ghost of Chad Mraz in that last high school game had entered the room.

Worse, the Ghost of Jordan in the "Flu Game" haunted him. Worst of all, the next Sick Guy Bound for Glory got there before James's eyes in Game 4. It amounted to the apotheosis of Nowitzki. Playing with a 101-degree fever because of a sinus infection, after a sleepless night and a morning shoot-around spent huddled in misery on the sideline, Nowitzki scored 12 of his 21 points in the last quarter, completing a 21–9 Mavericks charge, which ended when he made the net cords ripple one last time with 14.4 seconds.

The Associated Press reporter wrote: "What Nowitzki did grows in stature when compared to how meek a healthy LeBron James played."

James made only 3 of 11 shots—a tip-in during the first quarter, then a 15-foot jumper and a breakaway dunk in the third quarter. Not only did he fail to score in the fourth, he took only one shot while playing all 12 minutes. He finished with eight points, ending a double-figure scoring streak of 433 consecutive games, regular season and postseason. These were his fewest points ever in the playoffs. James's nine rebounds and seven assists were unnoticed, because the story everywhere was the Second Comeuppance of the self-styled "King."

As the series wore on, critics scoffed at any comparison to Jordan, saying James lacked the same "killer instinct."

"It was one of the hardest things I went through in my life," James said of the aftermath of Miami's 4–2 series defeat. "For two weeks, I sat in my room. Didn't do nothing, didn't go out."

Pundits were quick to place most of the blame at the royal feet.

"I judge by how many rings you've got on your fingers!" shouted the always fully decibel-loaded Stephen A. Smith of ESPN.

" I put 99 percent of the blame on LeBron James," said another ESPN talker, Skip Bayless. "That not only wasn't LeBron James out there, it wasn't LaRonda James or even L'Alfred James. He wants to be crowned without the rings."

The jab at women's basketball was too inviting to pass up, I guess, but I give him the credit he was due for "L'Alfred James." In view of James's favorite childhood superhero, Batman, it was an allusion to the butler at Wayne Manor, Alfred.

Included in the growing critical chorus was Mike Malone, the former Cavs assistant who saw the 2009 LeBacle in person. He said, "Everybody wants everybody to kill like MJ or kill like Kobe. But there are different ways of killing." James had to start killing them softly with the only figure of speech that turns sound into effect, the onomatopoeia. He had to turn to the swish of the jumper to complement the rip of the dunk. With the admission came the humility he had lacked until then. As the psychologists say, it's not who you were, it's who you become.

"I think it just gets to a point where you just say enough is enough. I think the Dallas series was the enough-is-enough turning point," James told ESPN's Chris Broussard, a former *Akron Beacon Journal* Cavaliers beat reporter.

Nothing, of course, to borrow the title of a novel by the late sportswriter and humorist Dan Jenkins, is "dead solid perfect." Or, as baseball pitcher Joaquin Andujar said of both America and the sports, "there is only one word for it, and that word is you never know."

I give you Game 5 of the 2022 NBA Finals, in which soon-to-be NBA champion Steph Curry of Golden State went 0-for-9 on the long ball. This is the same Curry who had made at least one three-pointer in 132 consecutive postseason games (which, incidentally, is every postseason game in which he'd ever played), and he'd made multiple three-pointers in 38 straight playoff games. Counting the regular season, Curry had made at least one three-pointer in 233 consecutive games. Those were all NBA records. Curry is not just better than other shooters, he is radically better in both range and accuracy.

Yet touch is a fickle mistress. It will have a temporary fling with someone else—James in Game 5 against Detroit comes to mind—and then drop him like a bad habit. There are so-called heat-check shots, taken and made at inexplicable and magic moments when it seems a shooter simply cannot miss. Those moments lead to enduring memories and to overheated prose in the press box, but the real power is in a sound base of technique.

James committed to rigorous shooting practice, took up meditation to calm his mind, and cut back on social media posts.

A little over three weeks before the playoffs started, James agreed to an interview with Kevin Van Valkenburg of *ESPN, the Magazine,* which published in an April 3, 2012, story, "The Mistrial of LeBron James." The former Cavalier played the sympathy card, portraying himself as everybody's scapegoat. "I'm an easy target; if someone wants to get a point across—just throw LeBron's name in there," James would say days later when asked why he's a lightning rod. "You could be watching cartoons with your kids and you don't like it, you say, 'Blame it on LeBron.' If you go to the grocery store and they don't have the milk that you like, you just say, 'It's LeBron's fault.'"

There might not have been a wet eye on anyone in Cleveland who read that.

2012 EASTERN CONFERENCE FINALS
Game 6, at Boston, Heat 94, Celtics 90

This was the tipping point in James's career, when the doubts about his resolve and resilience were at their highest, and he dispelled them.

Exactly one year after his disappearing act against Dallas, two years and a month after the LeBacle in Cleveland and the following closeout game in Boston, James was on the road again, at Boston again, trailing, 3–2 again. The Celtics, the team that broke his dream season, the team that chased him out of Cleveland, posed an old and seemingly insurmountable challenge. It was one of not only on-court adjustments and matchups but inner strength and mental toughness, intangibles that could not be physically touched but could be felt in the hearts and minds of his teammates as he refuted the doubters and responded to the pressure.

When James walked out of the tunnel to the court, as a storm of derision burst from the stands at the very sight of him, waiting for him was Pat Riley, Heat president, spectacularly successful former coach, ringbearer to the King and recruiter of his talents thereby. "BOAT," Riley said. "Best of All Time." Knowing the accolade was James's obsession, Riley said it with earnestness and conviction, repeating the acronym as they walked side by side. He was always a believer in positive thinking, making James's aspiration seem to be headed for inevitable affirmation.

The more common term is *GOAT*, "Greatest of All Time," an acronym that, clearly, had unfortunate connotations of blame, as in *scapegoat*—also of cheese and eventually of four-legged yoga participants, but it was hard to get by the blame thing.

Riley's words were motivational gold, but so was James's shooting after his off-season alchemy. James came out firing early, defying the reputation he was gaining for passivity, validating his off-season remake, and repudiating the "why can't Bronny shoot?" debate. He scored 45 points, garnered 15 rebounds, and made 19 of 26 shots overall, including two of his four three-balls, and a startling 7-for-11 on shots that might not have been considered midrange, meaning outside the paint, but still were inside the arc. It might as well be a distinction without a difference.

Miami had lost 15 of its previous 16 games against Boston. James was not about to let that happen again. The midrange shooting was crucial. The analytics wizards who would change basketball by making the their-pointer their trinity, a holy of holies for number crunchers, had not yet hijacked the game entirely. The reductio ad absurdum of their thinking would come on May 28, 2018, in the seventh game of the Western Conference Finals, when the Houston Rockets' long balls–and–layups philosophy reduced the midrange shot to the point of extinction and culminated in 27—twenty-seven!—consecutive misses from the arc. The odds against this happening at the NBA level were computed as 1 in 72,000!

Although Golden State was the face of the three-point revolution, with Curry and Klay Thompson sniping away, they had no problem with taking what the defense gave them. Nor did James. He dropped shots from 12 feet three times, from 14 feet, from 16 feet and from 21 feet.

The Heat's uncertain future and James's sketchy efforts in back-to-the-wall games in the past were fodder for debate around the sports world. But James was a one-man gang in the crisis of his career. He played 45 minutes, resting only in the final three minutes, when the victory over Boston was secure. In the game that was the fulcrum on which his career pivoted, he was magnificent,

"He was absolutely fearless tonight, and it was contagious," Heat coach Erik Spoelstra said. "The way he approached the last 48 hours, and not only LeBron, but everybody else. Nobody likes getting dirt thrown on your face before you're even dead. He showed great resolve."

"This was a gut check for us," admitted James.

Game 7, at Miami, Heat 101, Celtics 88

Winning the series was hardly a foregone conclusion even after James resurrected his big game reputation. In the Heat's Game 7 victory, he went to the paint the way Michelangelo did on his Sistine Chapel scaffold, leaving a muscular masterpiece that included 12-for-17 at the free throw line, 31 points overall, 11 of them in the last quarter, which Miami won, 28–15, and which began with the teams tied at 73. James's dunk gave Miami the lead for keeps at 83–82, and a majestic 30-foot three-pointer, off his fingertips just before the shot clock expired, plummeted through the net for a two-possession lead at 88–82. It was the only three-pointer James made in five tries, but it was the biggest shot of the game.

Boston is a fine city for colleges, seafood, and history. It is not so fine for its intractable traffic jams, the result of key roads being laid out along what had been eighteenth-century cow paths, the problem being, as wits said, it took an eighteenth-century cow to navigate them. But James was back on the path he had plotted so long ago, the one to that BOAT/GOAT thing.

As Julius Erving had said years earlier, you have to dare to be great, risking failure, withstanding criticism, ignoring catcalls. The paths of glory, despite what Thomas Gray wrote in his famous elegy about the grave, lead in sports to the brave.

CHAPTER 20

A King with a Ring at Last

Almost everyone—reporters, players, and ordinary tourists—loves Seattle, a city overlooked by Mount Rainier, bordered by Puget Sound, possessing magnificent views from the top of the Space Needle and, through a trick of perspective at the University of Washington's stadium high above Lake Washington, capable of providing the look and feel of college football played in the clouds.

Unlike the team thieves in Baltimore with the Cleveland Browns, Oklahoma City's civic fathers had clean hands in acquiring Seattle's SuperSonics. For two years in the early 2000s, in the wake of Hurricane Katrina's devastation, OKC was the site of the then New Orleans Hornets' games. Oklahoma City mayor Mick Cornett refused to compete against any Louisiana city seeking to give the Hornets shelter after the storm. The unexpectedly high attendance in OKC made it an attractive market for other troubled teams. Seattle's move there was a result of its inability to get a new arena built outside the environs of the Space Needle, with its memories of its 1962 World's Fair.

The nationwide perception of Oklahoma as a football state is because Bud Wilkinson, Chuck Fairbanks, Barry Switzer, and Bob Stoops coached at the University of Oklahoma. The state was always typecast by the words of an early school president, whose heart's desire was "to "have a university the football team can be proud of.""

Yet, Oklahoma has an illustrious basketball history too. It was not on the order of Indiana or North Carolina, but it had produced such players as Bob "Foothills" Kurland, a 7-footer who became the first player to dunk in college basketball and whose height and reach forced rules makers to outlaw defensive goaltending. The "first family of Oklahoma basketball" was the Prices from Enid, of whom the Cavaliers' Wall of Honor member Mark Price was a part. Add other Sooner luminaries such as Wayman Tisdale, Stacey King, Mookie Blaylock, Dennis Rodman, and Harlem Globetrotters' legend Marques Haynes.

Such great players as Bill Russell, Elgin Baylor, Pete Maravich, and Karl Malone played in the All-College Tournament in Oklahoma City, a Christmas holidays showcase the city started in 1935. The roster of head coaches or assistants at Oklahoma, Oklahoma State, Tulsa, Oklahoma City University, and other Sooner schools includes Hank Iba, a three-time US Olympics coach and defensive maestro; Eddie Sutton; Tubby Smith; Bill Self; Billy Tubbs; and Abe Lemons.

It even had a thriving six-player version of basketball for girls as early as 1935. The sport, created by James Naismith in 1891, was only "sweet 16" years old when Oklahoma and Oklahoma A&M (later Oklahoma State) started basketball programs in 1907.

The Sooner State got its name from the 1889 land rush, when the Indian Territory was opened for white settlement, and claim jumpers sneaked in "sooner" than the official starting time. The negative connotation has faded over the years, but the NBA team's new name—Thunder—was perfection.

Not only did thunderstorms frequently blast through the state, but OKC fans stood until their team made its first basket, a tradition also in Philadelphia's Big Five colleges. OKC fans were so loud in big games that the din made reporters' laptops jiggle and wiggle on press tables, just as Bill Fitch's locker-room blackboard had shimmied from the squall line of roars in the Cavaliers' Miracle of Richfield season. Consternation, exasperation and desperation were the reactions of visitors when the Thunder fans' storm exploded.

OKC had the home-court advantage in the 2012 NBA Finals, and the fans did not spare themselves a decibel of unspent exhortation. A championship would mean another unlikely triumph for small-town America against the NBA's coastal megalopolises (New York and Los Angeles), the Northeastern powers that are (Boston) or used to be (Philadelphia), the resort cities in both the snow (Denver and Salt Lake City) and the sun (Phoenix and Miami), the urban sprawl of Texas (Houston and Dallas), the bustling New South (Atlanta, Charlotte, and Orlando), the heartland industrial cities (Milwaukee, Chicago, Detroit, and Cleveland) dotting the Great Lakes' shorelines. Minneapolis, while not on a Great Lake, is on the "Father of Waters," the 2,340-mile-long Mississippi River. It deserves inclusion with the Great Lakes cities because Minnesota's state slogan is "Land of 10,000 Lakes"—actual number, 11,842—it can pit its "sky blue water," a term from an old Hamm's beer jingle, against almost any waterlogged area in any other state, including Florida and the Everglades.

2012 NBA FINALS
Game 1, at Oklahoma City, Thunder 105, Heat 94

The Thunder's dream of empire depended on the shooting touch of Kevin Durant, already a three-time NBA scoring champion, and the basketball firestorm that was Russell Westbrook. Durant scored 17 of his 36 points in another nightmarish final period for James and his team, giving the Thunder a 1–0 lead. He and Westbrook outscored the Heat in the second half by themselves, 41–40. While James finished with 30 points, his most in any of his 11 Finals games, he had only one basket over the first 8:15 of the fourth, when the Thunder, trailing for all but a few seconds, insistent in its persistence, suddenly grumbled and rumbled to the finish.

Despite Game 6 at Boston and the series victory one game later, the distaste for the way James had left Cleveland seeped into the game stories. ESPN took the kill shot with a statistic that all but left the erstwhile King with his own scarlet letter, A for *Abdication*, noting that James averaged just three points in the fourth quarters of the Heat's six-game loss to Dallas. He was far from the sole reason for the opening loss to the Thunder, but he was still taking the burn for opting for the Heat.

Game 2, at Oklahoma City, Heat 100, Thunder 96

The Heat tried to strangle the game as soon as it began, charging to an 18–2 lead. Urged on by fans, Oklahoma City closed enough of the gap and their fans conserved enough of energy for their team to mount a serious closing charge as the arena became a madhouse. Durant made a three-pointer to cut the Miami lead to 98–96 in the last 37 seconds. After

James missed a three, the Thunder went to Durant, who went to the baseline with James trying to Velcro himself to the opposing superstar. Thunder pealed from the stands, and a torrent of little *b*s and double *o*s rained down after Durant tumbled off balance from an apparent bump by James, but there was no foul called on his 7-foot-long missed shot.

James finished off the victory at the foul line, where he was 12-for-12. He scored 32 points, same as Durant, but had five more rebounds than his rival, with eight, and four more assists, with five.

Game 3, at Miami, Heat 91, Thunder 85

The scene shifted to Miami under the 2-3-2 playoff format for the Finals only. It was intended to reduce travel and allow more journalists to cover the league's signature event than the exhausting, often nation-wide crisscrosses of the previous 2-2-1-1 format. Fervent fans' fashion tastes changed with the venue: no more blue shirts making a meteoro-logical and competitive statement for the rising power, signifying Thun-der out of the blue and all that. Now it was white Heat tees on chair backs. Top of the world, Ma!

The Heat seemed a few BTUs shy of a hot or even lukewarm streak until a referee's whistle rattled and shrieked when it had been silent in the previous game. The Thunder were on the verge of snuffing out the Heat's pilot light when Durant went to the bench. This time, Wade was driving the baseline and Durant defending. This time, replays showed no contact by Durant, instead of the plenty of ignored contact by James in the previous game when Durant drove. The dubious call was Durant's fourth foul; and coach Scott Brooks, a former Cavalier player, took him out with 5:41 left in the third quarter and the Thunder leading, 60–54.

It grew to 63–54. But without their rudder, the Good Ship Thunder went a little overboard, fouling the Heat's Shane Battier and James on back-to-back three-pointers. The six made free throws cut deeply into the deficit. The lead rocked back and forth between both teams, with the Thunder's last lead at 77–76. A flurry by Wade gave the Heat the lead, then James crashed toward the basket, and Durant, trying desperately but unsuccessfully to get into position for a charge, drew his fifth foul.

James had turned into an unsolvable problem for OKC. It was the 20th time in the 2012 playoffs he had scored 20 or more points.

"He was great. He's been great for us all playoffs," said Heat forward Udonis Haslem. "I don't know if he looks up at the clock or score sheet, but he knows when we need him to make big plays and come through for us, and he comes through."

Game 4, at Miami, Heat 104, Thunder 98

The Ghost of Jordan's Flu Game knocked on the door again, and James opened it. Instead of dragging a chain of cash boxes as did Jacob Marley, the business partner of the grasping, covetous old sinner, Ebenezer Scrooge, in Dickens's *A Christmas Carol*, perhaps the Ghost of Jordan left behind it a trail of tubes of VapoRub, bottles of liniment, heating pads, electrolyte-enriched drinks and everything but a handy massage therapist.

Like Jordan, James would say afterward that his body almost shut down. A victim of leg cramps, which were to occasionally plague him in the future, James could barely stand. His running a crippled hobble, his face a mask of pain, his limp pronounced, his resolve was made up of everything he could scrounge together and put all out there on the floor, which included himself. Somehow, with his left leg threatening to betray him at every step, he managed 26 points, 12 assists, and nine rebounds and on one leg sank the biggest shot of the game.

James stumbled to the court on a drive midway through the fourth quarter, staying on the offensive end of the floor as the Heat regained possession, and then made a short jumper that gave the Heat a 92–90 lead.

After Westbrook missed a jumper, the Heat called timeout as James gingerly eased himself to the court. Unable to walk off, he was carried to the sideline in another foreshadowing.

(Two years later, in another such assisted exit, he would be the target of derisive Internet memes in an NBA Finals Yet to Come.)

He returned to the lineup in the last four minutes to a roar from the Heat fans that seemed not to engulf him as much as inflate the reputation he was rebuilding with each agonizing step. He walked himself into a pull-up three-pointer, because he could not drive past a fat man in a shirts vs. skins game in his condition, and bottomed it to break the last tie in the final 2:51.

"Of course, it's there to think about. Of course, it's there to think about. I'll be ready for it," said James, making it clear he planned to get his long-sought championship ring before the home fans in the last of the three straight games at Miami.

Game 5, at Miami, Heat 121, Thunder 106

James finished the Thunder with a triple-double of 26 points, 11 rebounds, and 13 assists in a 121–106 rout for a 4–1 series victory and his long-sought NBA championship. Not one, not two, not three, not four, not five, not six, not seven, not eight, but nine long years he had waited for one.

Asked how it felt finally to be champion, James said, "It's about damn time." Pause. "It's about damn time." He added: "I'm happy now that eight years, nine years later after I was drafted that I'm finally a champion and that I did it the right way. I didn't shortcut anything."

Blood pressure cups exploded in hospitals all over northeast Ohio among anti-James fans, as hardly anyone believed that part about not shortcutting. James, Bosh, and Wade colluded openly to play together. Details of their "Free Agent Summit" in Miami leaked to the sporting press and electronic media as if they were Churchill, FDR, and Stalin at Yalta.

In future years, James would be hailed as an exemplar of player empowerment, as he recruited other stars to other super teams. But this strategy came at the cost of fan estrangement. It had more than a whiff of being offered or denied a chance to sit at the cool kids' table in the lunchroom or to be in the room where the power brokers passed out choice assignments to the chosen few.

I believed that was the added spur to his later concerns about social justice and to his philanthropic efforts on behalf of disadvantaged children in Akron. He had walked those streets. He had been a have-not throughout the first half of his life. He wanted kids like himself to have a seat at opportunity's table too.

In basketball terms, he was certainly justified. He did not have to do it alone in Miami. Wade and Bosh scored 23 and 20 in Game 5. Sniper Mark Miller made no fewer than seven threes as Oklahoma City concentrated most of its defensive energy on James, and he was content to pass to wide-open teammates.

Holding the NBA Finals MVP award, although it belied what he had said earlier, he denied being badly shaken by the hate that came his way after the Decision. "I don't worry about what people say about me. I'm LeBron James, from Akron, Ohio, from the inner city. I'm not even supposed to be here. That's enough. Every time I walk in that locker room and see that jersey with the 6 on it (he had changed his number from the Jordanian 23 to the same number Bill Russell and Julius Erving had worn), I'm blessed. I ain't got no worries!"

The next two seasons would end in Finals against the San Antonio Spurs, who were both predecessors and exemplar of the small-town title dream that eluded the Thunder. The results and the timing of the pair of Finals would shape James's future in ways unknowable amid the confetti and champagne of his first championship in Miami.

CHAPTER 21

Leading the Heat through the Crucible

In *The Crucible,* Arthur Miller's play about the Salem, Massachusetts, witch hunt, the most admirable character is Giles Corey, a landholder indicted for practicing witchcraft. By definition, a crucible is a container in which materials are melted under fires as intense as any conceived in hell. Metaphorically, a *crucible* is a tortuous test, whether of physical punishment or moral choice.

Corey is "pressed"; heavy stones are placed on his chest, literally crushing the life out of him. But Corey refuses to confess. He is impervious to the weight of the guilt he does not feel, defiantly muttering as each additional stone is placed upon him, "More weight."

The "truth" of sports is revealed when all the chips are down, when the crucible glows with fire and fury, and when it is in Game 7 of the NBA playoffs. James could only end the witch hunt atmosphere in hostile cities by the assuming the burden of leadership and accounting for victories in not one, but two Game 7s. Sometimes he did so with dazzling solos, other times with brilliant orchestration of his teammates.

Before "the Decision," many fans had venerated James as the athletic embodiment of such prodigies as Wolfgang Amadeus Mozart in music and Bobby Fischer in chess.

After the Decision, James was vilified in some corners of the Internet and especially in some NBA cities—Cleveland comes to mind; Boston, too—because he still bore the stigma of Game 5 vs. the Celtics in Cleveland in 2010. This judgment, moreover, seemed set in stone. It had not changed that much in Cleveland after his 45 points in the Game 6 survival test at Boston, the most routinely hostile city in the league. It had improved slightly but not significantly after his Game 4 against Oklahoma City in the Finals, even though he became a champion at long last. In that game, he was at times an avatar of Jordan in the Flu Game. James, after all, hit the kill shot from the arc while effectively playing on one leg.

Nothing so far seemed capable of ending the criticism of his competitive heart, even though Game 5 was an aberration.

The 2012 championship night have been justification for the Decision to James and some of his fans. It was still an emphatic no-can-do with most Clevelanders, though. A second championship, in 2013, might provide an additional path to reconciliation with fans elsewhere. In Cleveland, however, the higher moral planes of atonement by James and forgiveness by the vast majority of fans would have to wait. And Clevelanders were used to waiting. It had been 49 years since the last city's championship in one of the three major sports, won by the 1964 Cleveland Browns. As was said of the Chicago Cubs, who ended 108 years of waiting by beating—who else?—the Cleveland Indians in extra innings in the seventh game of the 2016 World Series: "Anybody can have a bad century."

Make it "a bad half-century," and you had Cleveland and its greathearted, often heartbroken, ardent, and un-discourageable fans.

The Cavs fans' frayed patience was tested in almost unbelievable fashion by the stunning events of March 20, 2013. It was their own crucible, when those of wavering allegiance and weak mettle would have renounced their loyalty and melted down in despair. Before a Cavaliers home crowd still thirsty for revenge, James scored 19 points of his 25 in the second half, 14 of them in the fourth quarter, including 11 in a row.

With 9 minutes to play and Heat facing tissue-paper resistance from the Cavs, James Blair, a 21-year-old James fan from Ashtabula, Ohio, about 60 miles east of Cleveland, raced onto the court and approached James. "Popping" his James jersey, with "we miss you" scrawled on the front and "come back 2014" on the back, he and James shared a brief embrace, and in a friendly gesture, LeBron tousled his hair. It almost looked as if James were going to palm Blair's head and dribble it. It also struck me that the kid might never wash his hair again (Hunter Atkins, "Lost Stories of LeBron James, Part 3," *ESPN, the Magazine,* October 19, 2013).

James led the Heat back from a 27-point deficit, 67–40, with 7:27 to go in the third quarter, to a 98–85 victory. He hit the three-pointer to give Miami the lead, 80–79, and the two free throws to close it out.

But if James were to make any inroads at all with fans still feeling jilted and scorned, it would be through his steady, incremental, and at times radical improvement. A destitute kid from an Akron neighborhood called "The Bottom," as in "of the barrel," James had never allowed his almost unfathomable riches to deter him from his goal. It was a pursuit to which he dedicated everything—heart, soul, and sneaker soles—hiring a personal trainer for fitness, a massage therapist for pain, and a personal chef for diet, even installing a hyperbaric chamber in his house for oxygenation. He had a mind that was beautiful in its agility. He could juggle huge business opportunities, a budding interest in the movie industry, and endorsement possibilities and still study videotape of upcoming opponents with a coach's eye, and, incredibly, dredge up from it tactical adjustments buried deep in the past with his eidetic memory.

If he toned his body, he honed his mind too.

In a 2013 story, Brian Windhorst cited several examples, one occurring in Indianapolis when an exasperated coach Erik Spoelstra called time and the squabbling Heat players argued over how to defend a very effective pick-and-roll play run repeatedly by the Pacers. Spoelstra drew Xs and Os on his whiteboard, but James intervened with a better suggestion, bringing up a ploy that stymied the Pacers that the coach had last used in 2009. Spoelstra did not even remember it until he dug out the video hours later and confirmed James's recall. The Heat rallied to win on James's play plucked from the past.

Another example was when he corrected a reporter on the details of a step-back three-pointer he had just made over Andre Iguodala to win a game against the Warriors at Oracle Arena in Oakland. The newspaperman compared it to one from five years earlier at the same arena and the same spot over the same player. James begged to differ. Listeners who dug into the video file later confirmed his remembrance that it was over Ronnie Turiaf, not Iguodala; it was a two-pointer taken 6 feet nearer the basket, not a three; and it began a few feet down away from the 2013 game-winner on a side out of bounds play. Other than that, the inquisitor had nailed it.

In a world of instant messaging, analytical minutiae, and 82-game schedules, plus the playoffs, each game demanding a cascading series of decisions, these examples are a remarkable dig into basketball archaeology. James's biggest asset is his mind. He can not only recall the defensive schemes of the past but also apply them to crises in the here and now, illuminating the path out like a lighthouse beacon with its beams guiding a ship near a stormy shore.

By 2022, most experts probably ranked James as 1-A to Jordan's 1—as close as the hyphen is to each side of the alphanumeric designation.

In 2013, James would romance the cold stone in the hearts of his many critics. Loser of his first two Game 7's in 2007 and 2008, James had won his first seventh game in 2012 against the Celtics. Seventh games are the NBA's crucible, a test by the fires of competition which all the slag burned away, leaving as residue the truth.

As of 2023, James is 6–2 in seventh games, tied for the most such victories in modern NBA history with Larry Bird. Kobe Bryant was 5–1, Dirk Nowitzki 4–1.

In the old days, before player free agency, in a much smaller league with fewer games, Bill Russell had an unmatched 10–0 record in the Game 7 crucible. John Havlicek was 6–3. But without free agency, players were bound to one team for as long as the front office wanted them. This is why Boston's 11 championships in 13 years with Russell is a record that will never be challenged seriously.

Indiana, Miami's opponent in the 2013 Eastern Conference Finals, was still seeking its first NBA Finals. The Pacers would suffer as much as any team at James's hands, losing twice in the conference finals when James was with the Heat in seven and then six games and twice in the first round when he was with the Cavs.

Miami reached Stage 3 of the four-tiered playoff system with relative ease, sweeping Milwaukee 4–0, the victory margins of 23, 12, 13, and 11 points. James posted averages of 24.5 points, 7 rebounds, and 7.8 assists, leading his team in each category except rebounds, in which Bosh had an 8.6 average. Then the Heat excused Chicago from the tournament, 4–1. After a 93–86 opening loss, Miami ripped off victories of 37, 10, 23, and in the closeout game, only three in the face of Bulls' desperation. The final two stages would go seven games each and force James to dredge up all the mental acuity, physical stamina, competitive grit and gristle he had in him.

2013 EASTERN CONFERENCE FINALS

The topsy-turvy series was a bewildering jumble of a one-point buzzer-beating squeaker, two other single-digit decisions, by four and seven points, and four games that were decided by 18, 11, 14, and 23 points. The Heat won two of the three close games and two of the four blowouts.

It was not expected that Miami's "Super Team" would have to go all seven games against the Pacers. Indiana had won 49 games, its division, and all six of its home games in the first two rounds of the playoffs, both 4–2 series wins, against Atlanta and the New York Knicks. But still . . . the Heat won 66 games and lost only 16. Their 27-game winning streak during the regular season was a serious challenge to the Los Angeles Lakers' record 33 in a row in 1972, when they also won the NBA championship.

Game 5, at Miami, Heat 90, Pacers 79

Game 5 found the Heat and Pacers tied at two wins apiece. Early in the second half, the score was tight, the fans tighter, and, and the arena silent. The defending NBA champions were trailing 46–40 in the third quarter against a team from a state that revered underdogs.

Point guard Bobby Plump's last shot had kept the single-class, all-comers format of the Indiana high school state tournament alive for decades after his 1954 basket at the buzzer. It gave tiny Milan—a town whose school had only 161 students, the real-life Hickory Hoosiers—a 32–30 upset of the Muncie Central dynasty. Plump's Last Shot became the name of the restaurant owned by the plucky guard, who was only 2-for-10 before canning his game-winner from 14 feet out. Almost every Hoosier can pace off the spot on the court where Plump/David shot/slung the ball/rock and slew Muncie Central/Goliath.

One year later, Crispus Attucks, an all-Black high school, named for a Black stevedore, whaler, and sailor who was the first person killed in the Boston Massacre of 1770 and thus the first American to die in the revolution against Great Britain, located on what has been renamed Martin Luther King Drive, won the state championship under Oscar

Robertson's leadership. The "Big O" was then 16 years old and destined to be one of the all-time NBA greats. Tradition held that champions were accorded a victory parade through downtown Indianapolis, with a stop at Monument Circle for the players to hop off the parade floats and mingle with fans.

Tradition had no provisions for a Black championship team. The Crispus Attucks players were not allowed off the floats, made one orbit of Monument Circle, and were promptly whisked back to the Black area of town from whence they came. Sixty years later, at the 2005 Indianapolis 500, the injustice was finally rectified as the Big O and his surviving teammates were made honorary marshals for the Indianapolis 500.

Butler University, with only 4,000 students, came within a halfcourt buzzer beater that rimmed out of beating mighty Duke in the 2010 NCAA Championship Game. Moreover, Butler played in Hinkle Fieldhouse, where Milan's team became known as the "Miracles" in headlines around the state.

Larry Bird came out of little French Lick to become one of the great players in NBA history.

Why not the Pacers too? Why not another, in a state that cherished the game and rooted for the upstarts, another little giant rising up to do the un-doable?

Because LeBron. That's why.

Because LeBron James took over the third quarter and played basketball the way little boys and girls who shot at baskets on the sides of barns, on the gables of garages, and on the half-moon backboards in parks dream of doing. He scored 16 of his 30 points in the quarter and left this flamboyant statistical line:

In the 30–10 run that left the Pacers' hopes in flame, he scored or otherwise contributed to 25 of the points. He had four rebounds by himself; the Pacers team had six. He had four assists; the Pacers' entire team, degenerating into offensive stagnation, had one.

"That's LeBron showing his greatness and making it look easy," the Heat's Spoelstra said. "What we talked about was doing whatever it takes and competing for each other without leaving anything out there. His engine in that third quarter was incredible. He was tireless, he was making plays on both ends of the court, rebounding, covering so much ground defensively and then making virtually every play for us offensively. It's really remarkable."

Game 6, at Indianapolis, Pacers 91, Heat 77

Roy Hibbert played as if he hadn't heard the news of the approaching extinction of the low post big man. He had 24 points, 11 rebounds, more shot alterations than a tailor with a dieter's trousers, and a surly attitude after being fined $75,000 for criticism of the media members after Game 4. The scribes' sin, apparently, was in not giving the Pacers, winners of their first division title since, ahem, 2004, their due as one of the Powers That Be.

Hibbert was why Miami shot only 16 of 54, 29.6 percent when the Heat ventured inside the arc. He played the biggest part in a victory that forced a seventh game. James led the Heat with 29 points. No one else scored more than 10. It was a rinse and repeat thing, the Cavs teams all over again, with James playing dual roles as the King of hype and bastion of hope.

"Heat are floppers!" chanted the Pacers' fans in scorn throughout the game as the thespians from South Florida toppled theatrically backward when Hibbert bull-rushed the rim. James's nerves got so frayed after one swoon was ignored by the refs that he drew a technical foul.

If the Heat lost Game 7, it would be the flop heard 'round the basketball world.

Game 7, at Miami, Heat 98, Pacers 76

The seventh game was both a letdown, as James dominated with 32 points, and a lock up, as James put Paul George in handcuffs and shackles.

James's work recalled Phil Jackson's assistant coach in Chicago, John Bach. He once praised the defense of Jordan, who could be like a pit bull with a chew toy with the man he guarded. He was joined by Scottie Pippen, his wingman, another attack dog on defense. "They could just completely shut down the other team for two or three minutes. Just take everything away. I never saw anything like it," Bach said.

Everyone justifiably raved about Jordan's offense, just as they did James's.

And Jordan could both light you up on offense and turn out the lights on defense. There was flint in James's defense, too, and the sparks were flying.

A Heat solar flare in the second quarter in a 33–16 swing meant Game 7 was as good as over. The Heat won easily in the biggest rout of the series.

The Heat had survived a rival they had underestimated. Next up were the Spurs, whose arena might as well have been a haunted house of bad memories. James could recall the laughing San Antonio Spurs players and fans, many holding brooms or signs reading "LeBronzed"—after the 2007 Finals sweep. It gave him motivation, but by the very dimensions of the defeat, it also provided a challenge as daunting as any in his career to that time, except for the "BOAT regatta" in Boston on the banks of the harbor.

No matter how long native Texans have lived away (50 years, in my case), we are convinced that Texans play better football (How 'bout them Cowboys?!), cook better barbecue (brisket, thou art the food of the gods), tell taller tales (Pecos Bill and Sluefoot Sue), and have more illustrious history (the Alamo, aka the American Thermopylae) than anybody else.

Speaking of Greek things, the sporting gods of Olympus in Texas now, with the Dallas NFL team nearly 30 years removed from its last Super Bowl victory, are the Spurs. Only the second pro team in a one-sport market, after Portland long ago, in 1977, to win even one NBA championship, San Antonio had won four by the time of the 2013 Finals. They were led by an Air Force Academy graduate, fiery political liberal, basketball lifer, future coach of the 2022 Olympic gold medal–winning USA men's basketball team, and the Zeus of the pro basketball coaching pantheon, Gregg Popovich—at least, that is, until Steve Kerr and Golden State started a dynasty of their own before the decade was over.

2013 NBA FINALS
Game 1, at Miami, Spurs 92, Heat 88

Many Clevelanders, who seethed through James's enumeration of the eight championships for the "superteam," were heartened when the Spurs began their quest for their first championship since the sweep of the Cavs by stealing the home-court advantage in Miami. In fact, the

Heat looked in the opener like "not the Cavs again!" James's star was bright with an 18–18–10 triple-double that, as too often had been the case in Cleveland, did not result in victory.

The Spurs understandably looked fresher, having last played on May 27, when they won the NBA West, while the Heat went seven games with Indiana's rugged Pacers. Although center Tim Duncan, the posterized player in the photo in James's Cavs locker room dressing stall during the 2007–08 season, had 20 points and 14 rebounds, snappy totals for a basketball geriatric at age 37, the difference was a broken-play desperation shot by guard Tony Parker in the last 5.2 seconds. The game was close all the way. With San Antonio leading by only two points and the shot clock ready to expire near the end, Parker lost the ball, lost his footing, then made sure the Heat lost the game by banking in a tumbling shot that seemed more a computer-generated image than a flesh-and-blood play.

Referees reviewed the shot again and again to make sure it beat the clock, but the Miami fans were already filing out. They didn't like what they had already seen on the replay board.

Game 2, at Miami, Heat 103, Spurs 94

"The Spurs are the Spurs," James had said after the opener. "They put you in positions you're uncomfortable in on defense, and if you make a mistake, they exploit it."

And Miami's Mario Chalmers was still an "oh, no—oh, yes!" player often bawled out for missed assignments by coaches or lectured by his teammates, but sometimes capable of sublime shooting despite the ridicule. Two ready examples would be the tying shot he hit for eventual champion Kansas in the NCAA Tournament final in 2009 and the 25 points he scored in Game 4 in the Finals against the Thunder

"You have to have guts to play with our guys. If you don't, you get swallowed up," Heat coach Spoelstra said. "The good thing about it is the other guys were fine with him making plays."

"Honestly, for me, when I was struggling offensively, my teammates continued to keep it in range," James said. "I think 'Rio more than anybody kept us aggressive, him getting into the paint, him getting those 'and-ones' and making a couple of threes. It allowed me to sit back and wait for my time."

During a Heat rally in the third quarter, it was Chalmers who gave the battle cry and James who followed the often-maligned point guard's lead. James had only three field goals in the first three quarters, finishing with a subpar for him 17 points. Chalmers scored 19. As the Spurs reeled under the pressure of a Miami rally, Chalmers took charge.

"I felt like we had them on the ropes at the time. I told him, 'Let's go for the kill,'" Chalmers said. "He [James] said, 'I'm with you.'"

A breath-taking 33–5 Heat run followed.

Game 3, at San Antonio, Spurs 113, Heat 77

What was billed as a drama with a theme from ancient Rome of opposing triumvirates—Miami's Big Three of James, Bosh, and Wade vs. San Antonio's trio of Duncan, Ginobili, and Parker—became a showcase for Danny Green and Gary Neal. Both were Spurs' auxiliaries. Neither was a starter like Miami's Chalmers. But the Spurs two "rowels" (the pointy horseflesh gougers on a spur) proved the hypothesis that everyone on a team has a role and importance.

Green was no once-in-a-generation talent like James. He bounced around the NBA like a human blocked shot. He was a frequent recipient of rejection notices, similar to those authors and freelance writers have received, but his were more public and more demeaning. Still active in 2023, he had played with, in order, the Cavaliers; Spurs; minor-league Reno Bighorns; Spurs again; Union Olimpija in Slovenia; and, in his third stint, the Spurs. To alter the popular Cyrkle song of the 1960s, he "came bouncing back, like a Green rubber ball" for later service with the Raptors, Sixers, Grizzlies, and—whew!—Lakers. Danny Green knew how to pack light for any gig.

Neal had played collegiately at La Salle in Philadelphia, a power in the mid-1950s, when Tom Gola was there and some of us boomers were beginning first grade, and at Towson State in Maryland, where eventually he would return to coach. Neal, too, was familiar with visas and passports. He played internationally in Spain at Pinar Karsiyaka and Banvit in Turkey; Benetton Treviso in Italy; Barcelona, Malaga, and Zaragoza in Spain; in the minors for the Westchester Knicks, Reno Bighorns, and the Texas Legends in the unsung and not so legendary Dallas exurb of Frisco; and in the NBA with the Spurs, Heat, Charlotte, Washington, and Atlanta.

Their value lay in what former Ohio State basketball coach Thad Matta called the "million-dollar board." He meant a plank on the court in the either corner that served as the launching pad for the shorter three-pointer. It was there that the three-ball specialists ran, there that they staked their claim, there that they took the shot that launched a thousand pay days. By the 2010s, the three-pointer was bigger than almost any threesome in basketball.

In Game 3, Green shot 9-for-15 overall and 7-for-9 on threes and scored 27 points. He made only two two-point field goals. He added a 2-for-2 free-throw line. Neal shot 9-for-17 overall, 6-for-10 on threes for 24 points. He made three deuces. He was never fouled in the game, which clearly indicts the Heat defense in the stunning defeat by 36 points at home. It was the third-biggest rout in NBA Finals history.

James scored 15 points, missed 14 shots of the 21 he tried, and was outscored by Wade with 16 and by substitute Mike Miller, who had 15 on 5-for-5 arc bombing. For the first three games of his third Finals, James was 21-for-54, 38.8 percent. He was averaging 18 points. He had yet to score 20 or more in a game.

Game 4, at San Antonio, Heat 109, Spurs 93

James had rocked from side to side during the national anthem, his energy all but glowing from his pores. When the game started, the strength and speed that made him the player of his generation went to DEFCON 1, nuclear alert status.

As a team, the Spurs were much older than the Heat. The restful effects of their layoff until the Finals began had ended. The Spurs preferred a wide-open floor game, not Indiana's bump and thump. In Game 4, that played right into James's hands. James had 33 points and 11 rebounds; Wade hit his postseason high with 32 points; and Bosh matched his playoff high with 20 points, adding 13 rebounds.

"It was on our shoulders," James said. "We had to figure out how to win the game for us and play at the highest level. When all three of us are clicking, we're very tough to beat."

"When Bosh, Wade, and James score the way they did tonight and shoot it the way they did tonight, a team is going to have a difficult time if you help them like we did," Spurs coach Gregg Popovich said. "When those guys are playing like that, you better be playing a perfect game."

"The death of the Big Three was overrated," crowed Heat owner Mickey Arison as he entered his team's locker room after the game.

Actually, it soon looked as if it had just been put on hold.

Game 5, at San Antonio, Spurs 114, Heat 104

A one-man cavalry named Manu Ginobili came charging over the hill, bugle blaring, and saved the Spurs in his first start of the season. He scored 24 points and added 10 assists.

A former Sixth Man of the Year, Ginobli said, "I was angry, disappointed. We are playing in the NBA Finals, we were 2–2, and I felt I still wasn't really helping the team that much. And that was the frustrating part."

Ginobili wasn't just any Spur, or even just any part of the Big Three, no matter how large. Born in Bahia Blanco, Argentina, he was the only Spur who spoke fluent Spanish, which made him the team's most popular player among the San Antonio's Hispanic fans. After the game ended, he raced to the bench and soaked in the applause. It was the same greeting he got when he walked onto the court for the opening tap in the latest of, in what had been before the 2012–13 season, a long line of big games in the three championship seasons in which he had contributed.

Other ominous signs were the 60 percent the Spurs shot, the first for any Finals team in four years and the Finals three-point record of Green, another legionary who had now answered the call twice with powerful effects, sinking six more to go with his seven in Game 3.

After Miami got within a single point with 3 minutes left in the third quarter, Green's three-pointer and the left-handed Ginobili's daring abracadabra game of banked shooting angles, flips, floaters, runners and gunners made it 87–75 in favor of the Spurs as the period closed.

"Manu! Manu!" screamed the exuberant fans. All that remained was to play out the last dozen minutes of the fourth straight Finals rout.

Horns honked into the night in downtown San Antonio, a few miles from the AT&T Center in the middle of an industrial zone with trucks loading and unloading cargo, backing in with a squeal of brakes, or pulling out with their smoke pouring from their diesel pipes.

It was no place to end a dream, not that sunny Miami, site of the sixth game and, if necessary the seventh, was much better. Defeat and despair can visit anyone's neighborhood.

Game 6, at Miami, Heat 103, Spurs 100 (OT)

For all the statistically verifiable importance of Game 5 as a fulcrum on which a best-of-seven series tilts one way or the other, for all the obvious importance of Game 7, two Game 6s had enormous influence on James's career. The one on the road vs. Boston in 2012, down 3–2, was the making or breaking of his reputation as a clutch player. The one in Miami against San Antonio in 2013, down 3–2, was the crowning or uncrowning moment of his dreams of multiple championships. Further, its outcome affected the Spurs in 2014 and defined James's path for the four seasons that followed.

It was in so many ways the Spurs' game to win, except they didn't. Certainly, NBA officials felt that way, dispatching arena workers with yellow tape to cordon off the area of the court reserved for the trophy presentations once the formality of San Antonio closing out the game was complete. Except it never was.

The Spurs led 71–58 in the last 3:12 of the third quarter. Through three quarters, James was 3-for-12 from the field. Tim Duncan had 30 points by the end of the third quarter. He would not score in the fourth quarter. The Heat entered the fourth quarter trailing by 10. Playing with the edge desperation gave him in addition to his physical advantages, James went to the basket again and again and again and again and again and again—six times in all. He made four layups, dunked twice, missed only a 17-footer and one free throw—he made the second—and it still seemed not to be enough.

The Spurs led by five with 28 seconds to play. James clanged a three-pointer, but Wade outjumped, outreached, and outwanted the ball more than two Spurs, tipping the rebound to James. He nailed the second trey try, which would have taken the season with it had he missed. When future superstar Kawhi Leonard of the Spurs split two free throws, leaving it a one-possession game at 95–92, the Heat had their chance. Ray Allen nothing-but-netted a three from the million-dollar board to tie with 5.2 seconds remaining.

The Heat then got an enormous break when referees stopped the clock to make sure Allen wasn't a toenail inside the arc. He wasn't, but the delay kept the Spurs from inbounding immediately to Parker before the Heat could organize their defense. Instead, James dogged the San Antonio point guard the length of the court and forced an ungainly miss from 12 feet.

This was a different James than the one who couldn't get Miami to a Game 7 at home in 2011, when Dallas closed the Heat out and celebrated with a gigantic bottle of champagne. Just the thought of reliving the experience goaded him to new heights.

The Spurs took a three-point lead in the overtime, but James hit a cutting Allen for a basket and then gave the Heat the lead for good on an eight-footer in the lane with 1:43 to play in the overtime, 101–100. He stole Ginobili's pass 59 seconds later. Only 44 seconds after that, the Heat had won a game they seemed certain to lose.

"We seen the championship board [table] already out there, the yellow tape. And you know, that's why you play the game to the final buzzer," James said. "And that's what we did tonight. We gave it everything that we had and more. This was the best game I've ever been a part of."

He would get chances to rethink that, especially if he had to do it all over again in the ultimate sports climax, a seventh game.

Game 7, at Miami, Heat 95, Spurs 88

It is better to lose by a lot than a little. Despite the blow to the ego a rout delivers, it is better than fixating on the what-ifs in a narrow loss or wishing for the do-overs instead of confronting the did wrong, or obsessing over the "why us and not them?" The misery of a championship that got away is almost impossible to shed, even if you have one last grab at the acclaim and celebration before the victory parade starts without you.

Tough-minded as the Spurs were, Game 6 was their most confounding loss since 2004, when the Lakers' Derek Fisher took an inbounds pass with 0.4 left on the clock, faded and fired over a fast-closing Ginobili, and hit a 16-foot fadeaway shot on a play that began with the absolute minimum time to take a shot legally. Had it been 0.3, only a lob and tip-in would have been allowed. It gave the Lakers a 74–73 victory after Duncan had banked in a three-pointer for a one-point lead with 0.9 to play. Even worse, Fisher, a lefty, shielded the timekeeper's view of the ball, causing a 0.1 delay in starting the clock.

For James, the victory in Game 7, six years after the humiliation of the Spurs' Finals sweep of the Cavaliers, was the culmination of a magnificent run in 12 months with two NBA championships and an Olympic gold medal, with Duke's Mike Krzyzewski as coach, in which he was considerably more instrumental than in 2004 with Larry Brown as coach of the LeBronze medalists.

James scored 37 points in Game 7. He made five three-pointers, a result of all that puddle-hopping practice. He grabbed 12 rebounds. He defended Tony Parker when he had to, just as he had in hectoring him for most of the 80-something feet Parker covered on the last play of the fourth quarter in Game 6.

"In my case, I still have Game 6 in my head," Ginobili said. "Today, we played an OK game. They just made more shots than us. LeBron got hot. Shane [Battier], too. Those things can happen. But being so close and feeling that you are about to grab that trophy and seeing it vanish is very hard."

In the last quarter, with no more than six points, two scant possessions—separating the teams, James splashed three midrange jumps shots. They were the shots he couldn't make in 2007, the shots the Spurs dared him to take in the opening games of the series.

After Duncan, who finished with 24 points and 12 rebounds, with the Spurs trailing by only two and 50 seconds to play, missed from nearly pointblank range and then missed his own tip-in that followed, James made a 19-footer. Next, he repeated the killer "basket and casket" play of overtime in Game 6 by making another steal, this of a pass by Ginobili. James sank both free throws after being fouled, and it was all over except for cleaning up the confetti and streamers.

As of 2022, James would win two more NBA titles, one on the road in a joyless arena except for a small cadre of visiting fans, the other in Orlando's "bubble," from which fans were barred during the coronavirus pandemic.

He had had his last home-court championship confetti.

CHAPTER 22

The Spurs Strike Back

It seems incredible, given the firestorm his decision to leave Cleveland caused, but James had never demanded a trade, although he demanded that the front office acquire better teammates to complement him. He always left when he became a free agent, and he had every right to. The collusion at the so-called Free Agency Summit convened by what became the Heat's Big Three was not illegal by NBA rules. James honored his contracts even though he stacked his teams, empowering other superstars to each recruit his own posse, making competitive patsies of the teams that were unwilling donors. In years to come, former teammate Iman Shumpert said the team-stacking by James and other superstars had "ruined basketball."

As the 2014 NBA Finals began, the biggest story, creating the most outlandish speculation, was James's impending free agency.

Game 7 of the 2013 Finals affected James, an avid basketball historian, by giving the Heat a chance for the first NBA three-peat since the Lakers in 2001–03; Game 6 in 2013 affected Game 7 simply by making it, against all odds, necessary; and Game 7 affected Spurs coach Gregg Popovich with the agonizing plays that made the 13-point lead slip away—James's second-chance three-pointer when two Spurs lost the rebound to Wade, Kawhi Leonard's split of his pair of free throws, Allen's triple and the pause to review via videotape the placement of his feet.

It was like shaking the hand that shook the hand of John L. Sullivan, except the hand concealed a joy buzzer.

Every cell of Popovich's being might have been screaming to go all Bobby Knight chokehold / wrath of Khan on his players, but James's brilliance was as much a reason as anything for the loss. In addition, the grouchy man everybody knows as "Pop," whom James later called "the greatest coach ever," knew it is almost never the right choice to beat up a team that lost. Players with character will feel bad enough on their own.

Popovich did, however, keep the chase for what had gotten away foremost in his players' minds. The game clock at Spurs' practices was frozen with 3:12 left in the third period. The score was frozen at 71–58. Every single minute of work at practice was a reminder of how much the Spurs had let get away and of how incredibly thin was the Heat's resulting margin of victory. The difference was almost as slight as the nano tick of the clock when the Lakers' Derek Fisher hit the shot of a lifetime against the Spurs. The Spurs, moreover, were an aging team, with the time running out to do what they should have done before.

On March 4, 2014, the Spurs made their lone appearance in Cleveland of the season. I joined the cluster of reporters for a pregame session with Popovich in an alcove of the Cavs' arena near the visitors' cramped locker room. This is the case everywhere in the NBA, where creature comforts are for the home team alone.

Reporters share trade secrets, so I knew why my old rival and longtime friend Fran Blinebury had always enjoyed good relations with Popovich. Fran had helped me out on a Bill Fitch interview by, of all things, advising me to ask the then coach of the Rockets a question and then simply remain in front of him, preferably in his office, but up close in a mass interview if necessary. Eventually even Fitch would tire of the childish game and begin to talk. The same thing worked with Elvin Hayes.

With Popovich, the trick was to put up a brave front, avoid looking visibly intimidated, and hold your ground.

After I asked how he had handled the undoubted second-guessing and torment of the Finals loss, Pop eschewed former Marine Fitch's stonewall tactics and went to an Air Force flyboy's strafing of a reporter asking a dumb question. "Have you read or heard nothing of what I have said all season?" he asked, leaning into my space, an arm's length from his left side.

I stuck my digital recorder close to his mouth and said, "I want you to say it for my column."

There was a pause long enough for him to consider his options. Temperament went one-on-one with belittlement and then, to my surprise, amusement won out. He threw back his head and laughed heartily. "It's something that you get over because real life sets in. But it's always there, and you think about it from time to time—in my case daily," said Popovich. "But intellectually you understand that it's not the most important thing in life, and you move on. But it's something you never forget because you feel like you had one in your hand and let it slip away."

After the pregame interview ended, I walked down the corridor to the Spurs' locker room with Pop.

"Are you a baseball fan?" I said.

"Sure," he said.

"Do you remember the 1964 Phillies?"

He nodded.

"So you know who Gene Mauch is?"

"Sure," he answered. "They blew a big lead too."

"They lost 10 in a row of their last 12 and blew a World Series spot," I said.

I then related the details of a Q-and-A with Mauch and a gaggle of reporters in 1986. That season, his California Angels lost a playoff series they seemed sure to win, and there went another World Series berth. Before the playoff series ended unhappily for the Angels, however, someone asked, "Do you ever think about 1964, Gene?"

A heavy smoker, Mauch took a long drag on one of the cigarettes that would kill him. He repeated the question, while exhaling a long plume of smoke. "Do I ever think about 1964?"

Another drag, another gust of smoke. "Do I ever think about 1964?" he asked again, tapping his fingers angrily on his desk beneath a thickening smoky haze.

"Just every f—king pitch!" he said.

Popovich burst into laughter again, threw an arm over my shoulder in as close to a bro-hug with a reporter as he was ever apt to get, and said, "I'm close. I'm close. But I'm not there yet."

That night, the Spurs had a nearly unheard-of 39 assists on their 42 field goals in a 122–101 romp over the Cavs. Only one of their 25 second-half field goals was unassisted. That kind of ball movement was going to be difficult for any team to beat.

Popovich would not get to where defeat had taken Mauch. Instead, he and his team would get back to the NBA Finals that season. And this time, they would beat Miami soundly.

In many ways, the Spurs amazed me. Deep in the heart of football-mad Texas, the American Basketball Association's Dallas Chaparrals were dying from fan apathy. The name derives from thorny, tangled vegetation that is native to the Southwest. The chaparral bird is commonly called a roadrunner. We baby boomers, who loved Wile E. (for Ethelbert) Coyote on the television cartoon series, sometimes wondered why the stupid bird got top billing. because all it ever did was scamper around, making "meep, meep" sounds and foiling the array of powerful catapults, enormous magnets, jet skates, and even a hot-air balloon, from the last which Wile E. threw anvils. (Think about that one.) The coyote's touchingly misplaced faith in the products of the Acme Corporation—motto: "Quality is our dream"—was as much his undoing as the obsessive reliance on analytics had buried the Houston Rockets under a barrage of bricked three-pointers.

Of course, making the protagonist a wolflike predator with a taste for something close to squab might have been too upsetting to the impressionable tykes who watched it. Ornithologically, the roadrunner is a ground cuckoo. Clumsy in flight and rapidly tiring from the effort, it preferred dashing along the ground to flying.

Cuckoo was perfect for the slapstick ownership of the team. The basketball roadrunners were never going to get top billing in Dallas. The front office never put much wind beneath the franchise's wings until devising a birdbrained regionalization concept that denied the bedraggled team even a consistent home-court advantage. The word *Chaps,* as they were dubbed in headlines, was pronounced *Shaps.* They were renamed the Texas Chaparrals during the regionalization folly. They played not only in Dallas but in nearby Fort Worth and in Lubbock in the Texas panhandle, 346 miles away. It was a copy of the Carolina Cougars' decision to play in Greensboro, Winston-Salem, and Raleigh, all basketball hotbeds in the basketball-centric state of North Carolina. In Texas, the idea, like the bird, never got off the ground.

The *Dallas Morning News*'s beat reporter Randy Galloway tartly suggested they change names again to the US Chaparrals and just travel the land, playing wherever a town would have them, never to return to Dallas. In their death throes, the Chaparrals went rolling down Interstate 35 to San Antonio. I had reason to wish the coyote had caught the bird before it got there. I had a history in San Antonio, from my 76ers beat-man days.

It is never pretty when a game story or column goes into the shredder because a seismic change in the game at hand means the lede—again, not *lead,* in journalese, because it can be misinterpreted as a metallurgy thing—has to be Band-Aided and patched together in a tone completely at odds with the upbeat stuff written earlier during the game. On April 2, 1978, without aid of the three-pointer, which had not been legalized in the NBA, the 76ers let a sizable lead get away in San Antonio in the last two minutes and lost, 111–107. My piece had sprung more leaks than the dike the little Dutch boy plugged. I wondered later whether it might have been better simply to type: "Despite what you read below this paragraph, the Sixers hit the nail squarely on the thumb in the fourth quarter last night, when they otherwise forgot to hit anything from their shots to the dusty road."

Instead, after demanding access to the Sixers locker room when a television reporter was admitted and the print media members were stonewalled I got—well, *hogtied* is not the right word, maybe *subdued,* or *modified in tone and action*—or, more prosaically, *handcuffed.*

Sports Illustrated picked up what followed in the immediate moments after the game ended. My sad story was included it in its Scorecard Section in the April 17, 1978, issue, in which, even a John Peter Zenger in sportswriter's rumpled clothing, fearlessly championing the cause of a free and unfettered press, sometimes met stiff resistance from the police state. John Papanek's *SI* item about me read:

"NO RESPECT

"There was the case of Bill Livingston, pro basketball writer for the *Philadelphia Inquirer,* who was waiting to enter the 76ers locker room after a game in San Antonio. When a TV cameraman was allowed in and Livingston was not, Livingston took issue with the policeman guarding the door and wound up wearing a set of handcuffs. When the cuffs were finally removed (no charges were pressed) 76er Coach Billy Cunningham told Livingston, 'I wouldn't have bailed you out.'" This is exactly the kind of respect a writer expects from a coach.

The *Philadelphia Bulletin*'s Mark Heisler filed a brief story on it, quoting me: "Those things hurt," said Livingston. Unwilling to be scooped on what was in a very literal sense my own story, I dictated a short, embarrassing recap of my "Deadline USA" incident to the *Inquirer* copy desk. They took a jaunty approach to my near-incarceration, displaying the story in a box at the top of the first page of the sports section under the headline "Hold That Tiger!"

After the magazine came out, my unamused mother called, opening our dialogue, "What is this I hear about you being arrested in San Antonio?" I was nearly 30 years old then, but I still had to say words that no son, whatever his age, ever wants to say to his mom. "I was not arrested, mother," I protested. " I was released from custody, and no charges were filed."

Nicknamed "The Alamo City" for its biggest tourist attraction, San Antonio is known for Tex-Mex food, mariachi bands, and the old Spanish mission, the Alamo. Most Americans know "Remember the Alamo!" the battle cry after a Mexican army slew to a man its defenders during the Texas Revolution.

Almost all Texans and the vast majority of Americans remembered the Alamo. It resembled the sentimentality about the Confederacy when the statues of Rebel generals, memorials of a fratricidal war that ended in 1865, finally started coming down more than 20 years into the twenty-first century in states all over the South. The Texas Revolution against Mexico, like the later rebellion against the United States within a single generation, was fought for almost the worst cause imaginable: human slavery.

In my youth, schools were racially segregated. The old Southwest Conference, disbanded basically because of rampant cheating scandals, was not integrated until Jerry LeVias played for Southern Methodist University in 1966 and led the Mustangs to the conference championship that season, all while wearing the number 23 at the insistence of his grandmother—because his family feared racist reprisals, and the 23rd

Psalm is the one about walking through the valley of the shadow of death and fearing no evil.

Against this backdrop came Popovich, a political left-winger, coaching a team and building a dynasty with a United Nations roster of international players, including a taciturn leader in Tim Duncan, who went to Wake Forest but grew up in the Virgin Islands, and Ginobili, Parker, and Marco Belinelli, from Argentina, France, and Italy, respectively. The team Popovich built stood toe to toe with the big cities as the NBA made a mockery of the NFL's swagger about Green Bay's survival. San Antonio, Portland, Memphis, Salt Lake City, Orlando, and Oklahoma City all were one-sport cities that had thrived in the NBA.

In Cleveland, rooting against James and the Heat had almost become a civic obligation, the anxiety heightened by the realization that a Miami victory would complete a three-peat. During the previous season's 27-game winning streak, James had spoken openly of breaking the Lakers' record of 33. It was hard to imagine he would leave if the Heat had a chance to become the first team to win four NBA championships in a row since the Celtics' seven straight from 1959 through 1966. In those years, they played only two playoff rounds in each. The Heat faced four exhausting rounds every spring.

To the argument that the Spurs had "deserved" to win in the previous year's Finals, Popovich responded, "You don't 'deserve' anything. Just play." He knew that such thoughts might affect the team's desire for revenge. He knew no one gets his "turn" as a champion. There is no royal road to the big trophy. The anti-enabler of divas, Popovich gruffly tells young players, "Get over yourself."

James's response to the Heat's serious, no-entitlements culture had been overwhelmingly positive. In Cleveland, however, he had been treated like a favorite child pampered by overly indulgent parents. Every parent knows consequences are dire if you give a son or daughter everything they want. (Grandchildren are different.)

The Heat advanced to the 2014 Finals with only Indiana offering much resistance. The early rounds ended with a sweep of Charlotte; a 4–1 triumph in Brooklyn, where a tree grows, according to the title of a best-selling 1943 novel, but no champions have sprouted since the 1955

Dodgers; a 4–2 advance over Indiana, defiant as ever, but which ended with their season just as dead.

James wasn't back to square one, but he was in the Cavalier neighborhood, again burdened with teammates who, at least in comparison, "die down in the moment," his tart assessment of Mo Williams. Wade and Bosh didn't exactly die down, but the Heat's deep playoff runs had burned everyone's candles at both ends for four years and four Finals, and beautiful as their light had been in an Edna St. Vincent Millay way, they would not last the night.

2014 NBA FINALS
Game 1, at San Antonio, Spurs 110, Heat 95

The heat beat the Heat in the opener. The Spurs took care of the rest. "Beat the Heat" was the Spurs fans' mantra, but it became less a figurative allusion than a physical struggle. "Burnie," the Heat's *Sesame Street*-ish mascot, would have fit right into the sweltering, oppressive conditions inside the Spurs' AT&T Center when the air conditioning failed, with the outside temperature at 83. The sauna on the court was a steamy 90 degrees as ABC Television's sideline reporter Doris Burke reported in the fourth quarter.

"They're trying to smoke us out," James said during an early timeout.

Burke's report on the blast-furnace conditions came just after James slashed to the basket for a layup that cut the Spurs' lead to 94–92 with 7:30 to play in the game. James landed beyond the baseline on a good right leg and a left one stiffening as if made of wood.

Just as in Game 4 vs. Oklahoma City in 2012, he had gotten leg cramps at the worst possible time. Against the Thunder, he remained in the game long enough to hobble to the three-point and nail the game-clinching triple. It was as close as James had come to Jordan's agony in the Flu Game and a far hardier example of toughness than Paul Pierce's exit in a wheelchair after apparently suffering a knee injury in Game 1 of the 2008 NBA Finals, then returning after only 1:45 had elapsed on the game clock, under his own power, so badly hobbled that the blew by the Lakers' hoodwinked defenders again and again.

"You know, I think God sent this angel down and said, 'Hey, you're going to be all right, you need to get back out there, show them what you've got,'" Pierce said. Years later, he admitted he simply had to go to the bathroom, presumably, given the relatively short time that elapsed between roll-off and run-on, for a power pee.

Against the Spurs, James's only likeness was to Peter Stuyvesant, the Dutchman with a peg leg, in early America. James briefly returned to the game but was so restricted in mobility and gripped by pain that he went to the bench. After teammate Juwan Howard and a Heat official hoisted him up and lumbered to the sideline with their fallen star, James, whose progress resembled that of a French nobleman in a human sedan chair, did not return to the game. He scored 25 points but played only 33 minutes. The Spurs went on a 15–4 and ran up a 36–17 fourth quarter advantage in a resounding victory.

Perhaps James's unpopularity in some circles began after "the Decision," or maybe even earlier, after he crowned himself "King James" in high school. Much of the antipathy was in the eternal pleasure life's "have-not"s take from the downfall of a "have." He also, of course is Black, always an unpopular thing to be in some circles. The internet almost exploded with "LeBroning" memes. In one, the Spurs happily lazed in front of a huge courtside air conditioner as James was borne off. The meanest showed a trim blonde, doubled over in menstrual pain, crying, "OMG cramps," as James said, "Yes, lady. I know."

It was probably second all-time to a meme regarding the Delonte West–Gloria James rumors, in which James asked, "What's your favorite sit-com?" and West answered, *How I Met Your Mother.*

ABC's play-by-play man Mike Breen noted that old Celtics who were watching had to be saying, "What's a little heat?" because Boston Garden had no electrical capacity to handle air conditioning. An oscillating fan might have blown out every fuse in the tumbledown old wreck. The cameras spotted Heat president Pat Riley in the stands, still wearing a blazer, his blue shirt underneath so damp that the sweat delineated his man boobs, which were small but unmistakable.

The humidity and heat were so high, the sweat of the patrons so profuse, that after the game fans took mincing, cautious steps down concourses slick with sweat and heat condensation. Afterward, opinions were mixed on whether the Spurs—with 10 international players on their roster, none of them cosseted in climate-controlled arenas—had a major advantage. Ginobili said almost all of his games in Argentina had been played in stuffy, hot arenas. Tony Parker said Frenchmen liked it *chaud* (hot), not *froid* (cold). Duncan said that in the Virgin Islands, like Marilyn Monroe and the girls in the Sweet Sue and her Society Syncopators band, some liked it hot.

As for Miami players, Wade said his muscles were looser and he moved better in the hot environment. Chris Bosh, a native Texan, had played in such surroundings many times as a boy, so it was no big deal, in his view.

Game 2, at San Antonio, Heat 98, Spurs 96

With two days off before the next game, James had plenty of time to rest and hydrate. He took an 8:00 A.M. yoga class the day of the second game and wore shorter tights under his shorts. After starting 1-for-4 with three turnovers in the first quarter, James made 11 of his next 13 shots. At one stage, he scored eight points in one minute, enough to put the Heat on their way to victory. He finished with 35 points, 10 rebounds, a key strip of Tony Parker late in the game, and a pass to Bosh in the corner for a lethal three-pointer.

The Spurs again flubbed a good chance to win, with four straight missed free throws in the stretch run.

"For me, once I get into a good groove, I feel like everything is going to go in," James said. But everything wouldn't.

It was the 13th straight time the Heat had followed a playoff loss with a victory. But triskaidekaphobia and the revenge-minded Spurs ended that streak not once but twice.

Game 3, at Miami, Spurs 111, Heat 92

The Spurs had opened the second game by making 10 of their first 15 shots, losing only by dint of James. Incredibly, they were even deadlier than in the first game in hostile Miami.

The Spurs made 19 of their first 21 shots, a statistic that Gilbert Arenas, of video-game box-cover notoriety, would have envied. Teams have been known to do worse than that on the layup line. The Spurs made 13-of-15 in the first quarter for a 41–25 lead. They made 12-of-18 in the second quarter, for a 55–30 halftime lead. The 25-for-33 shooting for 76

The Spurs Strike Back   185

percent was an NBA playoff record. They led out of the gate, wire-to-wire, post-to-post, around the turn, down the backstretch, and through the home straight. They won easily with an efficiency of ball movement and shot conversion that gave them a lead it was impossible to blow.

The torrid shooting camouflaged the fact that the Heat shot 50 percent. That would end too. Kawhi Leonard, one of the culprits in the 2013 Finals between the teams, scored a career-high 29 points. James scored 22 points, as did Wade, but neither had a discernible impact on the outcome.

Game 4, at Miami, Spurs 107, Heat 86

Four straight Finals had emptied the Heat's tanks. Time and again, on-time and on-target passing and razor-sharp cuts gave the Spurs uncontested shots. Behind 20 points and 14 rebounds by Leonard, the Spurs coasted again. They also shored up their defense, holding the Heat to 35 percent in the first half, making James's 28 points overall a valiant but empty gesture.

To that point, no team in NBA history had ever come back from a 3–1 deficit in the Finals. Heading to San Antonio for Game 5, the Heat and their season were on a death watch.

Game 5, at San Antonio, Spurs 104, Heat 87

"I've said many times, a day didn't go by where I didn't think about Game 6," Spurs coach Gregg Popovich said of the turning point in the previous year's finals. "So, I think, just in general, for the group to have the fortitude that they showed to get back to this spot, I think speaks volumes about how they're constituted and what kind of fiber they have."

The Heat had no answer, at least after their 16-point first quarter lead vanished in the same old, same old of San Antonio's precision execution. "We wanted to redeem ourselves. I'm just glad we were able to do that," Parker said. At the head of the redemption line was Leonard. His missed free throw of a year earlier was a dim memory after his Most Valuable Player award in the Finals. Leonard finished with 22 points and seven rebounds in the rout. San Antonio won a record 12 playoff games by 15 or more points that season and was so dominant it blasted the Heat by 15, 19, and 21.

"They played exquisite basketball this series and in particular these last three games, and they are the better team. There's no other way to say it," Heat coach Erik Spoelstra said.

For James, it must have seemed at least a bit as if little had changed since Cleveland. Wade and Bosh combined for 24 points on 10-for-26 shooting. James's final contribution in Miami was to shoot 10-for-21 for 31 points and 10 rebounds on a team that scored only 87. The Spurs made his numbers the equivalent of a tree falling in a forest that was heard only by woodland creatures.

CHAPTER 23

Return of the King

The Heat in the off-season faced the impending free agency of each of the Big Three. In *Democracy in America*, required reading for any student of American history, Frenchman Alexis de Tocqueville had called Cleveland the Forest City for its woodsy setting. Should James return to Cleveland, it would be as big or possibly bigger news, given his championship imprimatur now, than when the lottery ball bounced the Cavs' way in 2003. In 2014, everyone in the Forest City would know if the sequoia fell where it was first planted. But that seemed highly unlikely reforestation.

ESPN's Stephen A. Smith called the Cavs a "mess" and said of Cleveland, "You look like a disgrace. What would LeBron be thinking about if he returned to Cleveland?"

Said the equally aghast Skip Bayless, "I would be astounded if LeBron James even seriously entertained the notion of going back."

In deciding whether to return to Cleveland or re-sign with Miami, James eventually reconciled with Gilbert against the wishes of the superstar's wife and mother. On the webcast *Uninterrupted,* James said Cavs owner Dan Gilbert's letter after "the Decision" "was loaded with insults—even referring to LeBron as the "self-titled former King." Gilbert had called James's decision to leave Cleveland a "cowardly betrayal" by a "former hero."

In the video, James said, "Gilbert completely bashed me and disrespected not only me as an individual but disrespected my name. And my name is not just myself, it's my wife, my kids', my grandfather's, my mother's, so many more people."

When he raised the prospect of returning to Cleveland, James said of his wife, Savannah, "My wife was like, 'F—k that. I ain't with that' . . . My mom was definitely like, 'F—k that. We ain't going back.'"

Nevertheless, Gilbert sat down with James in Miami on Sunday in the second week of June and apologized for the letter while the two met face to face to discuss their possible future together.

"We had five great years together and one terrible night," Gilbert told James and so started the process of reconciliation. "I told him how sorry I was, expressed regret for how that night went and how I let all the emotion and passion for the situation carry me away. I told him I wish I had never done it, that I wish I could take it back."

James told Gilbert he was sorry for the way he had handled the Decision. Although the two would never be close, James and the billionaire fart machinist made an uneasy peace / truce / diplomatic accord. James proved the bigger man, not only, obviously, at 6′8″ to Gilbert's reputed 5′6″ but also in spirit.

"How did I forgive?" James asked, in an interview with Dave McMenamin of ESPN. "I'm a man. Men, we all make mistakes. As a man, if you got a problem with somebody, you sit down face to face and you talk to them eye to eye. And you hash it out and move on. So, I think a lot of things that go on in life or in sports with people kind of holding grudges is because they're afraid to actually take a step forward. It's a fine line between pride and progress, and I'm on the progress side. I'm not on the pride side."

It is commendable that James wanted his own children and others not to hold grudges. Despite the defiance of his "I've done this before," commercials, alluding to spurning Akron Buchtel for St. Vincent-St. Mary, James, at heart, as a team sport player, is a good and decent man who wants to get along with others. He was almost surely uncomfortable with the torrents of hate, although he didn't admit it.

While he said "95 percent" of his decision to come back was about the location, playing with Kyrie Irving, whom he envisioned as an ideal wingman, was a "huge part" of it, per ESPN.

Lee Jenkins, *Sports Illustrated*'s top NBA reporter, wrote the story in James's voice. Ballyhooed on the cover, it ran on July 11, 2014:

Paraphrasing James's remarks, he spoke of the "special place in his heart" that northeast Ohio occupied and of the so-often dejected fans with their unquenchable passion for its teams.

The boos that rang in his ears when he returned to Cleveland with the Heat still echoed. The flames from fans burning his jersey on national television still singed his pride and fed his drive for atonement. He could imagine himself as a youngster, spirits crushed by an athletic idol who walked away. Atoning meant making that kid a fan again.

He wanted to make northeast Ohio a better place to live, with new infusions of opportunity he financed.

He concluded, "In Northeast Ohio, nothing is given. Everything is earned. You work for what you have.

I'm ready to accept the challenge. I'm coming home."

CHAPTER 24

World B. Flat

Winning comes with James, but so do distractions, wall-to-wall media attention, rumors 24/7 and inscrutable Twitter posts by His Mysterious Majesty. Also inescapable are the bruised egos of teammates balking at their smaller footprints on the national consciousness because of their sublimation to the prodigal, yet again favorite, son who had returned.

Still, the biggest problem was not James. It was a 6'2" combo guard who also provided the biggest opportunity for James finally to have an actual savior sidekick in Cleveland. Kyrie Irving, a deadly shooter who could also play the point, was one of the critical factors in James's return. Irving, despite having played only 11 games at Duke, due to injury, turned pro and was secured through the Cavs' lottery luck streak. He arrived at the top of the 2011 NBA draft lottery on James's departure. Irving was thrillingly dangerous with the ball in his hands.

He was also more than slightly daft, dreaming of being a franchise king in his own right instead of serving in a subordinate role or understudying for the lead. His world consisted of himself much of the time. Along with a grandiose and misplaced belief in his leadership qualities, his muddled head swarmed with crackpot beliefs that were a bit ripe for those of us who lived on planet Earth—which was flat, Irving insisted—despite satellite photos of our blue marble, spinning on the vast, dark playing field of space, accompanied by its solar running mates and their moons; some of them examined centuries ago by Galileo with his telescope.

Later in his career, Irving, happily ensconced in Cloud Cuckoo Land, was so against COVID-19 vaccination that he was ineligible to play most home games in plague-stricken New York, then sounded mystified in a postseason interview about why the team's disparate parts didn't cohere.

I called Kyrie "Cry Me," for his sense of grievance, but a fan on social media did better with his twist on Irving's wackadoodle beliefs, giving him the slightly but devastatingly altered name of the estimable 1980s Cavalier guard World B. Free: World B. Flat.

Free had saved the franchise by almost singlehandedly giving fans a reason to go to games in the 1980s at Richfield Coliseum, in the hinterlands around Akron.

Irving's professed beliefs were so ignorant that I thought of navigational charts on pre-Columbian maps on which, above seas patrolled by dragons, were signs that read: "Here be monsters!" For all he did, and it was plenty, to ensure the Cavaliers' eventual success, Irving would become one of the hazards of the voyage, like a reef unseen until the ship foundered on it.

Most of all, looming over everything and everyone, never lessening and ever tightening, was the pressure to win *now*. In charge of handling this soul-crushing job was David Griffin, elevated in February 2014 to the job of general manager, after the forgettable Chris Grant went down Gilbert's trapdoor. Griffin knew the drill and didn't much like it. Like so many coaches and general managers, Griffin trusted that process was crucial to progress. *Process* was the step-by-step cultivation of a new *culture*, another executive suite buzzword in sports and had little to do with visits to art museums or nights at the opera. Griffin used it to mean the customs, behaviors, and achievements of a nation, or, in this case, a team.

"We won despite our culture to a huge degree," he said to *Sports Illustrated*'s Chris Dodson in 2022. "And I knew it. I knew what we weren't doing. There were so many things during that period of time that I wanted to do differently. If you make everything about, 'It's a destination. Damn the torpedoes, I gotta get there,' that might be the only time you get there."

On June 11, 2014, the Cavs confoundingly won the first pick in the NBA lottery for the fourth time. Their luck was inexplicable, unless you believe in conspiracy theories. The first was when James, who grew up figuratively next door, in Akron, entered the NBA Draft straight out of high school in 2003. The second was in 2011, after James went to Miami in "the Decision," which netted Kyrie Irving. The third was in 2013, a year so bad that, had it affected French wine the same way, it would have tested the American taste for Gallic vinegars. It brought the only bust, Anthony Bennett.

The fourth, in 2014, netted Andrew Wiggins, the son of NBA player Mitchell Wiggins. The draft was held on June 20, three weeks before James's announcement, so the Wiggins lottery pick could not be considered part of any NBA solace for Cleveland's loss. The younger Wiggins was irresistible trade bait when Griffin started looking for a third member of another LeBron triumvirate. On August 23, Wiggins went to Minnesota in a trade for power forward Kevin Love, schooled at UCLA, teammate of Russell Westbrook, nephew of Beach Boy Mike Love, son of ABA and NBA player Stan Love, a three-time All-Star with the lowly Timberwolves in his six NBA seasons, and a man content to be the third wheel on a championship contender after years in Minnesota.

Griffin's next big move was not as successful. First, he fired Byron Scott, hired as coach in 2010 after James left. Scott had quickly become the captain of the basketball *Titanic* as the Cavs lost an NBA-record 26 straight games that season. After Griffin fired him, the general manager made a hire not just out of NBA and college basketball world but out of the country and the continent. His new coach was David Blatt, hugely successful in Israel and Russia, garnering enough plaques and certificates of excellence as to make wallpaper optional in his home, if he so chose. He was fresh from winning the EuroLeague championship and its Best Coach award.

Like almost everyone in the Cavaliers' organization during James's first stay, of seven years, however, Blatt was reluctant to confront James, who became increasingly and openly disrespectful of the first-time NBA coach. Unsurprisingly, this became a problem.

So did Irving's ego.

Said Griffin in a *Sports Illustrated* issue devoted to James's exorcism of Cleveland's devils and his own ghosts, "[The problem] was LeBron getting all the credit and none of the blame. People don't like that. They don't want to be part of that world."

Irving fixated on his own alpha-male status on his various teams and his celebrity, despite lacking both leadership skills, in the first case, and the chastening lessons of maturity, in the second. He would become a serpent, with a poisonous effect on all of his teams. "Cobra Ky," a play on the *Cobra Kai* television series title, fit him perfectly.

He played "Uncle Drew," a streetball legend, in the eponymous comedy film and in Pepsi-Cola television commercials. Unlike the old guy Irving portrayed, he was a prodigy. Like James, an NBA Rookie of the Year, the 6′2″ Irving would eventually share with James the Cavs' record for most points in one game, each scoring 57, James against the Wizards in 2017 and Irving, more impressively, against the Spurs in 2015. He was an expert marksman, going 7-for-7 on threes in the 57-point game, but his real glory was around the rim.

Deadly with either hand, Irving developed his ambidexterity by shooting reverse layups and hook shots with one hand, then the other, wheeling back and forth and then forth and back, under the basket on a New Jersey playground's baked concrete under a summer sun, all while being watched closely by his father, Drederick, lest he falter.

It is called the Mikan Drill, the workout regimen of DePaul's George Mikan, basketball's first great big man. Occasionally the young Irving's nose bled, and the world began to do whatever a Flat Earther believes it does at the onset of dizziness, since spinning is clearly not a possibility. Yet, he tottered back and forth, forth and back, as the drill became literally a pain in the neck whenever he twisted his head to look up and back at the rim and backboard time and time again.

Irving also developed a hesitation dribble that would freeze defenders the way Medusa turned the heroes of myth and legend to stone with a glance. He used a hard bounce of the ball before he would suddenly burst to the basket, taking the ball on the rise, chest high, in a basketball version of a defensive lineman's arm-over move in football. Donovan Mitchell, a Cavaliers star years later, used the same move, once scoring a staggering 71 points in a game, in large part because of his ability to get to the rim.

Alternatively, Irving had a staccato low dribble, with which he would tunnel through the defensive clutter. He played angles that Minnesota Fats and Fast Eddie Felson never knew about in pool halls. He could butterfly kiss the ball high off the glass, leaping left-footed or right- footed, using either his right hand or his left.

He was prodigiously good, utterly self-absorbed, unreasonably demanding and reliably truculent in interviews. Irving was probably the second-most talented player in Cavaliers history, but one whose legacy was marred by his selfishness and surpassing weirdness.

He and James did great things until Irving, by leaving, did the greatest harm since James had left years before. The difference between them is that James left trophies—in Miami, in Los Angeles, in Cleveland, the latter the first in over a half-century—while Irving left ruin.

CHAPTER 25

"Gassed Out"

One of James's greatest and least remembered shots brought the Cavs to Oakland for the 2015 NBA finals. On the play, in the dying seconds of the fourth game of a second-round series in Chicago, James beat a Bulls' double team, just as Chicago's Michael Jordan had beaten one against the Cavs on "The Shot" to win a fierce series over a quarter-century earlier. But James also had to overcome his own coach, David Blatt, who first called for a timeout in the last seconds that the Cavs didn't have. Referees missed his signal, which would have meant a technical free throw, possession of the ball in a tie game, and likely a daunting 3–1 series lead for Chicago.

Blatt compounded his error by designing a last play calling for James to inbound the ball. Instead, James "scratched" the play, as he said, demanded the ball, and did not miss the final shot even though he had burgeoning NBA star Jimmy Butler, then with the Bulls, in his face. The Cavs would scratch Blatt as coach on January 23, 2016. James clearly had lost all respect for the beleaguered NBA Neophyte. In retrospect, Oakland had been Blatt's last stand.

Oakland native Gertrude Stein said infamously, at least in the East Bay, "There's no 'there' there." She meant there was no sense of place, no defining landmark like the Golden Gate Bridge, and no towering hills scaled by little cable cars, climbing halfway to the stars. San Francisco had that, not Oakland. Tony Bennett left his heart in San Francisco, not Oakland. Humphrey Bogart as private eye Sam Spade gumshoed in *The Maltese*

Falcon in San Francisco, not Oakland. Steve McQueen was cop Frank Bullitt in *Bullitt* in San Francisco. Clint Eastwood was the .45 magnum-toting cop in *Dirty Harry* in San Francisco. Oakland could claim the great Bill Russell, at least in his younger days at McClymonds High School. Yet, when Russell was the cornerstone of consecutive NCAA basketball championships in 1955–56, it was at the University of San Francisco. Of course.

What was in Oakland were the Warriors, playing in a drab, dark arena next to a freeway across a vast parking lot from the Oakland A's baseball park. James was there too, where in the next four years he would achieve all kinds of unthinkable firsts—leading both teams in all of the important stats in one Finals and averaging a triple-double in another, making the play of his life in yet another, which ended a 52-year championship drought in Cleveland, thus making good on his vow to do just that. And in his last Finals there, playing with a broken hand in the last three games, he led the Cavs in scoring in each.

The NBA had a global reach by 2015, as shown in the anecdote about my frantic conversation with security personnel and their familiarity with LeBron in provincial Greece at the 2004 Olympic torch relay (see chapter 7). The Warriors certainly offered much for purists to like. Similar to the Cavs, the Warriors had hired a first-time NBA coach in Steve Kerr, who, unlike Blatt, knew the NBA and, having almost come to blows with no less than Jordan in practice with the Bulls, had a guff-resistant nature.

The Warriors had major stars in Curry and Klay Thompson, both sons of NBA players, both remarkable outside shooters, hence the "Splash Brothers" nickname, because on swishes they made the net strands fly up like water in a pool after a "cannonball" jump. Curry won the NBA MVP award in 2015 and 2016, but neither he nor Thompson, while certainly in the stellar firmament, was the Polaris of the league and the basketball world, as was James. The franchise had built through the draft but lacked the crazy No. 1 pick luck of the Cavs in the lottery. For example, point forward Draymond Green, a volatile leader, completely committed to the team, was a second-round pick.

Kerr had bright young assistants and gave them the freedom to make suggestions in game plans, increasing their visibility and prospects for a future head coaching job. Kerr wanted to replicate the Spurs' unselfish style because he was appalled when he saw that Golden State in its final season under Mark Jackson had made fewer passes per game, with 243.8, than any other team in the league, as Scott Howard-Cooper notes in his book, *Steve Kerr: A Life*. Kerr also liked big men who could pass, such as Chris Webber and Vlade Divac in the early 2000s, with the only Sacramento team that ever amounted to much. Green filled the bill perfectly, as did his backup at power forward, David Lee.

NBA FINALS
Game 1, at Oakland, Warriors 108, Cavaliers 100 (OT)

After Warriors fan Santana performed the national anthem as a guitar solo—good, but not Jimi Hendrix–at–Woodstock good—the series began with the allure of top of the marquee names in Curry and James and two straight pulsating close overtime games, in which the Cavaliers came within a frantic rim-out at the buzzer of winning both.

But the big news was that the Cavs lost not only the opener but also, with Love already sidelined after the first round because of a shoulder injury, what slim chance they had to win the championship, when Kyrie Irving went down for the series in overtime after his left knee collided with Thompson's, with the Cavs down, 102–98 and just over 2 minutes left.

Irving knew he was badly hurt, saying the knee "felt different" after the collision. He flew to Cleveland the next day and would watch much of the Finals from a hospital bed after orthopedists reassembled his kneecap, which had been fractured. Irving had been in and out of the lineup throughout the playoffs, drawing veiled criticism in print or sometimes pointed ridicule as a malingerer or wimp in the conversations of skeptical Cleveland reporters. The 43:37 he spent on the floor in the Finals opener and the 21:58 he played in the closeout of Atlanta drew questions about how badly he was really hurt. I strongly disagreed. Irving played only 11 games at Duke, because of injuries. Why would he malinger in his chosen profession's biggest event, the NBA Finals?

In 2017, on the *Short Story Long* podcast, Irving addressed the injury. Interestingly enough, he mentioned that while skateboarding as a kid, he had split open his knee, which was then sewn up. Turns out, he had a small fracture or crack in his knee, which widened dramatically after he collided with Thompson. This brings more context to what had unfolded, because their knees didn't make much contact on the play. In fact, it was the placement, not the force, of the contact that caused Irving to suffer a serious injury. The 25-year-old had never allowed his knee to heal properly, which essentially made the injury a ticking time bomb.

The opener almost never got to overtime. Irving made a spectacular block of Curry on a layup with 26 seconds remaining in the fourth quarter to preserve a 98–98 tie. After that, the Cavs ran the clock down and put James in the same isolation set he had remembered so fondly in Windhorst's story about his remarkable memory. This time, Andre Iguodala forced James into a closely guarded fall away jump shot with four seconds on the clock that glanced off the far side of the rim and bounced toward the corner. Iman Shumpert dashed off in pursuit of the ball, reaching it in a flash. A step in front of the arc, he seized the ball, jumped, and unloaded it like a trebuchet whipping a boulder at a medieval fortress. It looked good but spun out.

The demoralized Cavs went tamely in the lopsided overtime that followed. What would happen in the series was obvious. James would have to assume a massive load in both initiating plays and ending them with scores. How much Irving meant would be as obvious as a Mark Johnson remark. Irving shot 10-for-22 for 23 points in the opener. James was 18-for-38 for 44 points. In the game, they scored 61 percent of the Cavs' points and took 70.3 percent of the teams shots.

Game 2, at Oakland, Cavaliers 95, Warriors 93 (OT)

A change in psyche came in the change in the lineup, the Cavs' Australian Tasmanian Devil, whirling dervish, floor-burn fixture Matthew Dellavedova, with his fearless, reckless energy, came bouncing off the bench to replace Irving. In the next two games, which the Cavs and Warriors split, it was Dellavedova who lifted Cleveland fans' spirits, paradoxically, by diving on, crawling along, and staking claim to any part of the floor on which a ball of uncertain provenance was rolling. Because Dellavedova's kamikaze hustle had knocked Atlanta's Kyle Korver out of the East Finals, the Hawks protested long and loud that the Aussie was a dirty player.

Before the Finals began, I called Stu Jackson, the so-called Dean of Discipline, adjudicating plays that might be subject to player fines or suspensions. Jackson was unmoved by Atlanta's protests. "This nonsense about people calling Dellavedova a dirty player—I don't buy it," said Jackson. "What I do buy is that Dellavedova plays hard. He is very aggressive and—oh by the way—he is a role player. As a role player, if you don't play hard, and you don't play aggressive, and you don't create extra possessions for your team, you're not a very good role player. If you're a player, and Dellavedova is on the floor, you have to know where he is. You can't take him lightly."

The essence of Delly's game came in the last minute of the fourth quarter, with the Cavs desperately trying to stave off a furious Warriors comeback. Maybe the Cavs only got to overtime because the Warriors didn't get enough possessions to put up the game-winning shot. And that was because Dellavedova went down and claimed everything he could procure by dint or scratching, scrambling, and clawing for the vital inches Wally Szczerbiak had scorned against the Celtics years earlier.

Harrison Barnes had an open 16-foot jump shot in the last 42 seconds, the Warriors trailing, 87–85, but he missed it. Bodies-flying madness erupted under the rim. James knocked the ball loose as he, too, scrambled after it. Delly dived, wrestled it away, rolled over to put his body between the ball and the mayhem, and called time. Although Delly finished with only nine points, they all came in the last quarter and overtime. He calmly made two free throws to put the Cavs ahead to stay, 94–93, with 10 seconds to play in overtime. On the possession, James made one of his seeing-eye, rocketed passes, finding three-point specialist James Jones open in the corner. "Usually when JJ [Jones] JR [Smith] and Mike Miller shoot, we don't rebound, because most of the time, they make them," said James.

Dellavedova rebounded, though. Guys who live on loose change take nothing for granted.

Collegiately, Dellavedova had played 20 miles from San Francisco, at St. Mary's of Moraga, California. Suddenly he had become one of the most booed Cavs in the lion's den of Oracle Arena because opposing fans can live with James, or the lost Kevin Love and Kyrie Irving, beating them on athleticism and skill, but not on Delly going in among the trees and rooting the ball out. Extra possessions meant the Cavs got 10 more rebounds and six more shots than the Warriors.

Game 3, at Cleveland, Cavaliers 96, Warriors 91

The Cavs, surprisingly, took a 2–1 series lead in the third game. Leading the scoring was James, who accrued 39 points on relentless peppering of the rims, backboard, and everything but the stanchion. He made only 11 of 35 shots.

Validating the new hard-hat gritty game plan, the Cavs won, in part, because they got seven more shots and 11 more rebounds than the Warriors. It allowed the Cavs to shorten the game by possessing the ball longer and to play at their preferred pace, that of a stroll. Dellavedova scored only nine points, but seven were in the fourth quarter, second only to James's 10 in the final quarter.

With the Cavs trailing, 93–92 after three-point specialist James Jones uncharacteristically missed a wide-open corner trey off a rocketed pass by James. Dellavedova went in there against the trees and dugout the ball, drawing a two-shot foul with 10 seconds to play. He splashed both. It was not over until Curry inbounded after James made a free throw. Curry tried to rifle a bounce pass to Thompson, who was racing downcourt for three-pointer. Shumpert, chasing him, somehow saw the ball in his peripheral vision and picked it off as it almost bounced past him, then threw it to James, maybe just to give him something to scream about and then spike, both of which he did with gusto.

James said that Dellavedova, an undrafted free agent, "obviously is a guy who's been counted out his whole life. Probably people have been telling him he's too small, he's not fast enough, can't handle it good enough, and he's beat the odds so many times."

The third game had been played in Cleveland. But the location of any game didn't matter to Delly. His home was the floor, wherever the schedule took him.

In basketball, a *dig* is a swipe at the ball when an opponent is dribbling through defenders. It's particularly effective when a big man takes an unnecessary rhythm dribble, gathering himself for a dunk, an unfortunate tic the late Darryl Dawkins never overcame in Philadelphia. This made him vulnerable to smaller men. "Don't put the cheese on the floor. The mice will get it," the flamboyant, Cleveland State coach Kevin Mackey often said. Delly was the mouse who let James roar. He would dig his way to hell if it meant winning a game.

On his biggest play, Dellavedova slipped around James's pick on Steph Curry, then wheeled past Iguodala, who had to slide over to cover James. As Curry fought his way around James's screen, Dellavedova got a step on him. Now it was the little-known Dellavedova vs. the league MVP Curry. The Warriors' star dug at the ball and knocked Delly off balance behind the three-point arc. The next opponent was gravity, which seldom loses.

Either Jordan or Dwayne Wade is probably the all-time leader in "circus shots." (Teaser for events to come. James would soon sink similar shots from unlikely angles and contorted positions because he actually practiced such things as shootarounds.) Dellavedova got off a tumbling, legs-splayed shot fit for circus acrobats—admittedly clumsy ones—and banked it in. The Cavs' lead was down to a single point, with 2 minutes, 27 seconds left, before the bank shot went in. They led by 20 in the third quarter.

After the game, Delly was poked and probed, had intravenous fluids fed into him, and was whisked off to the Cleveland Clinic to rest and recuperate. Part of the problem was that Dellavedova guzzled heavily sugared coffee during timeouts and at halftime, looking for more fuel but instead becoming dehydrated.

A reporter from Australia raised the specter of knighthood for Delly after he set an Aussie NBA finals one-game scoring record. James thought long and hard about the possibility of "Sir Dellavedova" and said, "Whatever that guy wants to be, I'm all for it."

In the big picture, the Cavs' 2–1 series was as shaky as San Francisco in 1906, the year of the massive earthquake and fire. Iman Shumpert, whose steal saved Game 2, wrenched his shoulder and gutted out the last minutes of that game while wearing a harness on the wounded joint. Golden State had not only had a relatively smooth run to the Finals, but the attrition in the Cavs' ranks also made the Warriors' fusillade of three-pointers in mounting their huge, but unsuccessful comeback, even more ominous. They shot 7-of-14 on them in the fourth quarter, and Curry went 5-for-8. It was a reminder that as long as success or failure hinged on learning to love the bomb, the Warriors were never out of a game until the clock said they were.

The disparity between the teams in the final three games occurred because of two factors. First, without Irving, the Cavs had only J. R.

202 The Promise of LeBron James

Smith to try to match the Warriors on the long ball. Second, James was again in a slump with the perfidious three-pointer.

Game 4, at Cleveland, Warriors 103, Cavaliers 82

Remembering the effective lineup Popovich created by benching Tiago Splitter and inserting Matt Bonner, Nick U'Ren succeeded in convincing Kerr to sit Andrew Bogut and start Iguodala, a change that surprised the Cavs because Kerr had said in the mandatory pregame interview session, in a small, Red Auerbach–like bit of mischief, that the starting lineup would stay the same.

"I have proven that I will lie," Kerr said, puckishly, after the game. As Howard-Cooper pointed out, Kerr was still in his smart-ass persona and was not serious when he said, "As I told Nick today, he's gotten way too much credit. It's gone totally overboard. So enough about Nick."

Game 5, at Oakland, Warriors 104, Cavs 91

This was the year the NBA junked the 2–3–2 Finals format, initiated in 1985 to reduce travel and thus increase media attendance, and went back to the 2–2–1–1–1 plan—as no top seed that defends its home court in the opening pair of games should ever fall behind because the lower seed has the next three home games, potentially, pushing the better regular season team to the brink.

Of course, the change came just when the outmanned Cavs needed the 2–3–2 format most. It's a Cleveland thing. The Warriors won the next two games by 13 and eight points and were crowned champions.

Game 5, at Oakland, Warriors 104, Cavs 91;
Game 6, at Cleveland, Warriors 105, Cavs 97

Since the last two games were a rinse-and-repeat, same old, same old copy of the fourth game, little reason exists for an exhaustive examination of them.

Kerr's lineup changes and emphasis on ball movement resulted in a perfect 11-for-11 first quarter and 16-for-18 first half alone on assists and baskets. Late in the last game of the Cavs' season, waiting to report into the game, James sat on the edge of the scorer's table, his shoulders slumped, physically spent. "I gassed out," he said.

"I've been watching basketball for a long time, I'm an historian of the game," James said. "I don't know any other team that's gotten to the Finals without two All-Stars. I cannot remember thinking of it. I don't even know if it's ever happened, for a team to lose two All-Stars and still be able to make it to the Finals. There were a lot of points in those two suits on the bench (Love and Irving). I've had a lot of playoff runs, been on both ends, and I know one thing that you've got to have during the playoff run. You've got to be healthy. You've got to be playing great at the right time. You've got to have a little luck."

"Guarding LeBron James has to be the hardest job in basketball," Warriors coach Steve Kerr said, in what might have been the most meaningful compliment he received.

In the Finals, James averaged 35.8 points, 13.3 rebounds and 8.8 assists, becoming the first player to be the leading scorer, rebounder and assist man in the Finals, both teams included. No other player in postseason history averaged at least those stats in a series—not Jordan, not Bird, not Oscar, not Magic. The next season, the suits would be in jerseys and shorts. The Cavs wouldn't almost have to siphon the life blood out of Delly. They would meet the Warriors again. And the best player on the floor, regardless of what MVP voters thought, would make his greatest play in the greatest Game 7 of the greatest NBA Finals ever.

CHAPTER 26

Good Trouble,
Good Causes,
and Good Balance

"I always look at it, 'Would I rather not make the playoffs or lose in the Finals?'" said LeBron James after the loss to Golden State. "I don't know. I don't know. I've missed the playoffs twice. I lost in the Finals four times. I'm almost starting to be like I'd rather not even make the playoffs than to lose in the Finals. It would hurt a lot easier if I just didn't make the playoffs and I didn't have a shot at it."

He knew that the hurt he felt from the loss was attributable to attrition as much as the opposition; that it could only be healed by a championship; that the effort to do that would be enormous; that his atonement would not become absolution until he saved the loyal Cleveland fans from their trilogy of disappointment, defeat, and despair; and that their redemption would also be his own.

Before the games that count had even begun, *Cleveland.com*'s Chris Haynes, now an ESPN sideline reporter, broke the story that James had chided his teammates for their lack of seriousness. "You can tell if guys are messing around a little too much," James said. "Me as a leader, I'm able to gauge that and see where our minds are at."

Left unmentioned by everyone was the leader's tweet about Kevin Love the previous season and his growing disrespect for David Blatt, displayed through his body language and protracted scanning of the stands during timeouts as the previous season's playoffs wore on.

Even before training camp opened in September, the Cavs lost another player to injury.

Iman Shumpert suffered a ruptured extensor carpi ulnaris sheath "several days" before the start of training camp. "In training at a high school near his home, last week, he had an issue where he hit the rim with his right wrist. I believe he was trying to catch a lob [pass]," said David Griffin. The injury caused the tendon on the inside of his right wrist to become loose, and waiting on the injury to heal naturally without any surgery was not an option. He was expected to be out 12-to-14 weeks and miss at least 25 games.

"All I care about is raising banners," said James on Media Day as training camp began. "Nothing else. That's what I'm here for."

If a banner were to be raised, it should be tattered and shot-torn, just like the Cavaliers, as the Yuletide season approached and the three-month waiting period for Kyrie Irving and Shumpert ended.

The NBA makes a big deal of Christmas Day, which marks the first time many Americans, who have been tethered to their HD TVs, watching the NFL, really start to notice the league. The marquee matchup was a Finals rematch with Golden State in Oakland. It was forgettable except in the way epic defeats are remembered until they are avenged. The Cavs lost, 89–83. As a team, they shot 32 percent, the Terrible (on that day anyway) Triad of James, Irving, and Love shot 33.3 percent, or 17-for-57.

I wondered if "Remember the Day Santa Put Coal in the Stockings," would provide future inspiration. It did not. In the February 18 rematch in Cleveland, the Cavs took a 132–98 shellacking, falling to a record of 19–8, while the Warriors were an alarming 28–1. Dennis Manoloff summarized it in the *Plain Dealer* using boldface, black as the heart of midnight, subheads that provided not even a flash of hope in the midnight darkness. "Globetrotters vs. Generals," he called it, for the Globies' perennial Washington patsies.

But before that . . .

David Griffin, aware that the clock was near the halfway point the four seasons until James again became a free agent, chose the "shake well before using" approach to coping with the winter of James's discontent.

On January 22, 2016, Griffin fired Blatt and replaced him with assistant Tyronn Lue, who had done such commendable work in squelching Blatt's attempt to call an illegal timeout in the final seconds of Game 4 in the Chicago series the year before.

My column read:

"The body language of estranged player and embattled coach hinted of a break-up for a long time. And thus did King James and his Court, the Cavaliers' supporting players, finally send David Blatt to the unemployment line. Griffin spoke of a 'disconnect' in the locker room between the players and the coach. However, 30–11, the Cavs' record, is a 60-win season in the making . . . In Miami, Pat Riley commanded all of the players' respect with his record. Maybe Lue will too, although the record part is pretty thin. If so, that might be a first for a Cavaliers coach with James, but Lue had better work on it."

When Steve Kerr had arena workers play loud music at their practices, the team could have been dubbed, with apologies to the late Hubert Humphrey, the Happy Warriors. Whatever the secret Kerr found in Oakland, Blatt never discovered it in Cleveland.

A few days later came the announcement of the players who would participate in the All-Star Game in Toronto on Valentine's Day. James was the lone Cavalier selected. Replacing the fired Blatt, Lue coached the East because the Cavs had the best record in the conference. "I just thought in this league it's always been about winning, and winning has always been rewarded," Lue said. "Being No. 1 in the East and Kevin being one of four guys in the NBA to average a double-double on a winning team . . . I've just never seen a first-place team . . . getting only one guy in."

"It's definitely a kick in the rear end for our team, for sure, knowing all the work we put into it and knowing the other two guys," said James, speaking of Love and Irving.

It was far from James's best soundbite of the day. I pursued the quirky All-Star Game voting, which had been opened to players for the first time, with the caveat that they could not vote for someone from their own team. James and Kevin Durant, widely acknowledged as the best players in the league, had been spurned on many players' ballots. It was clearly a case of jealousy, but for some reason I did not use that word. "LeBron, what do you think of all the goofy votes on some players' All-Star Game ballots?" I asked.

James said quickly, "There's always a lot of goofy votes. Trump was elected."

Uproarious laughter. Mic drop. Walk-off. The man has timing.

(The same day, I presented James with a copy of my book *George Steinbrenner's Pipe Dream: The 1962 ABL Champion Cleveland Pipers.* It was Cleveland native Steinbrenner's first venture into pro sports. His behavior in the first league to use a three-point shot—at 25 feet, longer than the NBA's—prefigured his tumultuous time as "The Boss" of the New York Yankees. On the title page, I wrote to James, "The Pipers are the only Cleveland team ever to win a professional basketball championship. Make that statement obsolete this season." As I said, the man has timing.)

On January 30, 2016, Popovich brought the Spurs to Cleveland. As I stood with two San Antonio reporters, waiting to speak to him after the brief morning shoot-around at the arena, he smiled and said, "Gene Mauch!"

"How are you doing, Pop?" I said.

"He's still the president, isn't he?" Popovich replied.

Sometimes, I believed my role, as shown by James's wit, was to be the straight man for him and other NBA luminaries.

Everyone who covered James was aware that he knew sports history. Unlike Jordan, who spent his playing career doing and saying nothing that might dissuade any consumers from buying Air Jordans, James was interested in moving history by improving the present. His activities ranged from his philanthropic and educational initiatives to help children growing up under the same deprivation he experienced, to publicly backing Hillary Clinton, the presidential candidate who was far more likely to be a unifying influence on an increasingly divided country, to making his opinions known through the bullhorn he had because of his celebrity status. He weighed the effect of his liberal political beliefs against the loss of sneaker sales because of them and continued to speak out. Some things were more important than more and more money. Like Steve Kerr, James wanted a more inclusive society, one that, as Pope Francis I said in his rebuke of Donald Trump's "America First" policies, should "build bridges, not walls."

In 2018, the trouble an increasingly outspoken James had invited at least as early as his off-the-cuff Trump quip came at him when Fox News's conservative personality Laura Ingraham, enveloped by a fog of misinformation, tweeted "Shut up and Dribble!" at James. Calling James's comments "ignorant" and "barely intelligible," Ingraham also said, "This is what happens when you attempt to leave high school a year early to join the NBA, and it's always unwise to seek political advice from someone who gets paid $100 million a year to bounce a ball."

Indeed, James considered challenging the NBA draft rules after his junior year at Akron St. Vincent-St. Mary High School but never did. He graduated with his class in 2003. The words *ignorant* and *barely intelligible* are unfounded and derisive.

In reply, James defiantly posted on Instagram: "I AM MORE THAN AN ATHLETE." So was Bill Russell. So was Muhammad Ali. So were former NBA players and head coaches in 2016, like Golden State's Kerr and Doc Rivers, then the Los Angeles Clippers coach. James was in the "good trouble" advocated by the late congressman John Lewis, who was almost billy-clubbed to death by Alabama state troopers in Selma on Bloody Sunday in the March to Montgomery civil rights protest at the Edmund Pettus Bridge, which was named for a Confederate general. Lewis courted the kind of trouble that protests inequities and empowers the downtrodden.

And so did Colin Kaepernick, who began dropping to one knee during the national anthem in silent protest of police brutality. Simply for exercising his constitutional right to peaceful protest, he was blackballed by rigidly conservative NFL owners after then president Donald Trump addressed the issue in his usual nuanced way by roaring, "Get that sonofabitch off the field!"

James noted the actions of both the protester and the president. In time he would make his own views known more stridently.

In my column, I wrote: "James has his flaws. . . . Yet at the most fundamental level, James is no more or less than most of us. He wants his children to grow up in a better society and live in a better world than he had. He differs from many of us in that he had very little growing up. He also differs in that, now that he has a great deal, he gives a not-inconsequential amount back. The LeBron James Family Foundation has pledged to provide full scholarships to 1,100 youngsters from Akron, at the cost of approximately $41 million.

"If this is the mark of an ignorant, barely intelligible man, I say, where do we find more like him?"

The Cavs had no more marquee games until the playoffs began. They were the top seed in the East, although it took them until the 81st game of an 82-game season to clinch the spot. They did so against the Atlanta Hawks, their personal bop bag, who, like the inflatable children's toy, took a punch and reliably bounced back for more.

The Cavs finished 57–25, a single game ahead of Toronto, and, ahem, 16 (sixteen!) games behind the record-setting 73–9 record of the Warriors, the happiest team with Native American–themed mascots in the whole crowd of Chiefs, Braves, Blackhawks, Indians, and Redskins who were still tomahawk-chopping and war cry–bawling.

Clearly, the best approach to the first round, particularly for a top seed like the Cavs, was to get it over quickly and save the wear and tear. James's teams in Miami and Cleveland, after he came home, had swept three consecutive opening-round series. James had won 13 such games in a row since the Heat lost the fourth game against the Knicks in 2012 but closed them out in the fifth.

I tried not to be a victim of an April Fool's joke as the playoffs began in early spring and shied away from being too dismissive of the once-feared Pistons. I recalled the 1985 NCAA championship game. It was played in Lexington, Kentucky, where the *Herald-Leader*'s sports columnist D. G. Fitzmaurice wrote, "I can state, unequivocally and in public, that there will be a Martian in the White House before Villanova beats Georgetown. I realize Rollie Massmino [Villanova's coach] will probably read this to his players. I hope he does. It will take their minds off the game."

Final score: Villanova 66, Georgetown 64.

I did not want to be the press room's "D. G. Fitzmaurice Vomit on My Own Copy" winner.

2016 EASTERN CONFERENCE FIRST ROUND
Game 4, at Auburn Hills, Michigan, Cavaliers 100, Pistons 98

James had authored many epics in the agate type of the box scores with his triple-doubles, but the advance to the conference finals was so devoid of challenges that only two games in the opening pair of sweeps were close.

So I turned to some signature moments by the other starters.

The first was Irving, whose performance in critical situations rose to James's level during that playoff season and whose penchant for pettiness and petulance would make him a divisive presence with each of the four teams for which he would play in coming years. In the only close game of the Detroit sweep, the fourth, with the score tied in the late going, James dribbled on the arc in what was to be a 1–4 isolation set, with Irving flanking him on the left wing. As the seconds ticked away, James pointed emphatically to the left corner, where he wanted Irving to be ready for a three on a drive-and-kick. Irving rolled his eyes in exasperation, then moseyed slowly to the corner. It was individualistic in a sport with a collective purpose, but critics needed to back off. Moments later, Irving showed why he and James were the best tandem of closers in the league.

The Cavs led, 97–96 on a possession that began after a Pistons foul with 1:08 to play. With the shot clock only 0.7 from running out, Dellavedova inbounded from the baseline to the left of the Pistons' basket. He snapped the ball on a shallow angle to the right corner, to which Irving had raced from the top of foul circle for a catch (in an eyeblink)—and shoot (in an eyelash twitch)—three-pointer. His defender, Tobias Harris, was slowed by James's back screen, with James then cutting to Delly's side of the court, drawing every Piston with him except Harris. The latter was now frantically closing and flailing his hand at Irving, who faded away from the defender slightly and barely cleared Harris's straining fingers in the very last second of the 24-second clock. The shot went down with 43 seconds to play, 25 seconds from the play's start, one second after Irving's release, and it took the game with it.

Detroit's last spasm came with Cleveland leading, 100–98, and Reggie Jackson—not Mr. October of MLB and, come to think of it, not Mr. April of the NBA either—missed everything with a three for the win at the buzzer. Irving led the Cavs scoring with 31 points to James's 22.

The second player to get his exploits sung in the sunshine before the team went on their way to the Finals was the "Quiet Man" (no, not the movie about Ireland starring John Wayne, who was very dead by then). The player was starting center Tristan Thompson, whose dalliance with Khloe Kardashian made him bigger in *People* magazine than anywhere else. In the sports world, Thompson's shooting most foul at the line overshadowed the derivative celebrity that came with dating a Kardashian.

The oddity with Thompson is that he, like Judy Collins, looked at life from both sides now. I began a feature on him with: "If you look at Tristan Thompson the right way, as opposed to the left, which is the hand with which he used to shoot in the NBA, he is one of the most fascinating players in the league. The Cleveland Cavaliers' center is virtually ambidextrous. He changed shooting hands in 2013.

"Most NBA players decided which hand to use a wee bit earlier."

"Many people think it's crazy," Thompson said of the switch. "Anything in this world that's not been done before, someone gets the flak, or someone finds something negative to say because it's new. I won't be the only one to do that. Someone else may try it down the line. I didn't want to go through life with regrets. It was time to try something new. Couldn't get any worse. Why not?"

Certainly, Thompson could point to stats that supported the switch. In 2015–16, he had posted his fourth straight season of 60 percent or better at the free throw line. That is still very far from such near-automatics as Rick Barry and, in the very old days, John Wooden, both of whom used the two-handed, underhand "granny" shot. Barry, who ranked seventh all-time in free throw percentage, was its last practitioner in the NBA.

As for Thompson and granny ball, he said, in effect, "not no how, not no way." "I am a basketball player. I will never do that. I will shoot them like my peers do," he said.

Po-Shen Loh, mathematics professor at Carnegie Mellon University, who had conducted a study of the granny versus the overhand shot, argued in an email to me that fealty to the overhand shot amounts to "ignorance is bliss" hardheadedness:

"The arms are more stable in the granny shot, compared to the comparative clutter of the overhand stroke, reducing the variables involved in shooting. When you shoot granny style, your body is perfectly symmetric. Your left-right error on the basket is essentially negligible. You only have to make sure that you get your forward-backward ball placement correct, so that it goes through the hoop instead of in front of it or into the backboard. When you shoot the normal overhand, you have both types of error, because the overhand shot is naturally asymmetric. So, you not only have to get the forward-backward correct but also the left-right."

Po hypothesized that a 75 percent shooter, which is close to the NBA average, if left-right variance were eliminated, but front rim–back rim variance stayed the same, would jump to 90 percent.

The professor's remarks regarding the balance the granny-shot fere throw provides in stability and lateral accuracy was part of the larger picture of the evening, or "balancing," if you like, the playing field, which included Curry's knee injury when he slipped on a sweat-streaked floor where a player had fallen in the Warriors' seven-game series against Oklahoma City. It would be followed by Green's suspension for unseemly behavior and too many flagrant fouls. It culminated with Andrew Bogut's knee injury after a collision with J. R. Smith.

Attrition had reduced the Warriors' advantage just as the effect of injuries had diminished the Cavs the previous year. The scales had balanced.

2017 EASTERN CONFERENCE SEMIFINALS
Game 4, at Atlanta, Cavaliers 100, Hawks 99

The big story in the Hawks series was not Thompson's free throw shooting, though. It was his deterrence at the rim. He wasn't an underrated shot-blocker; he was a barely rated one, averaging 0.5 blocks per game, or one in every two contests. Yet interior defense was vital, given that the Cavs were committed to running the Hawks' shooters off the arc: someone had to be minding the fort, er, rim.

In the Atlanta series, the Hawks shot 9-of-41 when Thompson contested the attempt. Paul Millsap, their top inside scorer, was 5-of-24, 20.8 percent.

Most important was the obstacle he posed in the last minute of the only close game of another sweep. With the Cavs leading, 98–97, Atlanta's Dennis Schroder was proving more than either Irving or his back-up, Dellavedova, could handle. When he had an open lane for a go-ahead layup in the last 1:03, Thompson was the orange traffic cone and the "LANE CLOSED AHEAD" sign, knocking Schroder's shot away at the height of its arc.

Schroder tested him again in the final seconds with the Cavs ahead, 100–99. Irving's dig at the ball from the side made Schroder pick up his dribble, giving Thompson time to confront him at the side of the lane. Schroder pump-faked, then went up to shoot . . . too late! James tied him up from behind, won the jump ball against Schroder, who is seven inches shorter, and time ran out in the scramble for the ball.

The great Bill Russell's impact as a defensive force, rivaled in his day only by Wilt Chamberlain, was not only in the shots he blocked but also in the shots he altered with his menacing presence.

When Thompson's presence made Schroder hesitate and pump-fake, it gave James enough time to tie him up for the jump ball.

2016 EASTERN CONFERENCE FINALS
Game 5, at Cleveland, Cavaliers 116, Raptors 78

The third player to make the road to the Finals a smooth one was Love, who was still trying to "fit in or fit out."

Although James tweeted his preference for the communitarian values of fitting in, Love on the court was proving better at fitting out, adapting fully to the "stretch big" concept against Toronto in the surprisingly tough Eastern Conference Finals, which the Cavs won. 4–2. The Cavs' front office deep thinkers always expressed confidence in Love. Lue said after the sweep of Atlanta, "I believe Kevin is a top 10 player in the league, the one we'd all hoped we'd see."

So much praise seemed more of an attempt to shore up Love's confidence; otherwise, they would not have said so often how much of it they had in him. In the Hawks series, he had been upside down, shooting 19-of-40 on three-pointers, nearly 50 percent, but only 4-of-31 inside, an embarrassing 12.9 percent.

In the conference finals, the Cavs had won the first two games, but Toronto evened the series, 2–2, with back-to-back home court victories, in large measure because Love was 5-for-23 in the third and fourth games. "Northern Blight!" screamed the *Cleveland Plain Dealer*'s worried headline.

What came next was such a surprise that it was only fitting to use the slang meaning of *sick*, occasionally used for the moves of Irving and James. It was an enigmatic encomium for *awesome*. Love sick, Kevin hit his first six shots, went 8-for-10 overall, 3-for-4 on the arc, scored a team-high 25 points and led a colossal Game 5 rout in Cleveland. It was bigger even than the 31-point victory, 115–84, in the series opener.

Love's 4-for-8 on the arc for 20 points backed James with 33 and Irving with 31 in a 113–87 in the closeout Game 6.

James had the best comments afterward, which I was happy to use in the column:

"I know the guys [Irving and Love] have been waiting for this opportunity, being part of the postseason after what happened last year with injuries. Obviously, I can't say I haven't waited for them to get back to this moment because it's something we all envisioned when I came back and Love was traded, and, obviously, Kyrie was already here."

The Cavs were headed for a Finals rematch with the Warriors. In their 2015 championship, as Marcus Thompson II wrote in his insightful book *Golden: The Miraculous Rise of Steph Curry*, the opposing point guard had either been out or hobbled in every round in 2015.

In 2016, however, Curry tweaked his right foot in the opener of a first-round series against Houston, and a cautious Kerr held him out of the next two. Curry returned in Game 4 after the Warriors lost Game 3 in Houston. In the final seconds of the first half, Curry switched off James Harden to pick up Trevor Ariza. The Rockets' big man Donatas Motiejunas, trailing the play, tripped, and with his long, large, 7-foot, 222-pound body, did a midcourt to foul line impression of a sledless competitor in the skeleton, a Winter Olympics sport, with his belly-down headfirst streak down the hardwood. Curry's left foot slipped in the long trail of sweat Motiejunas left behind. Curry's legs spread as if he were going to a cheerleader's split; and his right knee slammed down near the three-point line he owned in every NBA arena,

He had sprained his medial collateral ligament. He would be able to play in the Finals, but the knee was never 100 percent. His movement and misdirection had lost the zip that made them effective.

As Thompson wrote, "The scales had balanced."

CHAPTER 27

"I Guess He Got His Feelings Hurt"

2016 NBA FINALS

Game 1, at Oakland, Warriors 104, Cavaliers 89

"Splat!" went the Splash Brothers, missing shot and touch, missing inside and outside, sometimes missing the entire apparatus at which they aimed.

Steph Curry, the unanimous Most Valuable Player during the regular season, the first ever to receive such an honor, and his fellow aquatic ace, Klay Thompson, scored 20 points. Combined. Yet Golden State survived, not only winning, but winning easily.

The Cavs came from 13 points behind, because of the Warriors surprising "Splatter Brothers," to take a 68–67 third-quarter lead. It stood for all of 45 seconds. It was the high point of a very low valley. All sorts of goats were available to be scaped on both teams, but Warriors substitute Shaun Livingston was the exception. To him, attention must be paid.

He was no relation to me, although if I could've had his game instead of writing about him and his teammates and their rivals . . . well, I didn't of course. But I could summon enough generosity to pay tribute to an athlete who suffered and then overcame a horrific injury fully nine years earlier. In an instant, at the age of 21, he seemed sure to have lost a promising basketball career that made him a top-five lottery pick in 2004. On an ungainly landing, without contact from the opposition, Livingston tore everything that needed to be intact to play high-level basketball or even walk normally. He tore his anterior cruciate ligament, his posterior cruciate ligament, and his meniscus cartilage; dislocated his left knee cap; and broke his left leg. *ESPNews* put a warning for viewers on-screen before showing the gruesome clip.

Doctors feared they might have to amputate his broken left leg. Many wondered if he would ever walk again. "The knee was all deformed, bloodied up, and leaking with pus," Livingston told ESPN's *The Undefeated* in 2016. "I just couldn't move it. Stiff. It was like I had a peg leg. All of my quad was skinny. It was like a pole with a pineapple in the middle of it."

It took 16 months before Livingston was able to resume basketball activities. He bounced around the league and even spent time in what is now the NBA G League, the new name for its minor league. His return from almost certain career oblivion was a wonderful story if you weren't a Cavaliers fan. He finally made the Warriors' roster and hitched along for the ride to the top in 2015, when he played in all six Finals games and averaged 5.0 points.

In the first game of the 2016 Finals, Livingston scored 20 points on 8-of-10 shooting after coming off the bench to play for 26 minutes, 34 seconds, and shoot 8-for-10. It is said that victory has a thousand fathers and defeat is an orphan. But in the hearts of Shaun Livingston's family, friends, teammates, and coach, it was clear, after he had waited so long and gone through so much pain and doubt, who the father of Game 1's win was.

Kyrie Irving (26), James (23), and Kevin Love (17) provided 66 of the Cavs' 89 points. Thompson tossed in an unexpected 10. That left 13 divided among the other Cavaliers.

One of them was Defeat's Designated Orphan, J. R. Smith, who saw 36 minutes and 16 seconds of incomprehensibly inconsequential action. He took three three-pointers, made one, got a single rebound and a lone assist, and committed a solitary turnover.

As an aging baby boomer. I could not forgo invoking another J.R., the villainous J. R. Ewing, the double-crossin', back-stabbin' varmint and oil baron on the hit television show *Dallas,* which ran from 1978 to 1991. It was supposed to be called *Houston,* for the oil-refining center city, not for Dallas, dominated by banking interests. The Dallas Cowboys, however, were winning Super Bowls in that era, and so the TV soap opera was named after America's Team.

After the reprehensible Ewing was gunned down by an unknown assailant in a season-ending cliffhanger, addicted viewers spent the entire off-season wondering "Who shot J.R.?" I tweaked that tagline and led with "Who shot? J.R.? Yeah, but only three times."

I wrote: "Smith loved his nickname of 'Swish,' although it had not served former Indians alleged slugger Nick Swisher well, on the sweltering nights when he swung, missed, and air-conditioned the area around home plate with the gusts his whiffs created.

"Like the dog that did not bark in the Sherlock Holmes story, J. R. was the shooting guard who did not shoot. Your dog might 'play dead' upon command, but the Cavs cannot afford for Smith to do so. The plain fact is that he must be much more aggressive in getting shots. Three attempts by a shooting guard won't ever cut it. His only basket was in 'garbage time,' in the last five minutes, when he made a 3-pointer to cut the Cavs deficit to 14. Much more was expected and must be provided. If the stars are struggling, the Finals might come down to the role players. Smith is a prominent one. He is also something of a headache carrier. It will hurt worse if he doesn't snap out of it."

Game 2, at Oakland, Warriors 110, Cavaliers 77

Boston's Kelly Olynyk effectively turned the lights out on the Cavs' championship hopes in 2015 when he dislocated Kevin Love's shoulder in a scuffle for an offensive rebound just past the midpoint of the first quarter of the fourth game of the first-round playoff series.

This time, Love took a Harrison Barnes elbow to the melon on another missed three-pointer as the pair pursued another offensive rebound with five minutes left in the second quarter of the second game. Down went Love, like Joe Frazier against George Foreman. After a quick check-up by trainers, Love was able to return long enough to sink a three-pointer. But in the third quarter, he became dizzy and disoriented and went to the bench again, with the NBA's concussion protocol awaiting him.

After the staggeringly one-sided defeat in the second game, the loss of Love for the rest of that game and the entirety of the third, it seemed fitting that another of the Warriors' lesser-knowns—this time Draymond Green, not Livingston, with a game-high 28 points—discovered his Midas touch at the same time as Curry and Thompson remembered where they had left theirs.

In Cleveland, the fans had seen this movie before. Players, coaches, managers, and general managers didn't win in Cleveland. They won their championship rings before coming to Cleveland—Lenny Wilkens in Seattle, Terry Francona in Boston, Mike Holmgren in Green Bay. They won after leaving Cleveland—Earnest Byner in Washington; Odell Beckham Jr. in Los Angeles, Bill Belichick (with more rings than he could fit on one hand) in New England; James in Miami; and Steve Kerr in Chicago, San Antonio, and as a coach, at Golden State.

You could go through all the uses of the definite article—The Shot; The Fumble; The Other Shot; The Blown Save; The Curse of Bobby Bragan, or maybe it was Rocky Colavito. They made up a year-round basketball, football, baseball photo album of disappointment. They were snapshots of midnight.

Would James returning change anything?

Even the *Plain Dealer*'s usually upbeat sports columnist Terry Pluto refused to turn his frown upside down: "The Cavs weren't even close to winning the opener. Then they disintegrated and embarrassed themselves in this game. It was unwatchable."

There were plenty of reasons to get dispirited. Among the many things that lowered Cleveland's chances were the Cavs' 37 percent overall shooting for only 89 and 77 points, low-lighted by the 5-of-15, 10-point Game 2 diminuendo of Kyrie Irving, the self-proclaimed LeBron-level closer. It appeared that the *Plain Dealer*'s Dennis Manoloff was right when he compared the Cavs vs. Warriors matchup to the Harlem Globetrotters vs. their patsies, the Washington Generals.

With the series shifting to Cleveland for the next pair of games, "The Warriors are coming! The Warriors are coming!" had some merit. We were not, however, in Boston or in every Middlesex village and town; Paul Revere was not on his steed to spread the alarm.

As for J. R. Smith, some imposter wearing his skin must have been responsible for the two-game totals affixed to his name of 69:40 in playing time, 3-for 9 shooting, eight points.

I pondered the biblical plagues of Egypt. But the 17-year cicadas were not due to come screaming and shrieking from their underground burrows until the next year, which put the kibosh on the plague-of-locusts theme. (The one time I need you, you go to sleep on me, you little layabout pests.)

I wrote:

"James does not talk about his mission as fully as he did last year, only saying, 'I'll give my all and live with the results.' Still, seldom has a championship pledge been made more openly in the name of ordinary fans than that of James now. All championships are extrapolated by the teams winning them into gifts for the fans, payback for their loyalty and other altruistic expressions that the team's public relations staff devises. James's mere return, of course, is part of his legacy. It is the treasure room of the old pharaohs' pyramids. The pharaohs thought they could take the riches with them into eternity. It would certainly work for a championship ring here, at least in the memories of long-suffering fans."

Dropping the King Tut angle after that, I recalled the 1973 Celtics went 68–14, second-best ever at the time to the 1972 Lakers' 69–13. Those Celtics won their last eight, even though the record was out of reach after their 14th loss, just because they didn't like to lose. Yet lose they did—to the 57–25 Knicks—mainly because John Havlicek played the final three games with a separated right shoulder, which was his dominant side.

The 2007 Dallas Mavericks were 67–15 and lost a stunning first-round series to eventual Cavalier Baron Davis's Clippers, who were 42–40.

I was sorely tempted to end with a segue worthy of late-night comedian Seth Meyers, such as "A repeat championship for the Warriors seems, but for the admittedly scant comfort provided by history, to be as inevitable as death, taxes, and the Cleveland Browns doing something stupid."

The Cavs, after all, had lost the first two games by a humbling aggregate 48 points. Asked if the Cavs were done, Stephen A. Smith said on ESPN's *First Take*, "Yes they are. I don't see that that's even a question. The Golden State Warriors have only lost back-to-back games once. and that was in the Western Conference Finals to Oklahoma City. And the Cleveland Cavaliers, this Cleveland Cavaliers team, is supposed to convince us they're going to win four of the next five. Their chances of winning this series is zero, as far as I'm concerned. If they lose one of these games [three and four, at Cleveland], this series is over in 5 at the most. They're not coming back to the Oracle and winning Game 5."

Game 3, at Cleveland, Cavaliers 120, Warriors 90

As I wrote: "The Cavaliers did not miss Kevin Love, often criticized, sparingly praised, while he was gone. Many of Love's critics would say they told you so. Injury is cutting into his postseason again. Love missed the Cavaliers' victory in the third game of the NBA Finals, a 120–90 rout, because he was undergoing the NBA's concussion protocol. A concussion, as even the cement heads in the NFL are learning, is nothing to mess around with.

"'There's probably people calling Kevin Love soft, and those people are idiots. You don't mess around with the brain,' said Warriors center Andrew Bogut, who suffered a concussion during the regular season. 'You can be a hero now in the NBA Finals in 2016, and in 2021 you will be sucking food through a straw. And you won't give a [damn] about what you did in 2016.'"

Despite Irving's unhappiness with being in James's shadow, for all his bragging that his pairing with James gave the Cavs "the league's two best closers," Irving knew better than anyone the psychic pain Love was experiencing after Irving missed the last five games of the Finals against Golden State in 2015.

"'I know he definitely wanted to play for sure,' said Irving 'Looking in his eyes, knowing in his heart that being at the Finals is what we've both dreamt of."

"I saw it on Kevin's face," said James. "It was that 'I hate that I'm going through this moment, I feel like I'm letting you guys down' moment, without actually even saying it."

In the locker room before the opening tip, James hugged Love, and so did Irving.

"'We dedicated that game to him,' said Irving.

"'That's what a team is all about, picking your brother up in time of need,' said James."

Love's brother triumvirs showed that the Cavaliers were a brotherhood like the Three Musketeers, only without capes, saucy plumed hats, swords (except for the blazing ones on the Humongotron), and that D'Artagnan guy.

Game 4, at Cleveland, Warriors 108, Cavaliers 97

Love came off the bench to score 11 points in 25 minutes of play, on 10 shots. It was one point more than J. R. Smith scored in almost 43½ minutes.

Curry scored 38 points, playing as loose and free as he had on the same floor in Game 4 in 2015, when the Warriors began a string of three straight victories to claim the championship. Those Cavs were hard-nosed despite being badly outmanned. These Cavs seemed soft of nose, soft in spirit, soft as Charmin. Mr. Whipple should've been their coach.

The Cavs' third loss in the Finals was their closest yet, at 106–97, so it wasn't really all that close. Nor was the 3–1 deficit they faced very close. It was a deficit no team had ever overcome in 32 tries in the Finals. The fans' morale around Cleveland in the wake of Game 4 went down like a mine shaft elevator.

In the game, Irving out-Jamesed James, scoring 34 to LeBron's 25. Together, they were 25-of-49, for 59 points. Could such a one-two punch possibly win it all? For three games and slightly over 45 minutes of the fourth, that had seemed unlikely.

Then, as the expression goes, s—t happened.

In the last three minutes, James tried to fight over a screen to defend a three-ball that Curry decided not to try. Green, who set the screen, barged into James, who took issue. He knocked Green down with one outflung arm, much like J. R Smith, when he could still hit anything, had decked Jae Crowder in the 2015 series against Boston. Off balance after delivering the blow, James became entangled with the fallen Green and tumbled to the floor, too.

Claiming he was simply "trying to get back into the play," James stepped over Green, the former nearly brushing the latter's head with the former's below-the-belt parts. Green, as he knelt before clambering to his feet, punched James in the King's crown jewels and threw a second, weak jab that missed.

A spirited debate between the two followed at the three-point arc as play continued with Iguodala missing a jump shot. Both James and Green ran to the basket for the rebound, while arm-wrestling every step of the way, eventually drawing a double foul.

Cavs substitute Channing Frye separated the two, but not before James appeared, in a closeup replay, to call Green a bitch. In turn, ESPN's Dave McMenamin reported later that Green had used the same word on James.

This had become quite a spectacle—two grown men, envied and idolized by millions of fans, resorting to the "am not, are too" school of dialogue favored by squabbling little boys on playgrounds around the country. I would not have been surprised had one of them fallen back on "I'm rubber, and you're glue. It bounces off me and sticks to you," which I considered comic and argumentative gold when I first heard it in the third grade.

The peril of the double foul for the Warriors was much greater than for the Cavs, because of Green's previous indiscretions, including a kick to the crotch of Oklahoma City's Steven Adams earlier in the 2016 playoffs. Adams astutely, if ungrammatically, noted that Green had at that moment "peaked with annoyingness." Going into the Finals, Green was two technical fouls or one Flagrant 1 foul on the NBA's aggregate annoyances list from being suspended for the next game.

"Draymond just said something that I don't agree with," James said. "I'm all cool with the competition. But some of the words that came out of his mouth were a little bit overboard, and being a guy with pride, a guy with three kids and a family, things of that nature, some things just go overboard, and that's where he took it."

Sir Charles Barkley, the very image of fox-chasing gentility in his Right Guard antiperspirant commercials and a well-known critic of the Warriors as a "jump-shooting team," weighed in with what amounted to a defense of crotch shots: "When a guy steps over you, you have a moral obligation to punch him in the balls. That's really disrespectful to step over a guy. You're supposed to pop him in his junk, if he steps over you. That's a perfectly fine response."

The NBA disagreed. The next day, Green was suspended for Game 5 after he was assessed a Flagrant 1, exceeding the limit.

Before the Cavs made the trip back to Oakland for what looked like the endgame, a defiant Lue said, "If you don't think we can win, don't get on the plane."

In a mandatory interview session the day before the next game, Klay Thompson fixated on James's objection to Green's tongue and not his fist: "Guys talk trash in this league all the time. I'm just kind of shocked some guys take it so personal. It's a man's league, and I've heard a lot of bad things on that court, but at the end of the day it stays on the court. I don't know how the man feels. But obviously people have feelings, and people's feelings get hurt even if they're called a bad word. I guess his feelings just got hurt. We've all been called plenty of bad words on the basketball court before. Some guys just react to it differently."

When James was at the interview-room podium several minutes later, a troublemaker whom I know very well (blush) relayed Thompson's "hurt feelings" comment. A question you know will get under an interviewee's skin is one of the real joys of being an interviewer, after which you sit back, waiting for his spittle-flying, furious response.

"What did you say Klay said?" James said, his eyes widening in surprise.

"He said, 'I guess he just got his feelings hurt,'" said the agitator.

"Oh, my goodness," James said, laughing.

"I believe the transcript will support that," said the quote-hungry scribbler.

"I'm not going to comment on what Klay said, because I know where it can go from this [interview]," said James, shaking his head. "It's so hard to take the high road. I've been doing it for 13 years and I'm going to do it again."

Clichés about playing hard followed, not that they mattered. Thompson had poked the bear, and the grizzly knew about it.

Out of the darkest night, years after the Decision's blight, came the brightest light.

CHAPTER 28

Seventh Heaven Straight Ahead

Game 5, at Oakland, Cavaliers 112, Warriors 97

Two for the show.

And what a show it was, put on in Oracle Arena by James and by Irving!

For James's part, he received more help from Irving than even Wade or Bosh had provided in Miami. As for Irving, the promise he had made before the 2016 Finals of playing "in a rage" had simmered along for four games at a degree warmer than "miffed," "irritated," or "annoyed" but well below an inferno of fury.

Now, sensing time running out and the chance for revenge slipping away, he kindled a fire and fed it with his resentment of the 377 days between his broken kneecap in 2015's Finals opener and 2016's fifth game, on June 16, the anniversary of the Cavs' demise a year earlier.

James and Irving both produced big-as-a-boxcar 41-point efforts, becoming the first teammates ever to score 40 or more in a Finals game, as the Cavs shocked Golden State.

The first challenge had been quieting the raucous, bellowing Warriors fans by recovering from a slow start—often fatal in a closeout game.

The Cavs dampened their expectation of celebration by not crumbling in the face of Curry's first fast start of the Finals with 10 points in the first quarter. Iguodala continued his usual Swiss Army knife work in points (8), rebounds (4), assists (3), and steals (2).

James had 12 points, but instead of the usual suspect, Irving, helping him keep deficits manageable, it was none other than J. R. Smith. Smith scored 10 points and kept the Cavs' first quarter deficits manageable. He held the Warriors' lead to only 32–29. This efflorescence stopped then and there with the baffling Smith, who finished the game with the same 10 points. By halftime, it was tied, 61–61, the most points in the first half of a Finals game since 1987.

The blowouts and lack of suspense in the first four games were forgotten in the first-half point sprees of the opinionated Klay Thompson, with 26, and James, with 25. Warriors fans placed blame for the nip-and-tuck half, justifiably, on Draymond Green, banned from even darkening the Oracle Arena's door until the game for which he was suspended ended. He instead glumly watched the game on television at the Oakland Athletics' next-door stadium.

On one play, Anderson Varejao, the former Cavalier, now a Warrior, missed a defensive switch and Irving walked to the free throw line for an easy two-pointer. That never would have happened with Green.

By his self-caused absence, Green was the most obvious scapegoat for the Cavs' resurgence. That was not accurate, however. The same factor, injury to a key player, as had afflicted the Cavs the previous year, was at work here; only it had been doubled for the Cavs, with Love out for most of the playoffs and Irving for most of the Finals.

The Warriors' amazing stretch of going unscathed by injuries except for Curry's slip on a wet floor changed in an instant. In Game 5, the score was tied just over a minute into the second half. Smith drove for a layup. Seven-foot, 245-pound Warrior center Andrew Bogut, a one-man blockade at the rim, knocked the shot away. Smith's momentum sent him crashing into Bogut's left knee. It buckled. Bogut crumpled to the floor in great pain, and the entire dynamic of the series shifted. Bogut was the Roy Hibbert of the Warriors. Hibbert had been a wall James and the Heat had to surmount on their way to the 2013 NBA championship.

With Bogut providing interior defense, the Cavs averaged 95.8 points in Games 1–4. Without Bogut for the remainder of the series, the Cavs averaged 106.7 points. James went from a 24.8-point average to 36.6. Irving went from 25 to 30.3.

No one on the Cavs team or in Cleveland felt the least bit sorry. Unlike the Olynyk–Love incident in 2015, there was nothing dirty about the play. Plus, the Cavs lost both Irving and Love, two-thirds of their triumvirate the year before. The Warriors took advantage of it. Now, it was the Cavs' turn.

But it was not easy. The Warriors' shooters and their golden touch got Golden State within six points, 102–96, in the last 7 minutes. In the NBA, this is a time-span equivalent to forever and a day.

Then, Irving, in the game of his life to that point, coruscating with fire as bright as the heart of a diamond, made more desperately needed jumpers than a lost driver with a dying battery in an in an uncongenial part of town and no cables with which to charge it. He started with an and-one on a drive and banked turnaround over Thompson, a far better defender than Curry. Irving's near-slip, recovery, and another turnaround over Thompson followed, and finally a three-pointer went down on which referees ignored an obvious foul by Iguodala. When it was over, Irving had shot 5-of-9 for 12 points in the quarter.

The series had come alive, as had the Cavs. The Warriors were going back to Cleveland, where they had won it all the year before. When they played for the rings and the rewards the jewelry brought, the Cavs had had only one money player left in James.

This time, there were two.

Game 6, at Cleveland, Cavaliers 115, Warriors 101

The Cavaliers and their fans wore black uniforms, in keeping with the black hole of noise and hopelessness down which the Warriors went, plunged there by the excellence of their inspired opponents.

James scored 41 points, including 18 in a row in the second half. It was the second straight playoff game in which he scored 41. It was also his most extended one-man display of excellence since he scored the Cavs' last 25 points in his 48-point, double-overtime masterpiece in the 2007 Eastern Conference Finals.

He scored or assisted on 35 of his team's 36 points at one time, with four assists for 10 points and 25 more on his own. The spree started with the Cavs at 72 points and ended them at 108. The lone other point came on Irving's technical free throw when Curry melted down and hurled his dog-bone chewed mouthpiece after fouling out.

Irving added 23, with Richard Jefferson scoring 15, Smith 14, and Iman Shumpert 13.

Also invited to the party was Dahntay Jones, usually the last man off Lue's bench. Jones took slumping Matthew Dellavedova's minutes after the Cavs' huge 22-point first-quarter lead dwindled to nine points. This amounted to three wrist flicks and three bottom-of-the-basket three-pointers for Golden State. Jones delivered five quick points. With the season at stake, he might have been expected to be seen on the floor more often than a unicorn, but not much else.

The definitive moment for many Cavs fans came in the last 4:32 when Curry sliced through the defense for a layup and James Stinger-missiled it away, then staring Curry down and spurning his effort with a smirk.

The past belonged to the Warriors and the Bay Area, which—since the Browns won the NFL championship in 1964—can boast five teams that have won a total of 15 championships in the three sports it shares with Cleveland. Many believed the future belonged to Oklahoma City. What was left is the present, the here and now.

"It's trio of the greatest words in the world, Game 7. I'll play it any-where," said James.

"I spent a lot of time watching Game 7s," Irving said. "Now that I get to experience it, I want to live in it."

It was time for the Cavaliers—all of them, from James and Irving to Dahntay Jones—to have their date with history.

CHAPTER 29

Swat, Shot, Stop

They are three short, sibilant words, each spoken with a snake's hiss at its beginning, together marking the joyous end of Cleveland's half-century-and-more championship drought and the sorrowful end of Golden State's joy ride.

The Swat and the desperate circumstances in which it was made became the signature play of James's career, although it was not as if he were a great shot-blocker, with a 0.8 per game average for his career. It will be as much a part of LeBron James's lore and legend as his relentless accretion of statistics and his seemingly inevitable domination of the all-time record books. In a career ablaze with highlights, it will be like the "One Shining Moment" song that is played at the end of the NCAA Tournament—except for LeBron James, because of the many sparkling plays and flashes of brilliance in his epic career, it will be "One Bright, Exploding Crab Nebula." It will be the ultimate expression of who he was and what he could do to make "unbelievable" untenable as a descriptor for him. In the sheer brevity of the split seconds in which it had to be accomplished; in the prodigious expenditure of speed, power, and lift it required; and in the will and character it showed it will be his Forever Moment.

The Shot—despite all the controversies Irving caused, teams he wrecked, selfishness he exhibited, fans he scorned, and jealousies he harbored—will live on as a breathtaking example of What Might Have Been in the career his delusions damaged. As for What Will Be, by the competitive circumstances of it, the brilliance of the player he outshone on it, and the sheer difficulty in making it, it will stand for years as what it was almost instantaneously and nearly universally called the Greatest Shot in NBA Finals History.

The Stop foiled Golden State's scheme for Curry to exploit Love in an isolation set. At 6'10" and not remotely comparable to Anderson Varejao or Tristan Thompson as a light-footed Cavs' big man, Love somehow managed to stay in front of Curry in the last minute; moving from side to side; dropping back on feints; rushing forward on pump fakes; zealously guarding the three-point arc from which a shot could tie the game; extending without over-pursuing to deter a shot from 35 feet out, which constituted the hinterlands before Curry came along; doing it all with no help, all of it up to him and the nimbleness he had to summon in the ultimate crisis of his career; recovering after every crossover, jab step, head fake, pump fake, behind the back dribble, and twitchy shooting finger possibility; always recovering as the shot clock ticked down; finally, in defiance of everything that was expected, forcing Curry to miss.

Typically for the third member of the Big Three, Love got no stats in the box score for what he did on the play.

Before the game began, Stephen A. Smith, undeterred by the opinion airball he had lofted after two games, said, "I suspect come Sunday night at Oracle Arena in Oakland, California, Steph Curry will make his presence felt emphatically."

Max Kellerman, his pontificate mate at the mic, compared James to Muhammad Ali, not for the principled and sometimes unpopular political stances both took but for the upsets by knockout Ali, the self-labeled "greatest," scored against Sonny Liston and George Foreman.

Said Kellerman, "You want to be considered the greatest of all time, LeBron, then do the impossible, like Ali. Beat a 73-win Golden State team on their court in Game 7."

It was an interesting inversion: James, the best player on a basketball court all his life, could only do it by imitating another King, David, against not one just giant but the NBA's all-time record-breaking team of Goliaths.

In the opening moments, it seemed as if a figurative little dark cloud had drifted over the Joy Boys by the Bay (per Steve Kerr's command that there be happy music in practices) and not the Cavs for once. J. R. Smith semaphored, telegraphed, and Instagrammed a pass from the corner to

James at the rim. Curry read it, was in the right spot at the right time, reached up to pluck the low-hanging fruit, and the ball went cleanly through the hoop of his arms.

No, you don't want to do that!

James with a second chance is like a cop at a just expired parking meter as you frisk yourself for change. You had the best of intentions, but he will make you pay anyway. The first of Curry's several Game 7 gaffes didn't get a lot of traction in the game coverage. But it was a four-point swing—the two the Cavs made after his interception that wasn't, plus the possible two the Warriors didn't get on the possession that wasn't. The game would be decided by exactly four points.

At halftime, the Cavs trailed, 49–42. They had made a pathetic 1-of-14 three-pointers. Iman Shumpert sank it from the right corner on a shot on which Shaun Livingston knocked him on his back. Shumpert celebrated briefly with fist-pumping, legs-shaking ecstasy while supine, then got up and calmly converted the free throw for a rare four-point play. Curry and the Warriors had missed what seemed a certain opportunity for such a swing. The Cavs had cashed their chance.

Although Golden State had made 10 of 21 first-half triples for a stunning 27-point advantage on the added value shot, it was not as though the surf was up for the Splash Brothers. They were a combined 4-of-12, the minimum acceptable 33.3 percent efficiency.

Draymond Green, his suspension served, had morphed into a Cannonball Brother, given the huge splash he made in the game. In the first half, he was 5-for-5 on the three. Again, Green, as I had written of Andre Iguodala the year before, was open for a reason: he could not shoot as well as Curry or Thompson. It was simply a statistical deviation from the mean, albeit one occurring at the worst possible time for the Cavs.

At halftime, James had 12 points, requiring, however, 11 shots to get them, to go with seven rebounds, five assists, and two blocked shots. Nevertheless, during the break, Lue went where few, actually probably no one but Pat Riley, had dared to go before. "'Bron, I need more from you," the coach said, speaking eye-to-eye, man-to-man, giving it to him straight, no chaser.

When James relayed the comment to James Jones, the veteran three-point specialist, an exemplary teammate in every way, whom James had respected in their time together in Miami, Jones wasn't lavish with the commiseration James sought. "Well, is he right?" Jones asked—which was another way of saying "Then prove him wrong."

James would do just that.

The second half began with Smith sinking back-to-back three-pointers in a flurry of eight quick points, the institutional memory of which helped keep him on the Cleveland roster for the next two seasons.

I recalled the Sixers' Fred Carter, mired in a shooting slump, relating before each game his jump shot's imaginary vacation in the sunny isles of the Caribbean and its stops as it slowly wended its way back to cold and snowy Philadelphia. At home at last, it got hot. I wondered what astral planes could the flighty and eccentric Smith have been touring? In his way, Smith, though affable and cooperative in interviews, could be as weird as the often sullen World B. Flat.

In the third quarter, World B. scored 12 points to James's four and made one of the damnedest shots I ever saw. It was worthy of mention with the best of Dr. J and Jordan, both of whom stood 6'6", and of the late Kobe Bryant, also 6'6", and LeBron, who had grown another inch to 6'9". The major difference between their shots and Irving's was that the 6'3" Irving had to finish below the rim, which he did with a flair that made him the best I ever saw at inveigling big men and defying long odds. And, yes, I saw the 6'3" Earl Monroe, who "had more spins than a Maytag," as the *Boston Globe*'s Bob Ryan wrote, and the 6-foot Allen Iverson, who could treat even the tallest trees around the rim the way a sawmill did. Jesus Shuttlesworth, the fictionalized high school basketball phenom in Spike Lee's *He Got Game*, learns from his estranged father that he was named not after "Jesus from the Bible" but after Monroe, known as Black Jesus on the playgrounds of North Philadelphia. Monroe received that title because his game was "the truth." The movie, which came out four years before James's *Sports Illustrated* cover, was eerily prescient about the clamor that would surround James and the celebrity he would create as a real-life phenom. Irving's shots around the rim were just as pure, celestial and true.

In the last 5 minutes of the quarter, Irving burst out of the pack after a Curry turnover. Challenged by Green, the only Warrior back on defense, Irving fended him off with a quick, short shove of his right arm. It was like Jordan and Bryon Russell in Jordan's Goodbye Game in Salt Lake City, only at full speed, not while dancing at the top of the foul circle, and just hard enough to get some clearance, not rough enough to push the defender down.

Irving poured all the Mikan Drill's blood, sweat, tears, and dizziness; all its tutelage in angles and arcs; the sum of the skills that he had suffered to gain; into his implacable belief that he could make any shot in the paint, no matter how high its degree of difficulty or how fierce his defender's resistance. Jumping off his right foot and shooting with his left hand, he flicked his wrist, and the ball was in flight, guided by his touch-perfect aim and his hours of plotting angles. It climbed high on its 5-foot-long journey to the rim, bounced off the backboard near its top, and fell into the net. He did it all while absorbing a slap to his right eye from Green's flailing hand.

Irving's momentum carried him to the baseline, where he craned his head back, as he had done countless times on the New Jersey playgrounds, just in time to see the shot go in. He walked to the corner, pointing his index fingers at the floor like gun barrels, fired a metaphorical shot with each, then rubbed his sore eye, walked to the foul line, sighted the free throw awarded for Green's foul, and swished it.

The game worried along, neither team able to take command. The Warriors held a 76–75 lead going into the final 12 minutes. What came next was the result of Kerr scrapping Nick U'Ren's small lineup suggestion because of the coach's fixation on finding a replacement for the insured Bogut. He played 6′8″ Harrison Barnes for 29:24 in the game and got 10 points, two rebounds, and an assist in return. At that, Barnes beat Nigerian American Festus Ezeli, who had started at center after Kerr moved Green back to power forward, where he belonged. The idea was to get size enough in the lineup to match up better with Tristan Thompson.

In 10:45 of play overall, Ezeli missed four shots, committed two fouls, and did little else but display his aerobic conditioning by running up and down the court to no avail whatsoever. Only 56 seconds after Ezeli's appearance, James baited the 6′11″ center into a big man's terra incognita, the three-point line. All-time All-Star against a player unsure of what the hell he was doing so far out of his comfort zone was a total mismatch. James up-faked, causing Ezeli to jump for a block and draw a foul on

James's missed three-pointer. James made all three free throws. An 87–83 deficit was now 87–86. Only 5:24 remained in the game.

Part of basketball slang is terms for victimized opponents. Using a pump fake to get an overeager and overmatched defender off his feet meant the player with the ball "got him a bird," as Cavs television analyst Austin Carr never seemed to tire of saying. When I covered the Sixers, coach Gene Shue admitted he conveyed his advantage in terms of marine life: "Give me the ball. I've got a fish!"

Fish or fowl, in a barrel or on the wing, Ezeli was soon stranded again on an island far, far from his home in the paint. Hesitantly backing off, lest he foul the devious James again, Ezeli gave James the room to bury his first three-pointer in five tries.

Jason Concepcion of the website *The Ringer* wrote that the three seemed to be the "result of sheer force of will" on James's part. (However, we can't rule out the amplifying presence of Festus Ezeli, a man with a fun name who graduated from high school at 14 and has much to offer the world as a person but with his every move, breath, and deed, killed his team like a human-shaped cyanide pill.) When, mercifully, Barnes replaced him, Concepcion called it "trading cyanide for arsenic."

In the interest of full disclosure, Ezeli attended Vanderbilt, albeit years after I did. He followed, among others, Will Perdue, a Commodores center with the Chicago Bulls, whom Michael Jordan called "Will Vanderbilt," because "You're not good enough to play for a Big Ten school." Neither the university nor its basketball program were the reasons Ezeli became James's foil in the midst of the tense drama, however. Kerr's counterproductive substitutions were.

Eight seconds after James hit his three free throws, in the middle of Festus's Festival of Flubs, Curry whipped up a spicy serving of stupid by throwing an errant, needless, behind-the-back pass that missed Klay Thompson and went out of bounds. Curry liked to show off with dance moves after sinking his intercontinental threes. He was such a *showboat* on the wild pass that I expected to hear Paul Robeson singing "Ol' Man River" from the 1936 movie *Show Boat.* In little longer than it takes to tap an iPhone screen and find an appropriate meme, Cavs fans flooded the Internet with pictures of Curry casually flipping the NBA's championship bauble, the Larry O'Brien Trophy, behind his back as an aghast Thompson reached for the unreachable. The trophy was named for the longtime Massachusetts political adviser to John F. Kennedy and former head of the Democratic National Committee, whose political connections as the NBA commissioner in the 1970s helped pave the way for the NBA-ABA merger.

"Yeah, I still think about that turnover," Curry said before the next season began. "But in thinking about that game, it's funny because I know the concept of making the right play, making a simple play, understanding that there are deciding moments in games and the difference between winning a championship or not could be one of those plays. I came out in preseason this year and threw a behind-the-back pass because I know I can do it."

Next in the spotlight was the touchy, feely empath Klay Thompson, a man sensitive to the injurious effect of an injudicious comment. *The Ringer*'s Concepcion, on such a creative roll that he deserves quoting again, wrote, "Ezeli may have shrunken down to the size of a quark under the black-hole gravity of the moment . . . but Klay Thompson sheds J. R. Smith like a loose cardigan and lays it up. Bucket. 89–89."

There were 4 minutes, 39 seconds left, during which the NBA championship was decided by cobblestones, bricks, and a whole lot of other schist, all of which the official scorer charitably ruled to be field goal attempts. It was as if a soccer game broke out and no one could score, or Nolan Ryan and Sandy Koufax were matching each other in no-hitters, inning by inning. The game was tied at 89–89 for so long that minutes seemed like hours, hours like ages. It was primitive stuff, as if the Original One Great Scorer had painted two sets of 89 tally marks each on the Altamira cave wall in Spain.

The bell rang for the 15th round of *Rocky*. Both teams were punched out, stressed out, worn out. Irving missed a shot that fell into the clash and crash of bodies in the lane. Iguodala emerged with the ball, streaking downcourt with Curry on his wing and Smith the only Cav back on defense. Iguodala passed to Curry, who flicked it back to Iguodala, who was closing fast on the outmanned Smith.

Coaches always stress that in fastbreak defense the first priority is to "stop the ball." Do not allow a straight line drive for a layup. Try to buy split seconds for a teammate to catch up, although that seemed impossible here. Try to force an extra pass, with its built in perils of being mistimed, mishandled, or misaimed like the Larry O'Brien trophy. Or try to take a charge. But how much time is there to check foot placement in relation to the telltale semicircle on the floor near the rim, which overrides a charge on even the smallest incursion by a defender? How much time remained to do anything but mark the bucket down in the scorer's book?

LeBron Time remained.

The science of the swat, as explained in ESPN's Sports Science feature, was almost unimaginable. The term for it is *chasedown block,* and James made one the likes of which Javert, pursuing Jean Valjean all through France in *Les Miserables,* would have envied. James was 88 feet from the rim in a game in which he would play all but 1:11 of its 48 minutes. Although exhausted, he summoned a tsunami of adrenaline from sheer desperation. It was the kind of crazy surge that earns soldiers medals in wars and enables fireman to run into burning buildings and rescue children. James covered the first 60 feet in 2.67 seconds, a time out of a comic book starring the Flash, not a real-world reading, and certainly not under the circumstances.

He was still 21 feet from the basket. Iguodala was 7 feet closer. James's acceleration rose to 20.1 miles per hour, a figure that seemed to have nothing to do with the normal space-time continuum. The almost imperceptible fraction, 0.15 of a second, according to ESPN, that Smith forced Iguodala to devote to stepping around him, enabled James to get there before the window of opportunity closed, only .02 of a second from slamming down. That twitch is shorter than the time it takes for a cork to pop on a bottle of champagne.

When he leaped, James's right hand was 11 feet, 5 inches above the ground, a height reached by tapping a reservoir of will only he had after covering a nearly inconceivable horizontal distance so quickly because of his resolve. His right hand spiked the ball off the backboard inches before it struck the glass after Iguodala's release. James's left hand was nearly as high, guarding against the possibility that Iguodala would try a favorite trick of his, a reverse layup. It struck the left side of the rim hard at the same instant.

NBA Rule 11: Basket Interference, Section 1 h (a) defines such a violation in part as "vibrating the rim, net or backboard so as to cause the ball to make an unnatural bounce," adding, "If it occurs at the opponent's basket, the offended team is awarded two points if the attempt is from the two point zone, three points if it is from the three point zone,"

But although all eyes—referees', Warriors players', and coaches,' ditto those of the Cavs and of the network broadcasters and the basketball writers—were on the convergence of James, his right hand, Iguodala, his shot, and the backboard, no one saw James slap the rim from the left, or *sinistral* side. (The word is derived from the same Latin root as *sinister*.)

James slammed the ball squarely off the glass, and it ricocheted to Smith without ever touching the rim.

Private prayers and public pleas were in the air at the congregation of the high church of basketball, located, in this case, before an outdoor screen of Humongotronian dimensions next to a parking garage near the Cavs' arena in Cleveland. In their happy, sad, cheering, cursing, always fervent devotionals, they asked, just this once for divine intercession. Hundreds of fans stood there for hours in sardine-tin confinement, and James answered each and every one of their prayers with the Block of Ages.

One possession later, James bulled his way across the lane, five feet from the basket, and did not have enough lift to get his jump hook over the rim.

Lue called time as the clock ticked toward the last minute. Doubt and fatigue increased the sense of unreality as two teams with some of the most feared scorers in the world stumbled brokenly to the finish line. The money was down, and the chips were at their height as Lue diagrammed the biggest play of the season. James caught Lue's eye and pointed to Irving. Lue agreed.

Few things said more about James than that moment. Although he had been criticized for his passes to Chad Mraz and Donyell Marshall, he was, like Larry Bird and Magic Johnson, all about winning and not about accumulating the individual awards or the glory that came with them. Irving seemed fresher and throughout the series had outplayed the hampered Curry, at whom the play would be targeted.

James was an All-NBA First Team member every year except his rookie season. The best Irving had done was the third string. But Irving certainly was familiar with the task at hand. He averaged 22 shots per game in the Finals and took only 10 fewer shots overall than James, but he made 12 fewer field goals.

Critics thought that was a wee bit too much shooting for a point guard, a position at which the traditional priority was passing. I wrote: "An old point guard named Jack McMahon, later the scouting genius behind the 76ers' championship team of 1982–83, called ball distribution 'passing the sugar.' On the sugar islands of the West Indies, beneath the burning sun in the cane fields, Irving would have been the worker slashing the stalks down with a machete, then incinerating the leafy residue under a pall of smoke from which black flakes fell like devils' snow, and finally going to work on the night shift at the refinery after that. He is the whole shebang. But from opponents' perspective, he is pure slasher and burner."

When play resumed, James inbounded to Irving, with Klay Thompson, taller and stronger than Curry, guarding him. James, Love, and Richard Jefferson, the last inserted because of his greater offensive potential than Tristan Thompson, ran to the corners to create more maneuvering space for Irving. The Cavs shuffled Klay Thompson into a screen with Smith, who cleared out to the left side of the court, taking Thompson with him and leaving Curry alone with Irving.

This was not the motion, pass and cut, big tent, come-one–come-all Warriors' offense. Ball movement is one of basketball's most basic principles. After three or four passes, as former Cavaliers center and part-time television analyst Brad Daugherty noted, teams don't chase the ball anymore. The key is to make an extra pass. Gene Hackman as the no-nonsense basketball coach in *Hoosiers* demanded at least four passes before anyone took a shot. His strategy clearly was sound. That way, everyone touched the ball, and no one harbored jealousies.

But the Cavs' ploy on the biggest play of the season was to run an isolation set, one on one, in a Cav vs. Dub elemental struggle. It was exactly the matchup they wanted. "Hell, we have the two best closers in the league. I'd be stupid not to put them in isolation sets," said Lue.

There had been 19 lead changes and 11 ties when the Cavs and Warriors trooped back on the court. The circumstances of the 20th lead change would compress the game into inches of thrust and parry in a duel fought at its conclusion in a space no bigger than a manicurist's emery board. The thrill of victory or the agony of defeat was dependent on Irving's hard-won genius with the ball. He shuttered the gleam from Golden State's gold-flinger Curry, dribbling 14 times, executing two between-the-legs crossovers, left to right, and back again. Next, he used his left hand so his quick sidestep had Curry briefly on his heels. Then he jumped and shot the fadeaway that broke the Warriors' dreams.

The scientists said Irving had created 5½ feet of separation, rather than the 4 feet of a straight step back. He needed every increment of every inch. Despite the bothersome knee, Curry was cuticle close. Perhaps he had pared his fingernails recently and that made all the difference in his challenge, for it was textbook perfect except for its failure by the narrowest of margins. It all took place in increments of time measured by blinking eyes. The crossover took 0.35 of a second. The ball release took 0.47. The ball did not create disorder among the strands of the net, in the manner of the Splash Brothers. It touched the rim and didn't go in all silky and smooth, but nothing else had been that way on the battleground of the fourth quarter.

Irving gave Curry a slight, deliberate bump with his left hip after hitting the shot. It meant, "Get off my stage, Steph."

Not quite yet, though.

Kerr eschewed using a timeout. Iguodala, who was Love's defensive assignment, screened James, who was guarding Green, forcing a switch. Then, Green screened Irving, who was guarding Curry, leaving Love, who had never quite been the player the Cavs thought they were getting in the Wiggins trade, in "Why me, Lord?" isolation outside the arc on Curry.

Two switches and a swish for three points was the Warriors' plan.

Instead, Love played the best 14 seconds of defense of his life after being isolated on Curry with 44 seconds to play. Curry went through all his tricks—jab steps and stutter steps; pump fakes and head fakes; a hurried pass, causing a near turnover to Green, who whipped it back as the deadly tango went on, probably for an eternity to Love; step backs and side steps—none of them enabling Curry to get past him. At last, Curry realized he had consumed too much time to try the two-pointer that had been there for the taking all along and, having passed up three better shots, finally lofted a three, one he certainly could have made and usually did. But it bounced off the left side of the rim. Only James was there for the rebound. Love was no longer the last option among the triumvirate in an emergency. He was the last man standing and pursuing and shadowing and tracking and contesting and finally preserving the precious lead.

With 30 seconds left in the game, James hot-potatoed the ball to Irving, one of the best free throw shooters in the league. By this stage, however, Irving no more believed in sensible and restrained play than he believed in NASA. Off he tore, one on almost everybody from Golden State, hellbound for the graveyard of Cleveland sports dreams.

This was the repository where fans had sadly buried their memories of "Red Right 88" and Browns quarterback Brian Sipe's interception on the play by Oakland; Jose Mesa's blown save in Game 7 of the World Series (pitching with "vacant eyes," according to Omar Vizquel), near the place where the ghosts of "The Catch," "The Drive," "The Fumble," and the other two Jordan shots still roamed.

Into the mausoleum of misery Clevelanders had also buried the NFL draft card with Johnny Manziel's name on it; the helmet Dwayne Rudd threw in celebration that cost the Browns a game against the Chiefs; and the package of the marijuana that Indians' reliever Chris Perez mailed to his home in the name of his dog, Brody.

What a festival of fools it had been!

In a continuation of the foolhardiness theme, Iguadala confronted Irving on the right side of the lane, blocking his layup. Irving executed a short, alarmed retrieve on the lane's left side and teetered precariously, a toenail from the baseline, before lobbing a long pass to Love at midcourt. He thus escaped the malignant goblins' influence in Cleveland.

Next, the Warriors' Barnes, as fuzzy on clock management as Irving, drew a deliberate non-shooting foul with 19 seconds to play.

No, you don't want to do that either!

By rule, the Cavs as a result had 14 seconds before the shot clock's expiration, three more than would've remained without the panicky foul.

James inbounded to the backcourt to Irving, who, like the little girls in the days of the Salem witches, had been infected by the derangement that was going around. Irving made another solo sortie toward the rim, James cutting diagonally behind him. The correct play was for Irving to kill more time with his dribble and maintain possession until fouled because of his free throw prowess.

But nooooo!

Instead, he dished to James, whose right arm was cocked back for another sepulchral slam, similar to the Dunk of Death years earlier over

Garnett. Green did the only thing he could do, committing a hard, but legal foul that spilled James to the floor with a splat.

"Nothing is given," James had said upon his return.

So, of course, James fell on his right wrist, thus affecting his shooting hand. He writhed on the floor in real pain, twice pounding his left fist on the floor, no histrionics now, the stakes were too high. Not only the trainers but the coaches and almost the whole Cavs team ran to the landing zone.

Kyrie Irving, however, who should have kept the ball, simply walked away, his back to the play, then turned and stood, bent over, his hands on his knees, at halfcourt.

Back at Cavs' Crisis Central, the situation was this: if James could not shoot his free throws, Kerr would pick the player to shoot them for him.

Hello, Tristan Thompson. Pick a hand, either hand.

James finally got up and went to the line and, shooting painfully with his right hand, clanged the first one off the back of the rim.

"Everything is earned," James had said.

The second went in hot, straight from the forge of his competitive fire, and rattled the rim on its descent. The Cavs led, 93–89.

After the Warriors called time to advance the ball, James stalked to the bench, raising the index finger on his shooting hand as he said, "One stop. One more f—king stop." One stop for the ring, one stop for the fulfillment of the promise he had made to win it all, one stop for the victory parade, one stop for complete redemption.

Eleven seconds were left, and the lead was two possessions, insuperable unless someone pulled a Shump and made a four-point play. After preliminary skirmishing, Tristan Thompson committed the foul the Cavs had to give without exceeding their limit and giving Golden State free throws. Seven seconds were left.

Before the Warriors inbounded, Coach Obvious, broadcasting for ABC at courtside, became Coach Still Pissed. Mark Jackson fretted about Shumpert, who would guard Curry on the inbounds play. "I lost a playoff game on a phantom foul and four-point play to [coanalyst] Jeff Van Gundy," Jackson said.

Shumpert, however, stayed a clear hand's breadth away from Curry, who missed his 10th three-pointer in 14 tries. Marreese Speights, an above-average three-point shooter, rebounded and tried to retreat to the three-point line in the corner to loft one. It was too late for that, though. His only chance was an immediate layup, after which the Dubs had to either force a 5-second violation under the Cavs' basket, for Cleveland was out of timeouts and could not advance the ball to the forecourt, or execute a steal and score on the inbounds pass. Time ran out before Speights could shoot.

It was so inconceivable that some players didn't immediately realize the impossible dream had come true and the unreachable star had been reached. Tristan Thompson had one of the most delayed reactions of all tardy responses. "We were getting ready for Game 8," he said. "And then it was like, 'Holy s—t, we won!'"

The box score showed:

Love scored only 9 points but collected 14 rebounds, second-most in the game to the 15 of the Warriors' Green. Love was the most efficient player on the floor, with a plus-19 in the plus-minus category, the difference in team points scored and surrendered while he was on the floor.

Richard Jefferson was scoreless but grabbed 9 rebounds in 25½ minutes of playing time.

Tristan Thompson was 3-of-3 from the floor, all on shots in the paint, and 3-of-4 at the line for 9 points.

Irving scored 27 points with 6 rebounds but had only a single assist.

Green narrowly missed a triple-double with a 32–15–9 line.

James's 27–11–11 was only the third triple-double in the seventh game of an NBA Finals ever, after Jerry West in 1969 at home against Boston (42–13–12 in defeat) and James Worthy in 1988 at home against Detroit (36–16–10). But James did it on the road, against a team that was 73–9 in the regular season. Indisputably, he was for the third time the Finals MVP.

James also led both teams in everything that was worth leading, averaging 29.7 points, 11.3 rebounds, 8.9 assists, 2.6 steals, and 2.3 blocks, No one had ever done anything like it before.

Curry was 6-for-19. The unanimous regular season MVP and the league's 82-game MVP for two straight years shot 1-of-6 for 3 points in the fourth quarter. His only basket was a 3-pointer with 6:57 to play, tying the score at 83.

Cleveland's 52-year championship drought in its three major sports had barely ended when Smith began jumping up and down under the basket where he had made Iguodala take the fateful sidestep, like a kid who had gotten a shiny new bike for Christmas. Love came racing off the bench to hug James, whose face looked more like a Greek mask of tragedy than one of joy, as every emotion burst out like flood waters through a broken levee—the sacrifice, the suffering, the second guessing, "the Decision," the bitterness that followed, and the cherry-picking, as ESPN called it, of his legacy. All the fit-in, fit-out controversy James started and the third-wheel status Love endured was forgotten and forgiven.

Their embrace was the physical expression of Paul McCartney's song about ebony and ivory, when all the metaphorical piano's keys were tuned in perfect harmony. It proved sports had the ability to bring people together. It proved that the Latin words engraved on the change in your pocket, *E Pluribus Unum*, meaning "Out of many, one," were not only the motto of the United States but also the legal tender of team competition.

On the Cavs bench, Tyronn Lue buried his face in the towel he was holding and wept unashamedly. He and his team had done the impossible.

James lay on the floor after the buzzer, bawling, tears streaking his face in outright, chest-heaving, breath-shuddering emotion. He arose, then spoke of the "hard road" he had taken and of the Man Above. He meant not only the road to tears and champagne but living on the edge of destitution, then putting in the work despite a future that was assured after his rookie year contract, before he ever played an NBA game.

In an interview with ABC's Doris Burke moments later, he said. "I made the decision two years ago to come back to bring a championship to the city. I gave it my all. I put my heart, my blood, my sweat, my tears into it, and against all odds . . . against all odds . . . against the best regular season team in history, everybody counted us out, but that's when we strive most. I know that's when I strive most."

Irving, too, reveled in the "against all odds" improbability of the championship, noting that the Las Vegas oddsmakers, when the Cavs trailed 3–1 in the series gave Cleveland no plausible chance to win it all. "A 1 percent chance," Irving said.

As the pent-up emotions spilled out of James, he could have added to the list of his deepest devotions to the Cavaliers' cause the hate he had come back to change and the love—for often the feelings are entwined—that was its alteration.

"I don't know why we take the hardest road. I don't know why the Man Above give me the hardest road, but the Man Above don't give you anything you can't handle. This is what he wanted me to do," he said.

Asked what made the Cavs' 2016 championship different from the two James won in Miami with the Heat, he said, "This is what I came back for. I'm home. I'm home."

"Cleeeveland!" he roared, holding the golden trophy high. "This is for you!"

CHAPTER 30

"Party Like It's 1964"

The victory parade was delayed for two days because the Cavs stopped in Las Vegas at the XS Casino on their way home. The goings-on were private, and coverage was skimpy, but going by my previous experiences with celebrating athletes and costly wine, I would be surprised if they did not play "champagne ball"—like paint ball, only with snooty, exorbitantly expensive French bubbly, and not Champagne SW 6644, the paint Sherwin-Williams advertised at its downtown Cleveland world headquarters, where the giant LeBron poster hung.

Alternatively, the Cavs might have performed baptismal rites on each other's heads with it. Perchance they could have even swallowed some of it.

They also almost certainly sampled games of chance, none of which offered any worse odds than 1-in-33, 0.03 percent chance the Cavs hit for the jackpot on Sunday, June 19, in Oakland.

Canadian Cavs fans—Tristan Thompson is a Canadian, and LeBron's appeal was worldwide—admitted to fretting nervously, while grimly silent, in bars, afraid to commit the cardinal sin of optimism. The feeling was natural when you've gone through the long haul of Elways and Jordans, of Marlins and Cubs, of a stolen NFL franchise and a shabby replacement team. The Browns' dive to Stygian depths ended two years after the Cavs' championship, when bitter fans held a lightly attended Cavs' parade in reverse on "Hue Jackson Day," as it was sneeringly called at the end of January in 2018. It was held in recognition of the beleaguered coach's record of 1–31 (January 31, get it?) for the past two seasons.

As for the actual Cleveland celebration, fans mobbed Hopkins International Airport, awaiting the Cavs' late Monday afternoon arrival on June 20. Traffic was so snarled on the roads leading to Hopkins that many abandoned their cars on the strips of grass along each side of the highways and walked as far as a mile for a glimpse of the King and his court.

The official parade, scheduled to start downtown at the Q the next day, was late out of the gate. An immense crowd, which general consensus estimated as 1.3 million, lined both sides of the downtown parade route. The 2020 census put the metropolitan population of Cleveland at 388,072 and Cuyahoga County's population at 1,264,817. All hands were on deck at the parade, apparently, and at least 35,183 more had squeezed in.

Downtown office workers banged on windows as the procession of cars and flatbed trucks inched along between the cordons of cheering fans around the perimeter of Public Square. J. R. Smith took off his shirt and President Obama chided him for it the next day. Tyronn Lue performed some rap lyrics. Kyrie Irving worked on acquiring a beer buzz. Kevin Love had two WWE championship belts slung over his shoulders, accouterments that went unremarked amid the rejoicing.

The Cavs' general manager, David Griffin, said to a thunderous roar of approval, "The shot, the drive, the fumble all must now be replaced by the block, the 3 and the D."

"The strength and determination displayed throughout the season, postseason, and championship game are truly the embodiment of our city and its people," Cleveland's Mayor Frank Jackson said in a statement before the parade. "A city and a people with heart."

Cleveland Browns sports heroes such as Jim Brown, Bernie Kosar, and Earnest Byner rode in open convertibles, as did Ohio State football coach Urban Meyer and basketball coach Thad Matta. The Ohio State marching band, which the school modestly describes as TBDBITL (The Best Damn Band in the Land), played the school's two fight songs, "The Buckeye Battle Cry" and "Across the Field," one being insufficient for THE Ohio State University. The band also played a third song, a game day Ohio

Stadium staple, "Hang on Sloopy," a 1965 Number 1 hit by the McCoys, a musical group from Columbus.

James was a big fan of Ohio State, consenting to have a placard with his name on it placed on an empty dressing stall in the basketball arena's home locker room, although he never played a second of NCAA basketball for Ohio State or anyone else. He and selected Cavalier teammates were occasional visitors to the Buckeyes' sideline at football games, where they joined the battle criers and field traversers in urging Sloopy to, for God's sake, hang on.

The parade route wound around the baseball stadium, Progressive Field, next to the Q, up East Ninth Street, down West Lakeside Avenue, and finally reached the Cleveland Convention Center and its pedestrian mall stretching for three blocks. It took four hours to do so.

Somewhere along the course of the celebration, an individual almost literally starved for attention at any cost picked up the droppings of a mounted policeman's steed and ate them. Besides being repugnant and disgusting, he got it all wrong. In sports usage, excrement is species-specific. Batshit means crazy, bullshit means a lie, chickenshit means cowardly, and horseshit means lousy, which the Cavs were, by acclamation, anything but.

On a stage erected for the purpose at the Mall, James and teammates addressed the fans. "I'm nothing without the group behind me, man. I'm nothing without the coaching staff. I'm nothing without the city. You guys are unbelievable, So I'm nothing without y'all. I love all y'all. I love all y'all, and, shit, let's get ready [to defend the title]," said James.

He also spoke about each teammate individually after introducing them. Some of it could have gone better, as for example, his remarks about Timofey Mozgov, the 7'1", 275-pound Russian who averaged in the five games in which he played only 5 minutes per game, 1.4 points, 1.6 rebounds, and 0.6 blocked shots. James called Mozgov "the biggest [Oedipal term first popularized in ancient Thebes] I ever saw." Some were offended. The vast majority laughed it off.

The Playhouse Square theaters were closed for the day because of the congested streets, mass transit stations were overrun, hotel rooms were sold out because fans were unable to get home, and souvenir shops sold

T-shirts that read, "Party Like It's 1964" and "You Can't Spell MIRACLE without the CLE."

James had said privately that he'd had a vision when he returned to Cleveland of "floats and boats" going down the streets to the continual, crashing surf sound of cheers. Incredibly, against all odds, he had fulfilled it. He was eligible for free agency after the season, but James had told Cleveland reporters before the parade began, "I ain't going no place else now."

The parade did not end until well past 4:30 on the afternoon of June 21. It was the summer solstice, the longest day of the year. No one knew it, but the sun would set on the Cavs' empire almost as soon as it had risen.

CHAPTER 31

Revenge Is Golden

In a pageant of irony, James was both cause and effect of the huge salary-cap expansion in the 2016–17 season.

As the face of the league with name recognition on a global basis that, because of the explosion of the Internet and social media, even exceeded Jordan's, James increased the popularity of the NBA. Accordingly, the NBA received a staggering new contract, with a $24 million salary-cap boost per team, with the ESPN and TNT networks.

Through his free agency collusion with other megastars and his great success in going his own way in business, James empowered other players. No one was immune to the lure of the once-in-a-lifetime windfall of a $24 million salary-cap increase. General managers had plenty of money to spend. NBA players had plenty of open hands to accept it.

As James said, "The first time I stepped on an NBA court I became a businessman."

The NBA had a $70 million salary cap in 2015–16, an increase of $6.935 million from the year before. Rather than gradually expand the cap, the NBA switched to a 10-gallon cap that would be $94.1 million for the 2016–17 season.

In response, Kevin Durant announced on Derek Jeter's website, *The Players' Tribune,* that he would be joining the Warriors. The decision shocked everyone and angered the Oklahoma City Thunder fans, considering that Durant had been playing for OKC for the last nine years. Even James in "the Decision" hadn't joined Boston, the team that beat him. Durant's jump was all the more galling to Thunder fans because he had failed to finish off the Warriors when the Thunder held a 3–1 lead in the West Finals the year before and was going to the team that had silenced the Thunder and turned off the lightning.

Fans there promptly castigated Durant as a frontrunner who couldn't beat 'em, so he joined 'em. Angry OKC fans posted on social media photos of Durant's face beneath which were the words "Never forget, never forgive." Durant signed a two-year contract with the Warriors worth $55 million. In Cleveland, sports talker Munch Bishop began calling him "The Parasite."

Ironically, James, who had the leading role in the rise of the cap and the making of the Cavaliers as NBA champions, also had a supporting role in breaking it. He was a popularizer, sure, but he was a basketball Guy Fawkes who actually did set the gunpowder off, blowing up a free agency structure that had stressed roster continuity ever since the invention of the Larry Bird exception to allow the Celtics to keep a megastar.

ESPN bloviator Stephen A. Smith called what Durant did "the weakest move I've ever seen from a superstar." Tuts were tutted on TNT's influential *Inside the NBA*. John Stockton, who played 19 years, all with Utah, all without a ring, had to at least wonder if stability was all it was cracked up to be.

Gone was the Warriors' "Strength in Numbers" philosophy, proclaimed in a banner atop the Oracle Arena. In a twist on what Shakespeare said of Romeo and Juliet, his "star-crossed lovers," the bright twinkle Durant brought to a team already sparkly with Curry and Thompson indicated that the Dubs now believed "the fault is not in our stars, but in our other guys."

In Cleveland, Griffin said James was "not the same animal" in his final two seasons there. James's problem was what to do about an encore after completing a feat almost as unimaginable as reaching the star closest to our sun, Proxima Centauri, 23 times farther from the Earth. The sun is a comparatively short hop, photon wise, at 93 million miles.

The Warriors came to Cleveland on Christmas Day, following a game in Detroit, 169 miles away over ground flat enough to convince World B. Flat he was right. It was the second straight year for the yuletide match-up. It welcomed casual fans back to the NBA with a rematch of the teams involved in the greatest Finals upset, greatest Finals comeback, greatest Finals swat, greatest Finals shot, greatest Finals stop, greatest Finals statistical dominance by one man since nets replaced peach baskets. The Dubs could be either angry avengers or feeble foils. The story worked either way.

The Cavs won, 109–108, rallying from a 94–80 deficit with 9:35 to play on the strength of Irving's 14-point final quarter. Playing all 12 minutes, he shot 6-of-11, including two threes. He won the game with a corkscrewing 13-foot fadeaway, landing on his butt with but 3 seconds to play. Irving finished with 25 points on 27 shots, six rebounds, 10 assists (to James's four), and seven steals. James had a line of 31 points on 22 shots, 13 boards, and four steals. In the last quarter, James made the only two field goals he attempted and played only 7:33. Durant was high scorer with 36 points, 15 rebounds—all of them defensive—and three assists.

In retrospect, this could have been Irving's forbidden fruit moment, when he was the man of the hour, taking almost half of his team's 23 fourth-quarter shots, making the biggest basket before the young season's biggest television audience. World B. was as hot as climate change.

The Warriors showed the ephemeral effect of the Christmas game, with a smashing 126–91 rout in the rematch in Oakland, one point more in victory margin than the thrashing they had administered at the Q in the previous season.

The Cavs posted a 51–31 record, second in the "NBA East" by two games to the Celtics. Golden State, in a tribute to their residual professionalism, went 67–15. The Cavs lost their last four games, were 10–14 after March 1, and looked shaky, vulnerable, and other terms indicating a shortage of puissance.

2017 EASTERN CONFERENCE FIRST ROUND
Game 1, at Cleveland, Cavaliers 109, Pacers 108

They swept the Pacers in the first round, but the point differential was only 16 overall.

A desperate, last-possession double-team, with James joining Smith and forcing Paul George to give up the ball, almost backfired. George found C. J. Miles, who had something of a "Cavs killer" reputation and was drifting lonely as a cloud. George later complained that he needed the ball back and should have taken the last shot. Miles, however, was wide open, and his 14-foot jumper looked good until it wasn't, bouncing off the rim as time ran out in a victory that so nearly was a loss.

Game 2, at Cleveland, Cavaliers 117, Pacers 111

The Cavs almost gave away an 18-point fourth quarter lead, despite 37 points from Irving, 27 from Love, and 25 from James, who attempted to put a smiley face on it by saying, "I'd much rather have an 18-point lead than not have a lead at all. We're right there on turning the switch on what we can really become."

Well, yes. And I'd rather be rich and a wastrel than never be rich at all. As for the "switch" idea, it seemed a mirage produced by wishful thinking. The Cavs had not looked or played like defending champions for most of the regular season, and the postseason was looking no different.

The Pacers had to believe they had a chance to get back in the series after the two close losses.

Game 3, at Indianapolis, Cavaliers 119, Pacers 114

They had to feel even better at halftime of the third game before their home fans. Indiana led, 74–49, beating the Cavs in everything with what amounted to a whuppin' stick. The Pacers shot over 50 percent in the half, the Cavs under 40. The Pacers shot just under 60 percent on threes, the Cavs just under 40 percent, a competent showing, but not in comparison to the Pacers'. The hosts also had more rebounds and assists and fewer turnovers. I wondered whether the Cavs would use the USPS or FedEx to mail the game in when it resumed.

Instead, Lue surrounded James with shooters, playing substitutes Kyle Korver and Channing Frye in the second half longer than he did Irving and Love. Korver had become a Cavalier in a January 17 in a trade with Atlanta of Mike Dunleavy Jr. and Mo Williams, plus cash and a first-round draft pick. James immediately nicknamed him "The Game Changer."

In the second half, James was a one-man stampede, attacking the rim on full-court drives time and time again, while Smith joined the two three-point shooters, who fanned out to the wings and corners for passes from James. Frye and Smith each made two of their three triples. Korver made both of his. Usual bench-sitter Deron Williams hit the only one he tried. James caught the fever, nailing half his eight threes.

The sheer dimensions of the bombardment made me wonder if I could get away with something like gonzo journalist Hunter S. Thompson's Super Bowl week evocation of power football years earlier. Thompson blithely went through life essentially hingeless, both in his person and in his prose. In the essay alluded to, his heedless rush of jackboot adjectives thumped along like a torchlight parade in old Berlin town: "The precision-jackhammer attack of the Miami Dolphins stomped the balls off the Washington Redskins today by stomping and hammering with one precise jackthrust after another up the middle, mixed with . . . numerous hammer-jack stomps around both ends."

It would have to be recast as the sheer, pulverizing weight of airpower because of the threes, I realized, and it would involve firebombings and carpet bombings, blitzes and rocketry. It was unpleasant stuff with Vlad the Invader (Vladimir Putin) in charge of Russia.

The problem was that it worked too well. As I pondered the prose possibilities of the Bankers Life Fieldhouse Blitz, the Cavs took their first lead since 13–11 on a James dunk, 100–98, in the last 6:30. In the last 3:29, the Pacers went to what I called the "hack-a-Bron" strategy. He went to the line to shoot six free throws and missed four. For the quarter he was 4-of-8, for the game 7-of-14.

The next day at practice at Hinkle Fieldhouse, when no one else selected the touchy topic for questioning, I said, "How'd it feel to get Hack-a-Shaq'd?"

"That wasn't no Hack-a-Shaq. They were just saving time [by stopping the clock]," he said, bristling.

"They weren't fouling Korver, were they?" I persisted. (Note to aspiring journalists: Always have your facts ready. Korver shot 89.8 percent at the line that season and was a perfect 10-of-10 in the playoffs. James is a miss or few below the average free throw shooter for an NBA player. He was at 73.5 percent in the regular season as of 2023, 74.1 percent in the playoffs.)

Game 4, at Indianapolis, Cavaliers 106, Pacers 102

This little discussion would have ramifications in the next round, which the Cavs reached with another stress-test finish, blowing all of a 13-point fourth quarter lead to trail 102–100. They regained it in the final scrums on a James three, then boosting that with two free throws by—what a surprise—Korver.

Smith, prepping for his command "brains of stone" performance a season later, intercepted Jeff Teague's pass with 11 seconds to play, then threw a Curry-like Larry O'Brien Trophy meme of an awful pass behind his back that Paul George intercepted with 8 seconds to play, George looked, locked, loaded, and let fly, missing a 27-foot tying three with 2 seconds to play. James then split a pair of free throws for the final margin.

2017 EASTERN CONFERENCE SEMIFINALS

The conference semifinals against Toronto devolved into another sweep. The Cavs threw the Raptors under the figurative Zamboni without leaving even a single chunk of saurian flesh behind. The Cavs won the first two at home, 116–105 and 125–103, then annexed the next two in Woe, Canada, 115–94 and 135–102.

The series also provided an edifying example of how to answer media critics. Not by cussin' and fussin' and finger-jabbin' to the miscreant's chest with each voluble objection to the scribe's screed for the day (George McGinnis vs. Livingston, 1976).

Nor was the proper corrective measure summarized in another case (Ernie Camacho vs. Livingston, 1987), in which the plaintiff's bull-rush of the defendant was halted by teammates Andre Thornton and Joe Carter, plus Cy Buynak, the rotund 5-foot-and-smallish clubhouse attendant. Stepping around the thrashing Camacho, who was pinned to the floor, I noted it took three men to hold him down. *Plain Dealer* colleague Paul Hoynes replied, "Two and a half."

As I advised Camacho before he tried to Pamplona me, "Prove me wrong on the field."

Or court.

James opened the first three games of the Toronto series by going 37-for-45, 82.2 percent at the line. Included was a 15-of-16 display of Korver-like accuracy in the third game. Computer problems that night forced me to dictate much of my column from the press box, thus missing the interview session with James.

After the interviews two days later, before Game 4, I walked back to the media workroom in what was then the Air Canada Centre, only to find James, lying on his back in the narrow corridor outside the visiting locker room, while a trainer worked with him in stretching exercises. As I tiptoed carefully past James, he looked up and asked, deadpan, "My free-throw shooting any better now?"

I turned and reported in an excited gabble my computer's treachery and my subsequent miss of his postgame discussion of his triumphant free throw performance. I continued, "I would say your free throw shooting was superb last night. I would also say it is time for me to face the music."

James laughed heartily, stood up, gave me a half-hug with his arm around my shoulders, and we parted as the best of chums, from all appearances.

2017 EASTERN CONFERENCE FINALS

Boston was next in the conference finals, led by its lone All-Star, 5′9″ guard Isaiah Thomas. This was the same Isaiah Thomas who made a sneak attack on James from out of bounds as he inbounded the ball in a raucous 2015 first-round Pyrrhic victory, in which Love was lost for the playoffs.

Thomas had been the "IT guy," a play on his initials and the "IT girl," Clara Bow, of the Roaring '20s. He was the lethal little man in a competitive universe of big men. The Cavs hounded, harassed, hassled, and hindered him wherever he tried to go. Iman Shumpert was his near-constant shadow. When they sicced James on Thomas in double teams, I flashed back to the Bulls' use of Jordan in the first quarter of the 1992 conference finals on a hobbled Mark Price. That game was effectively over then and there, as Chicago took a 37–18 lead.

Thomas's record was tangled. The very last pick of the 2011 draft, Thomas had refuted all doubts about his size and toughness, while raising doubts in Cleveland about his unscrupulousness with the brazen rules violation. In the 2017 playoffs, Thomas had flown to his sister's funeral, then honored her memory by scoring 53 points on her birthday. He had scored 27 points only two days earlier in Boston's Game 7 semifinal series victory over Washington, a game in which Thomas's availability had been in question because of a sore hip.

The Cavs led Boston by 11 after the first quarter and won comfortably, 117–104. As wrote Chris Fedor of the *Plain Dealer*'s Internet arm, *Cleveland.com*, "Teams with one star have a ceiling about as high as Thomas this time of year."

A lone star is a gone star. Tyronn Lue promised congestion, obstruction, and frustration for Thomas. "We've got to make it tough on him," Lue said prior to the game. "We've got to try to keep him off the free throw line. He's a great scorer; we know that. But we've got to do it by committee. Just keep him off the free throw line is the biggest thing. Make him make field goals and not free throws. He's going to get some calls; we know that. But we've got to do a good job of just paying close attention to him. No open shots, no easy threes. Just make it tough for him."

As Fedor wrote afterward, "The three numbers that mattered most were 17, 36.8 and three—Isaiah Thomas' point total, shooting percentage and free throw attempts."

My column compared working at TD Garden, despite the availability of trustworthy electrical wiring and indoor plumbing now, to the claustrophobic feeling Thomas must have been experiencing with defenders swarming him:

"Welcome to the land of the green goblins. Welcome to a Boston Celtics Eastern Conference finals playoff game.

"You've heard of sleeping with the enemy?

"It's not like that, because there's no room to stretch out here in Section 6, Row 11 of TD Garden. Medieval monastic cells have been roomier. I was back in the seat I seldom sat in during the playoffs two years ago, surrounded by Celtic fans behind and in front of the narrow press table near the Cleveland Cavaliers' bench. Fans craned their necks like construction equipment, trying to see what we sometimes acerbic, but usually grand Cleveland fellows, hardly worthy of a rude word, were writing.

"The fans were almost all wearing wristbands with LED lights that glitter and glow, as green as the lights on Thunder Road.

"Except the Cavs stole it.

"Emotion from the fans can't make up for the toll 13 playoff games, the last a tension-filled East semifinal Game 7 on Monday night, took on the Celtics. The Cavs played only the minimum of eight games in the first two rounds and had been off since early May."

I noted that James, isolated on the wee would-be giant-killer on one play, "forced Thomas to shoot an airball to himself, which is one of the seldom seen subsets of the traveling violation."

Thomas was done for the series by halftime of the second game, a grotesque rout in which the Cavs' 41-point lead was the biggest halftime advantage in NBA playoff history.

Boston managed to win one game. After reaching the Cavs' third straight Finals and the seventh of what would become a staggering eight in a row for James, the Cavs' leader had no wish to harsh his mellow with thoughts of what was ahead.

"I'm going to be honest, I'm not in the right mind to even talk about Golden State," he said. "It's too stressful, and I'm not stressed right now. I'm very happy about our accomplishment. Golden State, they've been the best team in our league for the last three years, and then they added an MVP [Durant]. That's all I can give you right now, because I'm happy and I don't want to be stressed."

He soon faced a more stressful issue, as he explained:

"No matter how much money you have, no matter how famous you are, no matter how many people admire you, being black in America is tough. Racism will always be a part of the world, a part of America. Hate in America, especially for African Americans, it's living every day. Even though it's concealed most of the time."

I wrote, "On the eve of the start of the 2017 NBA Finals, James solemnly spoke those words about the defacing of his $20.9 million Brentwood mansion in Los Angeles by one or more vandals, who spraypainted a racist word on its gates.

"The real LeBron James is not simply Playoff LeBron. That is only his persona in the spring, when he represents Cleveland, the city that gave the world Superman, in a way that fulfills our fantasies of flight and might.

"The real LeBron . . . is no more immune to the pathogen of racism than anyone else. . . . James is a target for the splinters of hate from broken minds. The gate to James's lavish second home in Los Angeles attracted one or more of those whose small minds are spiked by racism, resentment and evolutionary recidivism. This week, someone spraypainted there a hateful word we have all heard, one loaded with bigotry, one that should be from the past, like the Confederate battle flag, but never will be put away entirely.

"The word is usually either censored entirely or euphemized as the *n-word* nowadays.

"James recalled the martyrdom of a 14-year-old Black teenager, Emmett Till, lynched in Mississippi in 1955 for wolf-whistling at a white woman.

"Carolyn Bryant, the white woman who claimed Till raped her and whose husband was one of the two men who killed Till, recanted her testimony years later."

"I think back to Emmett Till's mom, actually," James said. "The reason that she had an open casket is because she wanted to show the world what her son went through as far as a hate crime and being black in America."

"He is always surprising . . . , in the expansion of his game, the persistence of his hunger, the scope of his dominance, and, as he has grown, the breadth, depth and eloquence of his social conscience today. The audience he commands comes from celebrity. The commitment he made in charity, activism, and courage comes from the heart."

Worried about his family's safety, gassed almost out by two seven-game series, after a Herculean effort to help his team win the East, he now faced a heavily favored Golden State team.

Golden State won, 4–1. The Cavs' losses were by 22 and 19 in the first two at Oakland, an aggregate 41-point clobbering that recalled the aggregate 48-point walloping in the 2016 Finals. The Cavs had then crawled out of the crypt by winning Game 3 at home, even without Love, who missed the game because he was recovering from a concussion.

The third game, the first in Cleveland, was the only close game of the 2017 series. The Cavs took a five-point lead into the fourth quarter but lost it in the last minute. Korver, my exemplar of center-cut, down-the-middle shooting, missed a wide-open corner three with the Cavs leading 113–11 with 53 seconds to play. Make it, and it's a two-possession game with nobody but Korver or Irving handling the ball and the prospective free throw duties.

Only eight seconds later came the shot James was still reliving months later. The play-by-play sheet said Durant swished his trey from 26 feet out. Perhaps time and memory have added a couple of extra steps to make its length more heroic. James said later he knew Durant was going to shoot from far out and that he simply had too much ground to cover to get there. Given that Durant is 7 feet tall, with a 7'5" wingspan, a high release, and an eiderdown shooting touch, blocking it might have ranked with the chasedown of Iguodala.

Irving then rushed a three and missed. Durant sank two free throws as the Cavs had to resort to that desperate tactic. Then vengeance was Iguodala's when he blocked a desperate James three that would have tied it at 116, and James was out of bounds on his retrieve. Curry closed it out at the line, 118–113. If 3–1 was being under a death sentence, 3–0 was toe-tag time.

Nevertheless, the Cavs postponed the inevitable with a 137–116 defense-optional Game 4 victory. The end came in Game 5 in Oakland, a 129–120 Warriors' win.

Durant hadn't simply put his finger on the scale when he signed with the Warriors; his addition might have unbalanced a truck-stop scale with a tractor-trailer parked on it.

In vain, James managed a triple-double in the Finals with averages of 33.6 points, 12 rebounds, and 10 assists. Durant, the Finals' Most Valuable Player, put up a line of 35.2, 8.2, 5.4.

Basketball, however, is a team sport. The Cavs were simply outgunned by a deeper, better team.

Who or what would it have taken to beat the Warriors of 2017 four times?

Time and/or scorekeeping by Renato William Jones? Known as Bill Jones, he was the damn fool British secretary general of FIBA (the International Basketball Federation) who helped steal the 1972 Munich Olympics basketball gold medal from the USA for the Soviet Union. A man who did not know the noun *treacle* from the verb *tinkle*, perhaps he could have given to the Cavs the ball on each inbounds play as many times as it took until they scored. It worked for the hammer-and-sickle crowd.

The Jordan and Pippen Bulls? Not in an era of enough threes bombing baskets to please Curtis LeMay.

The *Space Jam* animated movie gang?

Durant, aka "The Parasite," for jumping to the Warriors and feeding off the hosts' talent surplus, gave James a forthright compliment: "The man had a triple-double in the Finals, I ain't throwin' no shade," said Durant.

World B. Flat did instead.

Even before the next season began, the snakes in the muddled brain, the unsettled scores in the resentful heart, and the destructiveness of the enormous ego of Kyrie Irving drove the Cavs coverage. Although years later the Flat Earther renounced the inane belief, he was only saving his breath for other theories that were disgusting and not amusing.

But first . . .

ESPN's Brian Windhorst broke the news on July 21 that Irving had told the Cavs, "I want my own team."

Although it rocked the NBA world and blindsided James, the plan had been in the works for a while. General manager David Griffin parted ways with Gilbert earlier in the summer, to be replaced by Griffin's aide Koby Altman.

ESPN's Dave McMenamin, citing league sources, scored with a scoop, writing that Irving had acted "sullen and resentful" around his teammates during the 2017 playoffs and went days without talking to them during the sweeps of the Pacers and Raptors.

Former Cavalier Richard Jefferson, by then a network analyst, claimed Irving was upset the Cavs were shopping him after the 2017 Finals, leading to the combo guard ultimately putting in his trade request. "There was a trade," Jefferson said, apparently referring to a deal that never came to fruition. "And Kyrie believed, 'Oh you guys wanna make me the villain? You wanna say that I need to be traded? That's what it is? I'm the problem here?' That's why he wanted to leave. Once he found out that he was on the trade block and a trade almost went through, once he found that out, he was like, 'I'm gone.'"

This made clear the real meaning of Irving's exasperated eyeroll in the last minutes of the closeout game against Detroit in the first round of the 2016 playoffs: Irving never wanted LeBron James to come back to the Cavs. Irving believed he already had a team, sorry and noncontending as it was, and it was being taken away from him.

That was only the first kaboom in an off-season of fireworks, however.

On August 30, more pyrotechnics went off than would have been the case had the Humongotron exploded in flames and a hail of swords. The Cavs traded Irving to Boston for Jae Crowder, Ante Zizic, a 2018 first-round draft pick (Collin Sexton), and a 2020 second rounder (Skylar

Mars), plus the guy who put the "imp" in impudence, Isaiah Thomas, the Celtics' out-of-bounds pass deflector.

It was a trade that didn't help the Cavs that much, because they had lost a top-tier talent in Irving, who, in his inimitable, inimical ability to be dissatisfied and unlikeable, hurt the Celtics more.

By 2022, when he was two stops down the road from the Cavs— Brooklyn after Boston—Irving had been suspended by the NBA for retweeting a link to an antisemitic film, *Hebrews to Negroes,* and refusing to apologize for it. Irving thus took his small place in the long story of Jewish persecution, from banishment in Spain to pogroms in Russia, from Shylock to Kristallnacht, from, as the deplorable film says in its biggest lies, the international Jewish conspiracy to Holocaust denial. If Irving did not have a contract worth $36.5 million, the Nets would have purged him like the poison he had become.

An "idiot," Kareem Abdul-Jabbar, Charles Barkley, and Shaquille O'Neal called Irving.

James responded, "I don't condone any hate to any kinds or any race, to Jewish communities or Black communities or Asian communities."

By October 2017, Irving's image was on boxes of Wheaties, the "Breakfast of Champions," wearing his leprechaun-green Celtics jersey on the front. On the other side, he was none other than "Uncle Drew," Irving's TV commercial and movie alter ego in graybeard make-up.

Given my view of both Irving and Thomas, and admittedly stealing from a St. Patrick's Day sendup of drunken Irishmen in the comic strip "Bizarro," I thought the term "leprobates" fit both the former Celtic and the newly minted one.

My column about the team wrecker read, in part: "The NBA championship was not enough for Irving, who would no more have been totally eclipsed by James than Scottie Pippen by Michael Jordan or Kobe Bryant by Shaquille O'Neal.

"He had a cross-over dribble quick as a turncoat in the off-season. He could also tunnel under opponents' digs at the ball, but he had also developed a different style of 'dig' in praising Boston as a 'real sports city,' unlike Cleveland, which, I noted, 'was not only lacking in an NHL team now but struggled without his own august presence.

"Irving could score at the rim, despite his lack of size, from nearly every conceivable angle on shots that hip-hopped around the backboard as if Lin-Manuel Miranda had taken them."

I ended with a reference to Irving's inane, insane one-on-the-Dubs drive in the last half-minute of Game 7 in 2016, which could easily have resulted in a turnover and a resuscitation of the Warriors' chances:

"Because the Cavs won, Irving escaped the infamy of Earnest Byner and Jose Mesa. But jealousy and resentment ruined him. He wanted to be bigger, to have a team of his own. He diminished himself by the smallness of his jealousy and spite, although they were big enough to fill his whole world.

"Still, he has his breakfast. Eat up, chump."

CHAPTER 32

The Iconography of LeBron James

The biggest controversy before the games started to count came from President Donald J. Trump. His election was an almost unimaginable development that said a great deal about the appeal to many Americans of nativism, populism, racism, isolationism, and barely disguised fascism. All of those doctrines were part of the American Experiment as much as were the "better angels" Lincoln invoked after the conclusion of a fratricidal war of separatism fought by the South to defend slavery. The Founders' creaky Electoral College had the effect of continuing the subjugation of the Black population despite the Confederacy's defeat.

Trump was elected president despite a loss by 3 million votes nationwide, hardly a trifling number. The Electoral College system was born in the horse-and-buggy days when election results trickled into Washington for weeks and months over miles of bad road and across swollen rivers—hence, the March inauguration date for many years, allowing time for each state's votes to be tabulated.

A Rube Goldberg–like anachronism, the Electoral College originally was skewed to reward ballot victories in slave states. In the twenty-first century, its minoritarian bias excessively empowered conservative, rural "red" state voters.

Trump was a serial offender of everyone who did not look like him. The new president had only reluctantly visited Puerto Rico, a US territory with a predominately Hispanic population that had been devastated by Hurricane Maria. Upon arrival, Trump insulted the suffering people of the island by saying how "lucky" they had been not to have had a "real" disaster such as New Orleans had endured with Hurricane Katrina. He was flippant about the shortage of almost all household supplies, happily being filmed while residents jumped and scuffled for the paper towels he sailed into a crowd as if he were shooting basketballs at a hoop. Unknowingly, he had blasphemed the young James's socks shooting.

Trump was extremely unpopular around the NBA for his defense of the Ku Klux Klan members who descended on Charlottesville, Virginia, in a parade lit by tiki torches. They chanted their hatred of Jews, wore T-shirts celebrating the Holocaust, and mustered to the defense of statues memorializing Confederate generals.

After Golden State's victory over the Cavs, Trump invited the Warriors to visit the White House, an invitation that they found as attractive as a bout of intestinal flu. When most of the players, in particular Steph Curry, failed to be as rapturous about the prospect of meeting him as Trump believed they should have, he rescinded the invitation.

On September 23, he tweeted: "Going to the White House is considered a great honor for a championship team. Stephen Curry is hesitating therefore invitation is withdrawn!" The controversy came on the heels of Trump telling NFL owners to fire any player who did not stand for the national anthem.

Next, Trump complained that NFL football was no longer violent enough. That came after the stunning disclosures years earlier of the NFL's coverup of the brain damage players had incurred from chronic traumatic encephalopathy, repeated concussions due to blows to their heads. Worse was the NFL's unconscionable persecution of the Nigerian-born Pittsburgh forensic pathologist, Bennet Ifeandndu Omalu. He was the first to discover the effects of repeated blows to the head, when he performed an autopsy on the Steelers center from their "glory" years of the 1970s, Mike Webster.

As for the 2017 presidential invitation, Curry had said he did not want to go, but the Warriors had not made a collective decision and had planned to discuss it in the morning before Trump's tweet stiffing the Warriors as they were intent on stiffing him. Kerr said, "Not surprised. He was going to break up with us before we could break up with him."

James responded to Trump's comment with a tweet of his own: "U bum @StephenCurry30 already said he ain't going! So therefore ain't no invite. Going to White House was a great honor until you showed up!"

It became the most retweeted post by an athlete of 2017.

Said Curry: "That's a pretty strong statement. I think it's bold, it's courageous for any guy to speak up, let alone a guy that has as much to lose as LeBron does and other notable figures in the league. We all have to kind of stand as one the best we can. I didn't want to be applauded for an accomplishment on the court when the guy that would be doing the patting on the back is somebody I don't think respects the majority of Americans in this country."

Several hours later, James said Trump's comments were "something I can't stand for."

In a January 14, 2017, YouTube video that got 2,350,267 views in less than a month, James rode through Akron during a snowstorm, touring a recreation center, the apartment complex where he had lived as a child, and the high school that had meant so much to him. Along for the ride was Kevin Durant, and driver of the Uber, Tennis Channel broadcaster Cari Champion.

During the 16 minutes and 44 seconds of conversation, Champion said, "LeBron, you called the president a bum."

"Yeah. Straight-up, straight up," James said.

She followed that by asking, "How would you describe the climate for an athlete with a platform nowadays that wants to talk about what's happening in our world?"

Said James, "Well the climate is hot. The number one job in America, the point of [this] person, is someone who doesn't understand the people. And really don't give a f—k about the people.

"When I was growing up, there was, like, three jobs that you look for inspiration, or you feel like these were the people that could give me life. It was the president of the United States, it was whoever was the best at sports, and then it was like the greatest musician at the time. You never thought you could be them, but you can grab inspiration from them.

"I felt like I could be, you know, like if it was a neighborhood African American cop and he was cool as hell and come around, like, I could be him. I could be him . . . but I never felt I could be the president of the

United States, but I grabbed inspiration from that, and this time right now, with the president of the United States? It's at a bad time. And while we cannot change what comes out of that man's mouth, we can continue to alert the people that watch us that, listen to us, this is not the way."

Asked what could be done to improve ratings for the NBA All-Star Game, Durant, skipping blithely over his Golden State teammates and Splash Brothers Curry and Thompson, said of himself and James, "As the best two players, I feel as though we could definitely take it to the next level. Because everyone is just gonna follow our lead."

After James's excoriation of Trump, Durant's most quoted remark became the social and mainstream media equivalent of softball scores in tiny agate type.

By the time the actual season had started, James had become an icon in Black communities and among many fair-minded whites. In some commentators' eyes, he was the legatee of Muhammad Ali and Martin Luther King, both of whom had been heroes to James and others in his generation.

Icons should not be dismissed as products of hype. True icons, as Pulitzer Prize–winning historian Jon Meacham said, in his book *His Truth Is Marching On: John Lewis and the Power of Hope*, "show us glimmers of Abraham Lincoln's more perfect union. They are gates to a better path." The most inspirational ones, as James was now aspiring to be, "are part of an unfolding story they know is larger than ourselves."

The examples James had followed would become the examples he set. "Having three kids of my own and being around kids in my community, the one thing that they care more about than anything is that you care. And once they see that you really care about what they're going through or how they feel and things like that, their passion about what they want to become or what they want to do just sprouts out like none other. To be in a position where you can teach the youth is very key because, you know, we didn't have that. You know we had people in our hood who made money. . . . We know the local dope dealers, the local OGs and things but it's no end-game. It's not like we were out there with them."

OGs means *original gangsters*. James knew who they were and avoided them as much as disadvantaged kids today know who he is and follow his Tweets and his example.

Soon, James, via Twitter, showed his capacity for empathy with and respect for a troubled teammate by supporting Kevin Love, who was struggling with panic attacks.

In an ugly locker-room scene, James's old Miami running mate, Dwyane Wade, and Isaiah Thomas, both of whom had been Cavs for barely a half-season and soon would be gone—Wade amicably, Thomas less so—had derided Love and questioned his commitment to the team.

Love had been hospitalized following a November 5 loss to Atlanta because of stomach pain and shortness of breath. Said Love, "It's hard to describe, but everything was spinning, like my brain was trying to climb out of my head. The air felt thick and heavy. My mouth was like chalk. I remember our assistant coach yelling something about a defensive set. I nodded, but I didn't hear much of what he said. By that point, I was freaking out."

It happened again on January 20, 20018. The Cavs had lost a blowout on national television, 148–124, to Oklahoma City. It was their ninth loss in a dozen games. They would lose the next against San Antonio also.

After the OKC loss, ESPN's Adrian Wojnarowski reported:

"The Cleveland Cavaliers held a fiery team meeting in the practice facility locker room prior to practice, during which several players challenged the legitimacy of Kevin Love's illness that led him to leave Saturday's loss to Oklahoma City early and miss Sunday's practice. Several players were pushing for the Cavaliers' management and coaching staff to hold Love accountable for leaving the arena before the end of Saturday's game and then missing Sunday's practice, league sources told ESPN.

"The meeting was loud and intense, only calming down once Love spoke to those gathered in the room and explained himself. As usual, Love was the scapegoat. He had not been sleeping well, and he was distressed by the death of his beloved grandmother, to whom he had been unable to say goodbye."

Love spoke often with Channing Frye, whose locker was next to his and who was his seatmate on the team bus. A man with a quiet demeanor and a willingness to listen, Frye helped Love, as did the therapist Love began seeing. Like many athletes, Love had believed he could will himself through his problems, often giving himself private, emotion-charged pep talks: "Deal with it! Be a man!"

"It really makes you think about how we are all walking around with experiences and struggles—all kinds of things—and we sometimes think we're the only ones going through them," Love wrote in publicly revealing his struggles. "The reality is that we probably have a lot in common with what our friends and colleagues and neighbors are dealing with. . . . Mental health is an invisible thing, but it touches all of us at some point or another." Love credited Toronto guard DeMar DeRozan, who earlier in the season had divulged his own similar problem. Both had done much to destigmatize mental health issues.

Although Love was sidelined by injury then, James made a point to speak to him and lend him his support. It can be called various things. The next president, Joe Biden, called it empathy. Others have called it the ability to "walk in someone else's shoes," being able to see the world through the eyes of someone whose circumstaances might be completely different from one's own. James had big feet, as his first high school coach, Keith Dambrot, had noted. But they could still walk in another man's shoes.

"It was a special moment for me," Love said of James's kindness. "We sat towards the end of the bus. He kind of said, 'Hey, do you have a moment?' He stopped me, shook my hand, looked me in the eye, and said, 'You helped a lot of people today. It's important.' That was super powerful for me. Not only is he the best athlete in the world, the best basketball player in the world, but his influence and having my back with that was super important to me."

As for Thomas, after more rehab, he played in only 15 games with the Cavs, shooting 36.1 percent from the field and 25.3 percent from the arc and averaging only 14.7 points.

Perceptive viewers knew something was up, as opposed to the season, which was going down the drain, in the immediate aftermath of the Cavs' 140–38 overtime victory in Cleveland on February 7 against the Minnesota Timberwolves. After James, providing late help for Cedi Osman, rejected Jimmy Butler's driving layup, the Cavs called timeout in their own backcourt with 1 second to play. Jeff Green made a deep inbounds pass because of the absence of Love, who had broken his left hand in a January 30 loss to Detroit.

This was another area in which Love had an underrated influence. He was an elite outlet passer and long ball in-bounder, with an arm strong enough to throw a 90 mph fastball when he was in high school. In 2012, for an ESPN sports science feature, Love sank a 90-foot baseline to opposing basket bank shot for a world record on a two-handed shot, taken with a two-step approach. It was his 98th attempt.

Green, absent any of Love's 97 mulligans, whipped a two-handed overhead pass right on the money to James, who had sealed off Butler just outside the T-wolves' free throw line. James stepped back, faded further back, and released the ball, which barely eluded Butler's lunging challenge. As James landed just beyond the top of the foul circle, the ball went in and took the game with it.

James pranced down the sideline to the Cavs' bench in jubilation, as Osman gave him a celebratory chest bump, and Thomas, standing only inches away, tried to get close enough for a shared bro hug. That was a no-go. James never gave Thomas so much as a glance. I was almost certain Thomas no longer figured in the Cavs' plans. I thought James must have been consulted about plans to trade Thomas and had given it a "go."

The next day, Cleveland traded Thomas and Frye to the Lakers for Jordan Clarkson and Larry Nance Jr., each of whom became a contributor and did not assume the role of a team spokesman. In a Napoleonic gesture of ego, Thomas had done just that regarding Love and the team's struggles, drawing reporters' gobsmacked looks. Thomas simply had not been there long enough to assume any such role.

The Cavs finished fourth in the East with a 50–32 record, two games ahead of fifth-place Indiana. It was the worst record of a Cleveland team with James on it since back-to-back matching 50–32 marks in 2005–07, in his third and fourth seasons in the league.

They might have finished in the G League except for James, who made no fewer than 14 game-deciding shots either in the final two minutes or at the buzzer. It was the precursor to one of his greatest and least appreciated playoff seasons.

CHAPTER 33

Glory Road

Had it been the Browns, an incompetent franchise ever since it returned as an expansion team in 1999, tribute songs about James would have flooded radio airwaves. Those of us who lived through it will never forget 1986, when the Browns were the top seed in the AFC and playing on almost every radio station at some time every day was a song about quarterback Bernie Kosar with lyrics that seemed largely to consist of "Ber-nie, BERNEE! How you can throw! Bernie, BERNEE! Super Bowl!" The Super Bowl didn't happen, because of John Elway and because, even in that more adept mode, they were still the Browns.

Perhaps James had just been too good too soon and, frankly, too infatuated with the whole "King" thing early in his career, to capture some fans' hearts. But that would mean teenage fireballer Bob "Rapid Robert" Feller, and four-time Olympic gold medalist Jesse Owens, the "Buckeye Bullet," were not celebrated here in the 1930s, and both were, Owens with a memorable parade.

Probably, beating Golden State four times in seven games, should James somehow haul his teammates by their jersey straps into the NBA Finals, seemed as impossible with Durant on their roster as it had been the year before, indeed more impossible with World B. Flat now World B. Gone.

Without James, the Cavs would not have survived the first round against Indiana. Their three losses were by 18 points, 34 points, and the anomaly 2 points. Their four victories were by 3, 4, 3, and 4. They were outscored by 40 in aggregate points.

It was a statistical quirk that recalled the 1960 World Series, when the New York Yankees had lost four games by a total of 7 runs and won three by a total of 35, outscoring the victorious Pittsburgh Pirates 55–27.

2018 EASTERN CONFERENCE FIRST ROUND
Game 1, at Cleveland, Pacers 98, Cavaliers 80

Victor Oladipo, who played collegiately just down the road from Indianapolis at Indiana University in Bloomington scored 32 points as Indiana outplayed Cleveland from the start while pulling off a stunning victory.

It was the first loss for James and the Cavaliers in the opening round in eight years. Unaware of the stat until told of it after the game, James was also unimpressed by the single-game deficit.

"I'm down 0–1 in the first round," he said. "I was down 3–1 in the Finals. So, I'm the last guy to ask about how you're going to feel the next couple days."

The Pacers, who took a 21-point lead in the first quarter, won for the fourth time in five games in the regular season plus the playoffs against the Cavs.

James posted his 20th career playoff triple-double with 24 points, 12 assists, and 10 rebounds. The rest of the starting lineup—Kevin Love, Jeff Green, George Hill, and Rodney Hood—combined for 24 points. Hood and Hill arrived via trade on the same day that Isaiah Thomas, along with Jae Crowder and Iman Shumpert, were dispersed to the four winds.

"We believe that we can win," Oladipo said. "But it's only one game; it's only Game 1."

Game 2, at Cleveland, Cavaliers 100, Pacers 97

Well, no and yes.

No, the Pacers did not win. Yes, it was only one game.

James cut down on the ball distribution (only five assists), taking the ball, the game, and the Pacers' sense that they could do anything whatsoever to stop him into his own hands. He scored the game's first 13 points; helped the Cavs to a 33–18 lead after the first quarter, in which he outscored Indiana, 20–18; had 29 by halftime; and finished with 46—yet it was just enough, as the Cavs wheezed to the finish line.

The Pacers came back from an 18-point deficit, and Oladipo, with 22 points, had a wide-open three to tie with only 27 seconds left on the clock.

With the Cavs' defense consisting of hopes, prayers, and screaming, "Miss it!!" Oladipo missed it.

Game 3, at Indianapolis, Pacers 93, Cavaliers 90

The Cavaliers were 39–0 on the season when leading after three quarters. They were 39–1 after the Pacers overcame a 17-point halftime deficit.

The artistic center of the Indiana state capital is Monument Circle, with its 347-foot-high Soldiers and Sailors monument, commemorating the common soldiers who fought and died in the nation's wars, near the Pacers' fieldhouse. A year to the day after the Cavs' comeback from a 25-point halftime deficit, the Pacers had their own monumental moment.

Bojan Bogadanovic scored 19 points of his career playoff high of 30 in the second half. When he was not knocking down threes (7 of 9), he was helping harass James into six turnovers to go with 28 points, 12 rebounds, and eight assists.

Although he missed another triple-double by two assists, James did post his 100th playoff double-double, second behind Jordan's 109. James almost singlehandedly rallied his team twice from seven-point deficits in the final 3½ minutes. But Smith's 38-footer to win it at the buzzer was short. James scored 15 points in the second half. His teammates combined for 18.

The Pacers moved to 5–2 against the Cavs on the season and 3–0 in Indianapolis.

"A lot of teams have been close with LeBron, but he ends up winning," said Pacers' coach Nate McMillan, guardedly.

The question was: how much more could be asked of a player who was either making or threatening to make a triple-double in every game?

Objecting to that line of enquiry, James asked the members of the basketball press, "What are you guys looking for? I'm not going to throw my teammates under the bus."

Game 4, at Indianapolis, Cavaliers 104, Pacers 100

In a previously unexplored first-round landscape, in which the Cavs had mostly been playing from behind in both games and the series, James had seen his team lose the first game wire-to-wire, survive Oladipo's wide-open missed three to win the second, and lose the third to a Pacers' comeback that was more like an oncoming squall line of baskets.

Now the Cavs had to win on a hostile floor to avoid the 3–1 deficit that usually means the fat lady had sung, the lights were out, and the party was over. James contributed 32 points, 13 rebounds, 7 assists—and another milestone, his 100th playoff game with 30 or more points, second all-time to Jordan.

Korver, who finished with 18 points and four threes, combined with James to score all of the Cavs' points in a 10–2 run at the end, in which Korver sank two threes and James barreled, barged, slashed, dashed, muscled, and mangled every obstruction for two layups. "He's one of the all-time leaders in 3-pointers made," James said of Korver. "His four threes were huge. We needed every last one of them."

The same held for Smith's four threes, one of which was long enough to be a six. Smith's range is limited only by his passport. He will take any shot. He can make almost any shot. I would take him against both Larry Bird and Michael Jordan in the long-ago McDonald's commercial in which each made preposterously long shots in a game of H-O-R-S-E, ending with Bird's attempt from across a freeway and "through the window, off the scoreboard, nothing but net."

As the first quarter ended, Smith took an inbound pass near the Cavs' defensive basket, dribbled crosscourt to his left, leaped, and from the cold fringes of speculation, shot, with all his momentum carrying him left, across his body, at the basket in the distance to his right.

Nothing but net.

The play-by-play sheet called it 70 feet. I thought it was more like a *Star Trek* thing, going boldly where no man—certainly only few men—had gone before. The *Akron Beacon Journal*'s Marla Ridenour, seated next to me in the press box high above the court, had been writing her running column, that is, composing it as the game was going on. She looked up just as the ball plummeted into the net and asked me, "Was that from halfcourt?"

"No, that was from the three-point line. The Pacers' three-point line," I said.

Game 5, at Cleveland, Cavaliers 98, Pacers 95

James hugged teammate Cedi Osman, who had apparently become the designated greeter in such moments, then he leaped atop the scorer's table he had made his throne. The cheers LeBron James had heard in his head as a kid in Akron were real and roaring all around and above him in Cleveland.

It was every kid's backyard, city park, rec center dream basket. It had been mine when light burst from a Renaissance sky, and I sank a shot into a morning fireball of sunshine and ran back on defense, almost with angels singing in my ears. It had been LeBron James's too, except he was living it in real life and maybe forever more in the sport's lore after he caught the inbounds pass, took two dribbles and hit his winner over Thaddeus Young at the buzzer for the victory.

"As a kid you always have those 3, 2, 1 moments, and that's what it kind of felt like," James said. "I felt like I was a kid all over again, playing basketball at my house on makeshift hoops."

It gave the Cavs their first series lead against the resolute Pacers and, more, it had postponed for at least two more games the End—of the series, the season, and probably, James's last term with the Cavs.

Moments earlier, he had Iguodala-ed Oladipo with a chasedown block of a possible go-ahead layup, which brought Pacers coaches leaping to their feet, vainly screaming that it was goaltending. TV replays showed the ball appeared to hit the glass before James touched it.

"I got a step on him, and I felt I even got grabbed," Oladipo said. "It hit the backboard, and he blocked it. It was a goaltend. It's hard to even speak on it. That layup is huge."

"Of course, I didn't think it was a goaltend," James said with a laugh. "I try to make plays like that all the time. He made a heck of a move, got me leaning right and he went left, and I just tried to use my recovery speed and get back up there and make a play on the ball."

James finished with 44 points, 10 rebounds, and eight assists and went 15-for-15 from the line. (Frankly, the guy seemed intent on showing me up. Wasn't one apology about his free-throw shooting in a whole different country the year before enough?)

"He does it at both ends every single night," said Cavs forward Love. "That's why he's the best player in the world."

Game 6, at Indianapolis, Pacers 121, Cavaliers 87

Oladipo had gone 12-for-50 after his Game 1 burst of 32 points as the Cavs relentlessly doubled him. With the Pacers down in the series, 3–2, he suddenly went off like Krakatoa with legs, scoring 28 points on 11-of-19 shooting, 6-of-8 on threes, with 13 rebounds and 10 assists. It was his first triple-double, and it got so bad that Tyronn Lue kept every starter on the bench in the fourth quarter, including James, because the Cavs trailed by 25 on their way to a lopsided embarrassment.

Lue said. "I don't even remember [what happened to start the second half]. I really don't. It happened so quickly."

The Pacers would be confident going to Cleveland after their 34-point rout. Could the Cavs, who had just gotten kicked around as if the Pacers were using them to play hacky sack, come back one more time?

Of course, the answer was yes. The Cavs had James. And home teams traditionally have a major advantage in Game 7s.

Game 7, at Cleveland, Cavaliers 105, Pacers 101

James played through leg cramps in the second half, his face sometimes contorted in pain. He scored 45 points despite everything.

Following the game, an exhausted James said the series took a physical toll. He was like that in 2012, when I had seen him limp into the interview room in suburban Detroit after the 48-point playoff game against the Pistons. He was young then, had been hooked up to IVs in the locker room, and still could barely speak through his exhaustion. When asked how he felt, he responded, looking exhausted and barely able to croak out an answer, "Awful."

"I'm burnt right now," an older James said in 2018. "I'm not thinking about Toronto right now until tomorrow. I'm ready to go home. Can we? I'm tired. I want to go home."

James added nine rebounds and seven assists and played over 43 minutes. In a bewildering series of blowouts and squeakers, it often seemed to be the Pacers vs. James.

Fads had come and gone, like Oladipo from conqueror to conquered and not quite back again. There had been one-offs, like Smith's shot from the wrong three-point line, his "Magellan," as I thought of it, comparing him to the Portuguese captain of the first ship to circumnavigate the globe.

What there had not been much of was help. In Game 7, however, Love hit four triples, and Tristan Thompson played in a clearly unsatisfied Lue's 34th different starting lineup of the season and chipped in a 15–10 double-double in points and rebounds. Lue had decided to go with the players he trusted most, the holdovers from the Finals of the pass: Thompson, Love, Smith, Korver, and, of course, James.

Amid despair and its repair, the flair of big plays and the scare the Pacers gave Cleveland, there had always been James.

"Amazing," said Oladipo of James. "He did what he always does. It's not really shocking. He's the best in the world."

"We had the better team. They had the best player in the world," said Pacers substitute Aaron Brooks.

EASTERN CONFERENCE SEMIFINALS
Game 1, at Toronto, Cavaliers 113, Raptors 112 (OT)

"The basket didn't want it."

Philadelphia 76ers assistant coach Jack McMahon said that on February 25, 1978, after the damnedest miss of a dunk you'll never see again. The Sixers' Darryl Dawkins, who missed it, had turned 21 only a month earlier. A mischievous 235-pound, 6'11" man-child, Dawkins was the father of the power dunk, acknowledged as such by no less than Shaquille O'Neal, who said, "I am only his son."

Dawkins dunked with such power that not only did he discourage attempts to block his dunks because that came with the risk of broken bones, but he also broke two glass NBA backboards. This led to the installation of collapsible, snap-down rims to lessen the effect of the detonations by the self-described "Dunkateer."

In a game at Denver, Dawkins was the recipient of a pass within "sighted glass, smithereen-ed same" of the backboard. Leaping, with the ball held high behind his head in both hands, he slammed it over the rim with the force of one of Thor's ragnarokin' and sockin' hammers. The ball hit the nylon latticework of the net and simply . . . trampolined . . . back . . . out. The Sixers fell as if beaned by a stray hammer and lost the game. No one ever saw anything like it.

But the final minute of the fourth quarter of the first game of the Cavs–Toronto series came close.

The Cavs traveled to Toronto, the NBA East's top seed with a 59–23 record, the day after James described himself as "burnt," like bread in a faulty toaster. I drove to Buffalo the day after Game 7 against the Pacers, spent the night with in-laws, and drove across the Peace Bridge on the two-hour trip to Toronto on the morning of the series opener.

At the border checkpoint, a Canadian customs agent asked why I was visiting Canada.

"Business," I said. "I'm a newspaperman from Cleveland. I'm going there to cover the playoff series Toronto."

"It happens every spring," the customs guy said.

"Just like baseball starting," I said.

"And Cleveland always wins," he said.

Perceptive guy, it turned out.

While Indiana pushed the Cars and their leader to the breaking point, the Raptors had rested for three days after eliminating Washington in six games.

When Toronto took a discouraging 33–19 lead after the first quarter, a Raptors victory took on all the aspects of a slam dunk, which, as Dawkins had shown, was not absolutely, positively a done deal, even when the ball was proceeding toward the net at a snappy pace.

The Cavs behind James's 21st career playoff triple-double—26 points, 12 rebounds, 13 assists, almost unthinkable numbers under the circumstances—came off the mat. Smith scored 20 points, Korver 19.

The Cavs never led in regulation, which ended in a 105–5 tie amid a mad flurry of Raptor follies—including Fred VanVleet's missed three with 7 seconds left; DeMar DeRozan's offensive rebound and miss at the rim at 4 seconds; C. J. Miles's two offensive rebounds and two misses on layups as two seconds ticked off; and finally 6'11" Jonas Valanciunas's offensive rebound and miss from two feet in a spasm of futility. The Raptors shot 5-for-25 in the quarter. The basket's bias had never been clearer. The ball, unwanted, had been orphaned.

Elmer Fudd never missed as many bunnies with his blunderbuss.

Korver hit a three-pointer 37 seconds into the overtime for the Cavs' first lead. Smith hit a three, and Tristan Thompson mastered what Valanciunas could not, scoring with a hook shot from two feet.

The victory marked only the second time in the past 20 playoff seasons that a team had won a game in which it never led during regulation time. The other was Oklahoma City's win in 2011.

The opener also affected the entire series, planting seeds of doubt in the Raptors' minds, where they grew into tangles, thorns, and thistles of inadequacy.

Game 2, at Toronto, Cavaliers 126, Raptors 110

After the second game, the temptation was almost irresistible to start the column with the dateline "ToBronto," which I liked better than "LeBronto," although the latter was gaining more traction among the press-box pundits.

I was dissuaded from doing that by memories of the *Philadelphia Daily News* hockey writer, whose name shall be concealed, lest blight, scorn, rolled eyes, and a journalistic chorus exclaiming, "Good grief!" blight the concept any more than it already had been tarred. The occasion was the Philadelphia Flyers' first victory in Montreal since, apparently, the invention of the Zamboni, which the scribe hailed with a cringeworthy game story that began with the following celestial dateline followed by a seraphic chorus:

"Heaven—And the angels sing."

The printers' devils, meanwhile, threw up.

Love said he knew something special was coming in Game 3 during the morning shootaround, when James kept pouring in fadeaways that made all attempts at obstruction disappear. James had 43 points, making 19 of 28 shots, rendering Love, for the moment anyway, the guy to ask for stock market tips and lottery numbers. James added 14 rebounds and finished only two assists shy of a second straight triple-double. It was the first 40-point, 14-assist game in NBA playoff history.

Game 3, at Cleveland, Cavaliers 105, Raptors 103

At 2:00 A.M., I stopped on the American side of the border after Game 2, en route to a night's sleepover in a Buffalo hotel. The customs agent at the border noted the press pass still dangling from a lanyard because I had been in such a hurry to leave.

"Who won tonight?" he said.

"Cleveland, easily," I said.

"So, it's 2–0?" he said.

"It'll be 4–0 soon," I said.

Not exactly Kevin Love's level of foresight, but a few days later, I believed I had deserved some points for accuracy.

One of the things I most liked about James, besides his social and political activism, was his genuine love for the game, which he spoke about with great passion. "I've been doing that since I was like six, seven, eight years old," James said. "Maybe even before that. There's a picture floating around of me beside a Little Tikes hoop with a saggy Pamper on, and I was doing it back then and all the way up until now," said James,

Seldom, however, has he done anything like what he did in making the fifth playoff game–winning buzzer-beater in his career and his second of the 2018 playoff season. None had a degree of difficulty that was so far off the charts of reasonable feasibility.

Toronto rookie O. G. Anunoby tied it with a three in the last 8 seconds. With no timeouts remaining, the Cavs had to go the length of the floor. Again, James simply did whatever it took to beat the odds, the opponents, and time itself. His level of play seemed to grow ever higher.

"Tie game, [or] one down, those are moments I live for," he said.

Toronto coach Dwane Casey wanted to trap James on the right side in the backcourt near the baseline on the game's final play, but James took the inbounds pass and went by defenders at, said Casey, "100 miles per hour."

Raptors point guard Kyle Lowry thought all along that James would take the ball up the left side, but he lacked the size to alter or bother the shot. James jumped after racing past the Toronto bench, affording the Raptors subs an up-close-and-personal look at despair. He banked the ball high off the glass, and it went in with the game clock reading 0:00 and the crowd exploding into bedlam, with his teammates running from the bench, hugging and mobbing him until finally he hopped atop the scorer's table, just as he had done against Indiana in Game 5, basking in the love of fans who had once hated him.

"I always wondered why he messed around at practice, taking crazy shots like that," said Love. "And now I know."

Game 4, at Cleveland, Cavaliers 128, Raptors 93

I dated the end of what had seemed to be top-seeded Toronto's year to the opener, which the Cavs stole because four Raptors missed a flurry of shots in the last handful of seconds, three of them failing at point-blank range.

Others might have pointed to James's superlative second game after the being-burnt feeling was gone. The Game 3 buzzer-beater rendered moot any comeback chances for a team that James had physically and mentally dominated.

He went 29–8-11 in a fourth game that was a formality. The Cavs led by four points after the first period, 16 after the second, and 28 after the third and won by 35.

Dwane Casey compared the defeat to trying to get over the hurdle of Michael Jordan. Soon after Casey's team was eliminated, he was named NBA Coach of the Year. Shortly after that, he was fired.

2018 EASTERN CONFERENCE FINALS
Game 1, at Boston, Celtics 108, Cavaliers 83

The Celtics' very presence on the NBA stage was astonishing, in the absence of Gordon Hayward, lost with a broken leg for the whole season 4:35 into the opener at Cleveland, and of World B. Flat, who struggled through much of March with a knee injury, then had season-ending surgery. I entertained the notion of wondering in print whether he hurt himself while trying to karate kick a globe on a stand and screaming, "You lie!" I refrained though, because of, you know, civility and inherent class.

(Aside: Hah! Yeah, right!)

I remembered the Boston writer who, before Game 7 in the 2008 conference semifinals, played off coach Rick Pitino's comment that Bird, Kevin McHale, and Robert Parish weren't walking through that [locker room] door, but LeBron would be doing just that.

Ten years later, it was a case of same door, different LeBron.

With the Celtics down to an eight-man rotation because of injury attrition, Marcus Morris drew the unenviable assignment of trying to keep James from blowing the Celtics into nearby Boston Harbor. Added incentive for James was Morris's boast that he could guard James better than anybody in the league except future star Kawhi Leonard.

The evidence in the opener was that it wasn't brag, just fact. Morris held James to a 2018 playoff low 15 points while scoring 21 himself. James still contributed with seven boards and nine assists. He shot 5-for-16 from the floor, missed all of his five threes, and committed seven of the Cavs' nine turnovers. He committed only eight in the four-game sweep of the Pacers.

"I have zero level of concern," said James. "I've been down before in the postseason, but for me there's never any level of concern—no matter how bad I played tonight, with seven turnovers, how inefficient I was shooting the ball," he said. "We have another opportunity to be better as a ball club coming into Game 2, and we'll see what happens."

Game 2, at Boston, Celtics 107, Cavaliers 94

More of the same is what happened, at least on the scoreboard. Things were different in the box score, as James scored 42 points with 10 rebounds and 12 assists. It was his fifth 40-point game of the playoffs. He scored 21 of Cleveland's 27 first-quarter points, tying his one-quarter career playoff high. He was shot 8-of-13 from the field, 4-of-7 from the arc. But the scoreboard disparity remained.

Boston's record at home in the playoffs was ominously perfect at 9–0, just as it had been in 2008, the Celtics' only championship season since 1986. The Celtics also had never lost in the 37 times they had taken a 2–0 playoff lead.

As if that weren't enough, Boston's Jayson Tatum hit James in the jaw, spraining his neck, when Tatum tried for a steal. James went to the locker room for treatment. The Cavs went down, 55–48 at the half and were outscored by 20 points in the last two quarters.

Perhaps just for old times' sake, J. R. Smith shoved Al Horford in the back, sending him hurtling over the baseline on a layup attempt. Marcus Smart got in Smith's face, and both were assessed technical fouls. Smith drew an additional Flagrant 1, recalling his backhanded knockdown of Jae Crowder back in the 2015 playoffs and Smith's resulting Flagrant 2.

As summer drew nearer for the Cavs, the Gang Green was proving to be a pain in the neck.

Game 3, at Cleveland, Cavaliers 116, Celtics 86

A quote often reprised after the death of the British Queen Elizabeth II in 2022 was Victorian writer and critic Walter Bagehot's insistence on maintaining an air of mystery around the monarchy: "We must not let daylight in upon the magic."

It applies to sports in our time, when anything that moves is parsed as closely as the feet and meter of a line of poetry. In the twenty-first century NBA, geeky stats have proliferated. These include each player's usage rate, grade by pluses and minuses during playing time, rebounding and turnover percentage, points in the paint, points on the arc, and on and on into a labyrinth of numbers at the end of which stands Daryl Morey, the analytics minotaur.

And yet for all that, no one can measure the mystique or in the case of Earvin Johnson, the Magic in nickname and deed, whenever the Lakers were in a tight spot. James was his team's magician, capable—in his physical presence, skill level, and record—of giving teammates shelter in his reputation and confidence in his example.

If James wasn't dazed and shaken after taking the figurative, and, in the matter of his jaw and neck, all too literal punches, why then should they be? After the decisive victory in the opener, Boston coach Brad Stevens had said of the second game, "I think we have to be very aware that we're going to get a heavyweight punch."

It didn't happen in Game 2. But it was coming soon afterward.

In the arena corridor in Cleveland before the third game, James thumped his chest with both fists in a harbinger of things to come. He strode toward the tunnel that led to the court, out into the bright lights, the fiery swords, the loud roars, the photographer's clicking and flashing cameras, bringing with him the heavyweight punch the Celtics had been expecting all along.

James had 27 points and 12 assists in Game 3, as the Cavs led by 19 in the first quarter, won by 30, played cohesively on defense and with the chemistry on offense that had been lacking all year.

The Cavs not only weren't dead, the presumed corpses were frolicking around.

Proof of the revitalization was the backcourt of George Hill and Smith, who scored 13 and 11 points, after being outscored 41-3 by Boston's backcourt in the previous game. Perhaps best of all, James only had to play 37 minutes in the rout.

"They took it to us," Celtics coach Brad Stevens said. "Point blank: They just outplayed us."

Only 19 of a possible 300 teams had ever overcome a 2–0 deficit in the playoffs. James and the Cavs had done it in 2007 and again in 2016 in their epic, unprecedented comeback from a 0–2 and then 1–3 deficit to win the championship on Golden State home court. Now they were trying to make the third time their charm and the Celtics' curse.

Game 4, at Cleveland, Cavaliers 111, Celtics 102

The Cavs had 19 turnovers. In the second half, they had two assists. James had them both. It was double their assist total of the first half. James committed seven turnovers, but he shot 17-for-28, bullied his way to 44 points, and surpassed Kareem Abdul-Jabbar in total playoff field goals, scoring 2,356 of them, all without benefit of a skyhook.

"He's a big body. Ultimately, you just have to stay in front of him and hope he misses," said 6'1", 190-pound Boston guard Terry Rozier.

In one voice, the basketball world could have said, "Well, good luck with that."

Late in the game, James made his only three to go with as many misses, which finally put away the Celtics, who were lingering on the verge of a comeback.

"Ultimately, anybody that didn't think this was going to be tough, I mean, everything is tough. In this deal, it's a blast to have to grit your teeth, get up off the mat and go after it again," said Stevens, the 37-year-old Boston coach who looked young enough to take his team to the Tastee-Freez after victories but was an accurate appraiser of James's heavyweight punch.

Tristan Thompson had a 13–12 points-rebounds double-double. Kyle Korver, as old as Stevens, added 14 points and once outran three younger Celtics and, no Szczerbiak he, dived on a loose ball.

"We have to just have our same mindset we had when we came home for these two games. If our minds are there, we put ourselves in a position to be victorious," said James, looking ahead to the fifth game in

Boston and apparently denouncing mindlessness in basketball, as if anyone needed to.

"He's the best in the game at evaluating the court and figuring out what he wants and where he wants it. You just have to make it as hard as possible, because he's going to find a matchup that he ultimately wants," said Stevens, also refuting the concept of airhead basketball.

Game 5, at Boston, Celtics 96, Cavaliers 83

James looked tired. Korver had tossed and turned all night with a sore leg and elbow after his hell-for-leather ball dive. Boston's younger players, with their fresher legs, won their 10th straight home playoff game as a result. Celtics' rookie Jayson Tatum posted his ninth playoff game of 20 or more points, scoring 24. It was one fewer than Abdul-Jabbar's rookie record string.

James had 26 points and 10 rebounds but also committed six turnovers and managed only two points in the fourth quarter. He was 1-of-6 on threes. "I had my moments, but I think everybody at this point is tired, worn down, whatever the case may be," he said. "I was still trying to make plays, put our team in position to win."

Game 6, at Cleveland, Cavaliers 109, Celtics 99

Win or go home. Or in James's case, as an upcoming free agent, go elsewhere. If this was the last game of his four-year-long second term in Cleveland, his 11th overall, his last tour—OK, make that tour de force—through the playbook, the record books and the scrapbook, it was going to be a memorable one.

He played most of the game without Love, lost in a violent head-to-head collision with Boston' s Tatum in the first quarter.

James played the first 35 minutes without a break, then gutted out eight more minutes after Larry Nance Jr. ran into his leg and sent pain shooting up from the right side of his ankle. And yet he still had enough left to make back-to-back threes in the last three minutes, clinching it. After the second, he pounded his chest and screamed into the tumult from the stands, as he had done in the hallway before Game 3.

He scored 46 points with 11 rebounds and nine assists.

With Game 7 in Boston at TD Garden, where the Cavs had lost Game 7 eight years earlier, with Boston unbeaten at home in the playoffs as it had been all the way to the championship in 2008, the post–Game 6 comments had an elegiac feel.

"Greatness," Cavs coach Tyronn Lue said. "Championship pedigree. Giving it his all. We needed that, especially when Kevin went down. We had to play 'Bron as many minutes as he had to. He delivered. He was up for the challenge. He carried us home as usual."

"I've been in the league for some years and ran across him on the other side and really hated his guts," said Hill, who was on the Indiana teams James had eliminated. "But to have him on our side, it kind of lets me take a deep breath of fresh air. It's just something that you really can't explain, what he's doing night in, night out. It's just something special."

Asked about his scream after the consecutive triples, James said, "The love of the game. It's something you can't explain."

How long does love last? Certainly, at least on the fans' part, through his first seven seasons in Cleveland. Then it was rekindled in his next four. Forever is a long, long time. But if James stayed and took the $35 million contract in the offing, and maybe—even if he left after this extended YouTube marathon of his playoff highlights—they were willing to give forever a shot.

Game 7, at Boston, Cavaliers 87, Celtics 79

By 2018, Cedric Maxwell was deep into his career with the Celtics' broadcast team. Called "Cornbread" in college for his supposed resemblance to the character nicknamed that in the movie *Cornbread, Earl and Me*, he had been dubbed "Mad Max" as a player.

Maxwell would do a lot of unethical, but not quite illegal, Auerbachian things to win. In an overtime playoff game in the 1984 Finals, he was continually walking across the free throw lane, both hands wrapped around his neck in the time-honored "choke" sign, before the Lakers' James Worthy, struggling with his confidence, could shoot the ball.

Before the seventh game at Boston in steamy old Boston Garden, in one of the iconic moments in Celtics' history, Maxwell, a few hours later named the series' Most Valuable Player, was quoted as saying to his teammates, "Get on my back, boys. I'll carry you."

This version of his remarks had been sensitivity cleansed, like many an athlete's quote, including many in this book. As he admits today, he actually said, "You bitches get on my back. I'll carry you."

The problem, as Maxwell discerned in 2018, was the lack of a Maxwell in the Boston locker room. Being on the cusp of the NBA Finals was a new experience for most of the players. In the press work room, Maxwell said to a couple of Cleveland reporters, "They are pretty tight in there," nodding toward the Celtics' locker room, down a corridor only a few steps away.

I wondered just how tight they were. I related the comment of the Cleveland baseball team's traveling secretary, Mike Seghi, before they walked out into the Seattle Kingdome to win the 1995 American League pennant against the Mariners' towering, almost unhittable "Big Unit," the 6'10", intimidating, very hard-throwing lefthander Randy Johnson. Said longtime Major League Baseball executive Phil Seghi's son, Mike, "They're so tight, you couldn't pull a pin out of their ass with a tractor."

Maxwell burst out laughing. Minutes later, ducking out to get a cup of coffee in the media dining area, I caught Maxwell's eye as he leaned against the wall of the corridor, waiting for the Celtics to emerge. Glancing at me, Maxwell exclaimed, "With a tractor!" As the game wore on, it began to become obvious that John Deere was overmatched by the pin embedded in the Celtics' butts.

In the only close game, the lowest scoring, and the only breakthrough by a visiting team in the series, under the highest level of expectation and tension, James was spectacular. Playing all 48 minutes, he had 35 points, 15 rebounds, and 9 assists in the Cavs' win.

No one on either team surpassed his numbers. Tatum had 24 points to lead Boston, Marcus Morris got 12 rebounds, and Marcus Smart got seven assists. Marcus Aurelius got a DNP-HD (Did Not Play-History's Decision).

"He's had a lot of gaudy games," Cavaliers coach Tyronn Lue said. "But I just think Game 7, in Boston, all the circumstances that surround Boston, the history . . . to come here in a hostile environment: [it's] right there."

"Our goal going into the series was to make him exert as much energy as humanly possible and try to be as good as we can on everybody else," Celtics' coach Brad Stevens said. "For the most part, I thought we were pretty good at that . . . but he still scored 35. It's a joke."

"We have an opportunity to play for a championship," James said. "It doesn't matter what the storyline is going to be; it doesn't matter if we're picked to win or not. I'm the wrong guy to ask. I just like to compete."

He would put all of that in jeopardy in a colossal but, under the bizarre circumstances, understandable loss of composure and temper that destroyed his team's chances in the very first game of the upcoming NBA Finals.

CHAPTER 34

Dead-End Road

The 2018 NBA Finals had just begun.

The Finals were over.

James had been otherworldly.

James was only human.

Journalists live by the tenet of objectivity.

The Cavs were robbed.

In everything that happened before the refs' controversial decision in the opener, James was unstoppable, scoring 51 points, making 19 of 32 shots, sinking three of seven triples on his way to becoming the only players in Finals history to score 50 or more points—yet lose.

The Cavs were hindered by a last-minute replay review of a call on James, who attempted to draw a charge on a driving Kevin Durant. It was initially called as one but later changed into a blocking foul. The referee crew determined James was indeed outside the restricted area but also drifting left toward Durant, deemed not in legal position to take the charged.

The Cavs, holding a two-point lead with only 36.4 seconds left to play, were poised to enjoy the sweet perfume of victory and the swing in home-court advantage it brought.

The canker in the rose was a five-year-old amendment to the block/charge rule that allowed officials to go to video replay in the last two minutes of the fourth quarter or overtime. After the game, as the distraught

Cavs denounced the overturn of the original charging call, the NBA rushed out a press release that was only about, oh, five years too late.

It read: "Clarity on blk/charge review: The trigger is that if in the last 2 minutes of the 4th or overtime officials have doubt whether the defender was in the restricted area. While reviewing, they may also confirm if the defender was in legal guarding position when the contact occurred."

It is a stain on the Cavs' front office and coaches that no one knew about this revision. It is also a stain on the on the NBA, which did not emphasize the change. Lue was utterly unaware of the change. "LeBron was clearly four feet outside the restricted area. He wasn't close. What are we reviewing?" He said after the game, "For our team to play their hearts out the way they did and compete the way we did, it's bad. It's never been done before. It ain't right."

In the locker room, the Cavs' fury was directed toward Ken Mauer, who with Ed Malloy made up the rest of the officiating crew. Mauer had been the referee who watched the replay and made the decision to reverse the call.

ESPN's Dave McMenamin tweeted: Four words I've heard more than once being muttered under Cleveland personnel's breaths in the Cavs postgame locker room: 'Ken Mauer f—ed us.'"

What made it worse for the Cavs was that the head of the three-man crew was Cavs nemesis Tony Brothers. In the close-out game of the sweep against Boston in 2015, Brothers was the blind mouse who should have been given a cane and a guide dog after he somehow missed a flagrant and nearly unprecedented interference violation by Isaiah Thomas, although Brothers was *looking right at him.*

Thomas had nearly run into the first row of spectators after making a layup, then had quickly run up behind James, who was inbounding the ball. With a slap of the unwary James's wrist, he deflected the ball to a Boston teammate, who sank two free throws after being fouled. The illegal play ignited an unjustified but in the end unsuccessful Celtics rally.

It was four years now, and Brothers was still working big games.

James called the overrun of the block/charge call a "huge play" and said "I knew I was outside the charge line. I read that play as well as I've read any play in my career, maybe in my life."

"I was ready to shoot the free throws and run down the clock," said James.

Instead, the comedic stylings of J. R. Smith sent his team spiraling toward a disheartening overtime loss. With four seconds to play in the fourth quarter, the Warriors' Klay Thompson fouled George Hill. He made his first free throw, tying the score at 107. His second bounced off the front of the rim, where the far shorter Smith got inside position on Durant for a possible game-winning tip-in.

But wait!

To tweak the *Dallas* soap opera line about oilmen and homicidal tendencies, Who shot? JR?"

Incredibly, no.

Thinking the Cavs led by a point—a contention Lue made but Smith denied—the Cavs' shooting guard dribbled away from the basket. James stared in disbelief on the wing, first screaming at him to shoot, then begging for the ball. "I just thought we were going to call a timeout. Because I got the rebound, I'm pretty sure I couldn't shoot it over KD," Smith said. "If I thought we were ahead, I would have just held on to the ball so they could foul me. Clearly that wasn't the case."

"I can't talk about a situation that way because I do some dumb stuff on the court," Durant said. "I don't know what was going through JR's head. He made a great rebound and gave them an opportunity to win the basketball game."

Draymond Green gave Smith cover, saying Smith was simply looking for James, adding, "I would have looked for LeBron, too."

Time ran out without the Cavs calling timeout, although they still had one. It was not as if Lue, positioned at the far end of the court on the Cavs' bench, had made the time-honored gesture of a *T* with his hands, which might have been missed with the refs so far away and their eyes on the last-second frenzy. Nor did Lue desperately shout for one, which might have been swallowed up in the fans' din. Lue had saved the season in 2015 by preventing Blatt from calling the timeout the Cavs didn't have against Chicago. Unfortunately, a second incarnation of Lue was not sitting beside the coach to call the timeout the Cavs did have.

A stricken James became utterly distraught when he asked Lue if the

Cavs had had a timeout, only to discover they did. James slumped on the bench, his head buried in his hands, a towel draped over it as if he were in mourning. It was hardly the posture you expect from a great leader. But in the next instance, you had to admit few leaders had ever led such a ragged team so far.

The unfathomable sequence of blunders led to overtime and a 124–14 walloping for the disheartened Cavs.

In the locker room, James savagely smashed a whiteboard with his right fist in rage, causing a "deep bone bruise." The Cavs did not disclose the injury, nor did James wear any protection on it in the next three games, keeping the Warriors in the dark about the injury until after what began as James's tantrum had turned into a nearly inevitable sweep.

In everything that came after the punch, James was still, unimaginably, transcendent. The Warriors won the next three games by scores of 122–103, 110–102, and 108–85. James missed a total of only one quarter plus 40 seconds of play. In Game 3, he scored 23 points and added 10 rebounds and 11 assists for an almost inconceivable triple-double under the circumstances. Burdened by pain and a nearly unfathomable workload, he was—and still is, as he nears the age of 40—a marvel.

No one was the wiser about the injury until James faced media members after the sweep, wearing a dark brace on his hand. "Pretty much played the last three games of the Finals with a broken hand," he said.

It was not the way anyone wanted it to end.

The cheers when Lue took him out of the fourth game lacked the wild glee after his buzzer-beaters. The applause was respectful. It was like an elegy in remembrance of "just a kid from Akron," who had won their hearts and broken them, then rewon them. It was he who puffed with pride the chests of so many Clevelanders who so often had been disappointed. It was he who gave them a parade, which, no matter that it was officially in honor of the Cavs, was really, like the championship, for them.

CHAPTER 35

Requiem for a King

With his own hilltop Xanadu in Los Angeles, minus the loneliness and the undisplayed treasures of the world still in crates of the newspaper mogul in *Citizen Kane,* LeBron James was nearly certain to sign with the Los Angeles Lakers as a free agent.

Given the long downturn in Celtic fortunes, the Lakers were the NBA's royalty now. The franchise was the home of a constellation of stars who signed there after beginning in cities less prominent in publicity and financial opportunities—Kareem Abdul-Jabbar, from Milwaukee to LA; Shaquille O'Neal, from Orlando to the City of Angels; and later, Anthony Davis, from New Orleans to La-La-Land. As a basketball historian, James was fully aware of that. He was ready to take his place as the next Lakers icon.

Also, James was in the movies by 2018. He had received positive, even glowing, reviews for his role two years earlier in *Trainwreck,* in which he played himself as the best friend of Amy Townsend's (Amy Schumer) boyfriend, Aaron Conners (Bill Hader). "The Greatest Movie Performance by an Active NBA Player," the *New Yorker*'s Ian Crouch wrote, praising James's "gently bizarre version of himself" and using his stinginess in the movie as an example of "playing against type." As described in chapter 6, however, this was absolutely true to James in the early years of his NBA career.

(Less kind were reviews of his 2021 performance in *Space Jam: A New Legacy,* the sequel to Jordan's bravura 1996 performance.)

On July 2, 2018, local television programming was interrupted in Cleveland for the news bulletin that James had signed as a free agent to play in the shadow of the big HOLLYWOOD sign. Two days earlier, I had retired after 34 years as a sports columnist in Cleveland, 10 years, primarily as the *Philadelphia Inquirer*'s 76ers beat man, and two years at my journalism alma mater, the *Dallas Morning News*.

Part of retirement involved turning in my laptop. The *Plain Dealer* called me on my cell phone that night, just after I had showered and donned pajamas. They needed a column PDQ (pretty damn quick). Rather than peck away with an index finger on my cell phone, I used my wife Marilyn's iPad, which only reluctantly booted up after a long time of non-usage. As I banged away with my hard-typing stroke, the tablet bounced all over the lapboard on which I had placed it.

Any anchor in any port in a storm, I say. I commandeered the food canister of our dog, Archie, and slapped it down on the lapboard to weight it more securely. I resumed furiously typing, as the container inched along the lapboard and almost fell to the living room floor.

My wife refused to take the photo I requested of the ridiculous scene, saying she would be too embarrassed if anyone ever saw it.

I had to dictate it. Still, the column got published. It was an ode in prose to the man I hailed as "inspiration, icon, activist and ring-bearer."

"Four years ago, LeBron James yanked the sword from the stone and said the magic words that opened fans' hearts that had seemed forever shut to him.' I'm coming home,' he announced through his media confidant, Lee Jenkins of *Sports Illustrated*.

"Nothing was the same after he returned from a four-year stay in Miami."

For both the player and the fans, respect replaced recrimination, and boos became cheers.

"Because of the Browns' supremacy in the All-America Football Conference, it is forgotten that the Detroit Lions had much the better of their meetings in NFL Championship Games. They played for three straight years, 1953–55, for the NFL Championship. Detroit won two of them and made the final margin 3–1 with a rout in another title game in 1957.

"It was Golden State and the Cleveland Cavaliers in cleats. But Hannibal did not win. Napoleon did not win. Lee did not win. Rommel did not win. Their genius lives on. Unlike some of them, James's reputation is not tarred by the brush of unpopular causes. James has consistently been on the right side of history, championing the causes of the disadvantaged and the down and out.

"James brings with him a vast media presence, a global scope of fame and fortune, and a name recognition that tops maybe every other athlete in the world except Argentina's Lionel Messi or Portugal's Cristiano Ronaldo. But who follows them avidly in America except in the quadrennial World Cup?

"No one, not Lou Bourdeau, Bob Feller, Rocky Colavito, or Albert Belle; not Jim Brown, Otto Graham, Frank Ryan, or Bernie Kosar; not Mark Price, Brad Daugherty, Kyrie Irving, or Kevin Love, ever did so much for one team as James in his second tenure with the Cavs.

"More of a Magic Johnson distributive type with the ball than a Kobe Bryant monopolist, more of a multitasker than Michael Jordan, James epitomized a generational advance in strength and speed since Jordan.

"James became the all-time leading scoring champion while looking first to empower his teammates and pass. James has become the most dominant NBA record-book presence since Wilt Chamberlain, in part by extending his prime to the unthinkable extent in what should be the twilight of his career.

"'I think maybe the greatest testament to LeBron is that five years ago he was one of the top five players of all time,' Warriors coach Steve Kerr said. 'From five years ago until now, it seems like he's 10 times better, because he's added so much skill to his game.'"

"Off the court, James has been a role model, never in trouble with the law; a philanthropist, opening doors to the impoverished and downtrodden by funding college scholarships; a devoted husband and father; and the legatee of the political activism of Kareem Abdul-Jabbar, Muhammad Ali and Jim Brown.

"As a long-time NBA executive said of James: 'When you've been around the league as long as I have, you hear things. "One guy is a hound on the road. Another guy is into drugs." But I have never heard a thing about this guy.'"

"In the 2018 playoffs, James twice leaped atop the scorer's table after buzzer-beating shots. His arms were upraised to embrace the fans' cheers and symbolically to hug them in what seemed to be each side forgiving the other.

"Goodbye, LeBron. Thanks. Have a great rest of your life."

He is doing just that. In 2020, during the COVID-19 pandemic, James won his fourth NBA championship. He and newly arrived Anthony Davis led the Lakers to a 4–2 victory over Miami in the Orlando "bubble," in which no fans were admitted and the media presence was scanty. It had all the spectacle of an extraordinarily skilled pickup game in an empty gym.

TNT's Charles Barkley immediately threw shade on it. "There's a bunch of bubble gangsters there. I'll never say anything against LeBron, who's a great player and a greater guy. But the bubble doesn't count. Stop it."

Barkley's criticism never gained traction. History would count it.

Just as history might determine in the future that we will never see—in Cleveland, Miami, Los Angeles, or any other place where he had been King—the likes of LeBron Raymone James again.

CHAPTER 36

A Midwinter Night's Dream

Chalk dust hung in the air above LeBron James's head and his widespread arms at the NBA's 75th All-Star Game in 2022 in Cleveland. The powder throw was back, sprinkling his hair, including the growing bald spot, with what was merely talc but might as well have been stardust. Perhaps the greatest athlete in Cleveland history, for there are always Jesse Owens and Jim Brown to consider, James brought with him his boyhood friends from Akron, his signature pregame gesture, and his flair for the dramatic.

True, he copied the chalk throw from Kevin Garnett, who copied it from Michael Jordan, who . . . Wait, wait! This sounds like a list of "begats" from a book in the Bible. But the frame of reference fits, chapter and verse. In this case, it was 1 Corinthians 13:13. "And now these three remain—faith, hope, and love. But the greatest of these is love."

In the pregame celebration, the fans' cheers pealed like thunder as a camera flashed a shot of the Cavaliers' 2016 NBA championship banner on the Humungotron. This was followed by a crescendo of music and cheers, drowning out everything after the public address announcer's words, "He's just a kid from Akron . . ." Head flung back, eyes staring into the darkness before the spotlight took its customary place on him, James screamed happily from a welter of emotions swirling within him. Surely, they included memories revived, familiarity renewed, and joy rekindled. It was a stark contrast to his cheerless, injury-plagued season 2,000 miles away with the Los Angeles Lakers.

Clearly, James saw himself as the next in line to become a legendary Lakers icon, like Jerry West and Elgin Baylor, Wilt Chamberlain and Kareem Abdul-Jabbar, Magic Johnson and Kobe Bryant—James and the wingman he recruited Anthony Davis.

But the Lakers' 2019–20 NBA championship was literally a cheerless event, held during the coronavirus pandemic in a shuttered arena in Orlando, a virus-free "bubble," with no fans present, few reporters, and no victory parade in in its wake through the streets of the City of Angels. The next season, the Lakers humiliatingly missed the playoffs entirely.

At the All-Star Game, James seemed reenergized after he spent the weekend in Akron and in his Humongotron-worthy mansion in Bath, roughly midway between Akron and Cleveland.

He and his mother, Gloria, had been the focal points of a fashion show on Friday night at the State Theater in Playhouse Square. Both looked elegant. LeBron wore a camelhair coat big enough and long to have been shorn from a member or two of Lawrence of Arabia's Damascus *camelry*, a term coined for want of a better equivalence to horse cavalry.

In a pouch slung from his belt, LeBron brought a bottle of his luxury tequila brand, 1707 Lobos; apparently, you are not A-lister in either in the movies (Matthew McConaughey's Longbranch bourbon) or sports without your own brand of an ardent spirit. *Tequila*, for those who are curious, is said to be the Spanish term for "I don't remember doing that."

James had been corralling investors, including his business partners Rich Paul and Maverick Carter, his Lakers' teammate Davis, and nether-region knockout puncher and rival Draymond Green, for the launch of his brand in 2020. It all paid off.

Lobos 1707 bested Michael Jordan's Cincoro, also launched in 2020, in the finals of the prestigious San Francisco World Spirits Competition. They were two of the three finalists for the Best Reposado Tequila award, meaning the Montezuma's lightnin' of both had been aged 2 to 12 years in oak barrels. The third finalist was Don Nacho Tequila, which, at least going by its name, was just the thing to complement tortilla chips with jalapenos.

The Lobos brand stands for "celebrating the strength of the pack." It is, in short, a nod to togetherness and unity, the values James esteemed most in basketball.

Continuing that theme, the boyhood friends who predated the group's controversial collective choice of high school—the ones who were by his side in the Central-Hower game and the Roger Bacon game and the Oak Hill game, and the ones before and after—were with him again as they posed for a group photograph on the eve of the All-Star Game at Rocket Mortgage FieldHouse.

It had been a quarter-century since the 1997 Golden Anniversary NBA All-Star Game was held in Cleveland. Its centerpiece was the selection of the 50 top players of all time. On its 75th anniversary celebration, the list of greatest players would grow to 75, their names announced in a halftime ceremony. The historical touch was moving, particularly when James and Jordan, the two top alphas—by unspoken but general agreement in a room in which there were no admitted betas or gammas—embraced during the ceremony.

Player salaries, television rights, marketing resources, and audience popularity had increased exponentially in the quarter-century since the previous Cleveland All-Star Game. That is because NBA athletes are gifted enough to compete on the highest level of human possibility. Such spectacle sells everywhere.

The three-point revolution has made the outside shooting contest every bit as popular as, if not more so in some years, the Slam Dunk Contest. On cue, enter Steph Curry, whether from stage right, stage left, or, to parody Austin Carr's three-point call, "from deep, d-e-e-e-e-p outside."

Curry sank threes with the nonchalance of a motorist tossing change into a tollbooth basket on a turnpike. Curry scored 50 points, his second-best ever, and won the inaugural Kobe Bryant Trophy as the All-Star Game Most Valuable Player. In all, he sank 16 triples, once turning his back on the ball as it reached the peak of its 37-foot flight, racing back on defense because he knew he had pured it. His total would have broken the NBA record of 14 treys in a game, held by his fellow Splash Brother, Klay Thompson. But of course, Thompson did it in an actual game with discernible defensive efforts directed against him.

Alluding to current Cavaliers Darius Garland and Jarrett Allen, both first-time All-Stars, James told a roaring crowd before the opening tip, "Cleveland has a third All-Star, and it's me."

The biggest prize was also the most generous. A huge amount of charity money was to be divided between the Cleveland Hunger Bank and James's charity, the I Promise School for disadvantaged kids in Akron, which he had helped fund. Its graduates are eligible for tuition grants at nearby Kent State University. The program says much about James's own growth and his urge to make a difference, turning the problems of his own youth into the current generation's promise.

Under the revised format, the first team to reach a targeted point total, which was 163 in the game's mostly defense-free precincts, would win the lion's share of the charity money. James scored 24 points overall on as many shots. But with the game on the line, his team leading, 161–60, in the last seconds, James, as so often he has been, was the man made for the moment and our memories. He posted up on the right side of the floor 18 feet from the rim and demanded the ball.

Defender Zach LaVine stuck to him like adhesive tape. Joel Embiid made it a double-team a few ticks of the time clock later. James faded away from both, his right leg cocked at the knee, as he lifted off from his left.

The FieldHouse was by then a madhouse. It was easy to imagine the almost palpable unity of support for him spreading, as fans watched the shot on HDTVs and on cell phones; followed it over car radios, where it grew even bigger in the imagination; imitated it and replicated it in the days ahead on inner city playgrounds, polished gym floors, and on baskets alongside driveways and maybe some nailed to telephone poles, in all parts of the world that were besotted with basketball,

Of course, the shot went in as time ran out. It is what James does. Final score, 163–61, I Promise school $450,000, Cleveland Hunger Bank $300,000. James and the way he plays the game of basketball had surpassed the hype again.

The kid from Akron, who dreamed of playing on the NBA courts 35 miles away from his home, who grew up without the money or the transportation even to watch a game in person, had had a night that only grew better in Cleveland when he refused to close the door on the chance he might enjoy a last hurrah in Cavaliers colors. To a delighted audience, first as a teenage draft pick and then as a seven-year veteran, the Messiah had experienced these hello-goodbye, hello again–goodbye again moments.

"Just hearing the ovation I got from these fans here, they've seen 11 years of my NBA career, and they saw four years of my high school career, and some even saw me when I started playing basketball at the Summer Lake at the ARB (Akron Recreation Board)," said James. "These guys have followed my journey. So for me to be back here today and for them to give me that welcome, that didn't only mean something to me, that meant something to my family and friends that are here. How much more can a man ask for, really? When you have the opportunity to live this moment, with everybody that has seen you come up ... We all spent All-Star Weekend together, and I don't know if that will ever happen again. So, there's no reason for me not to have joy."

The night was a gesture of faith, fueled by James's philanthropy, in the future of his hometown's poor children, a future many presumed to be reserved for the sons and daughters of wealth and privilege. It also was a gesture of hope that the reunion of the city of Cleveland and its shining star would be repeated so James might return and play for the third time, the charm time, in a Cavaliers uniform.

That is unlikely to happen.

But after the years of acclaim for his success and of antipathy for his Decision, the fans' acceptance and appreciation in his return was, simply, a tender gesture of love, both received and requited.

Index

Oklahoma Thunder, 212, 222, 248–49, 266, 276; 2012 NBA Finals, 154–59, 161, 168, 182

Oladipo, Victor, 270–71, 273–75

Ollie, Kevin, 34

Olympics, 18, 29, 36, 108, 121, 174, 269; 1936, 133; 1972, 258; 2004, 42–51, 196; 2012, 113; 2020, 48; 2022, 167; Dream Team, 46, 49; Pan Am Games, 47; Team USA, 44–50, 74, 129

Olynyk, Kelly, 217, 225

Omalu, Bennet Ifeandndu, 263

O'Neal, Shaquille, 18, 48, 66, 91, 121, 123–24, 127, 260, 275, 291; injuries, 122, 126, 129

Oracle Arena, 162, 199, 220, 224–25, 229, 249

Orlando "bubble," 174, 294

Orlando Magic, 110–16, 121, 155, 291

Osman, Cedi, 267, 272

Ostopchuk, Nadzeya, 113

Owens, Jesse, 133, 269, 295

Pacino, Al, 103

Painter, Curtis, 107

Palace, the, 62, 64, 71

Papanek, John, 179–80

Parish, Robert, 92, 101, 279

Parker, Anthony, 121, 168–69, 174, 181, 184–85

Parker, Candace, 121

Paul, Chris, 76

Paul, Rich, 26–27, 29, 296

Pavlovic, Sasha, 75, 77, 87, 103, 121

Paxson, Jim, 35–36, 55, 137

Peace Bridge, 276

People magazine, 210

Perdue, Will, 233

Perez, Chris, 239

Petticoat Junction, 63

PGA, 67

Philadelphia Bulletin, 138, 180

Philadelphia Daily News, 106, 277

Philadelphia Eagles, 32, 77

Philadelphia Flyers, 277

Philadelphia Inquirer, 19, 77, 97, 105, 138–39, 179–80, 292

Philadelphia Journal, 90

Philadelphia 76ers (Sixers), 17, 19, 31, 33, 36, 54, 57, 71, 80, 86, 90, 92, 95–97, 104–5, 115, 129, 137, 154, 179, 180, 231, 233, 275, 292; 1975 Finals, 21; 1976 ticket campaign, 50; 1981 Eastern Conference Finals, 73, 106; 1982–83 team, 237; 2001 season, 91

Philcox, Todd, 134

Phillips, Frank, 12

Phoenix Suns, 74, 155

Pierce, Paul, 93, 98, 101–2, 104, 116, 127, 182–83

Pinar Karsiyaka, 169

"Pinball Wizard" (The Who), 74

Pippen, Scottie, 80, 84, 258, 260

Pitino, Rick, 24, 101

Pittsburgh Pirates, 270

Pittsburgh Steelers, 113, 263

Players' Tribune, The, 248

Playhouse Square, 246, 296

PlayStation, 61

Plump, Bobby, 164

Pluto, Terry, 218

Ponte Vedra, 44

Pontiac Silverdome, 64

Popovich, Gregg, 48, 90, 129, 167, 170–71, 175–78, 181, 185, 202, 207

Portage Path Elementary, 3

Portland Trail Blazers, 21, 74, 129

Posey, James, 99, 103–4

Potapenko, Vitaly, 54

Power Memorial, 22

Powers, John, 95

Price, Mark, 139, 154, 254, 293

Prince, Tayshaun, 51, 64–66, 71–72, 81–82, 84, 86, 89–90, 146

Private Lives (Coward), 36

Progressive Field, 246

Providence Steamrollers, 97

Ptolemy I, 146

Public Square, 245

Putin, Vladimir, 252